MY COWORKERS THINK I'M A PRO

My Coworkers Think I'm A Pro

Musings Of An Age Group Triathlete

Brock Gibbs

Bottom Bracket Books

ISBN: 978-1-7771473-0-3 (Paperback)
ISBN: 978-1-7771473-1-0 (Electronic book)

Cover photography: Anne D'Avignon
Cover design: Christopher Gibbs

FOR OWEN

TABLE OF CONTENTS

FOREWORD

I was at mile three of my run and I knew that if I could hold it together I would possibly get my first 70.3 Age-Group win. Feeling strong and confident, I knew there were a few guys behind
me chasing with their fire-within, and I knew that I would need to
keep fighting hard.

In that pack was a young-looking guy with blonde hair bouncing under his hat, that I was certain was not in my age-group. As
we approached the turn-around, I caught a glimpse of the back of
his calf, and he was most certainly my age and surging fast. We
fought hard together right down to the finish-line, and I managed
to hang on for dear life to get the win.

Triathlon is such an individual sport requiring hours and
hours of practice, training, and working on the skills needed to

compete and finish, yet it also gives back so much. The sport develops friendships, memories and challenges, not only on the race course, but also in our everyday lives. Syracuse 70.3, 2016 was the day I met Brock Gibbs and thus our friendship began. We spoke for quite some time at the awards ceremony, and I was quite drawn to his motivation, humbleness and humour.

In the pages ahead, Brock brings you through his adventures, his ups and downs, highs and lows, bringing us through his mind and body connection in his world of triathlon, all with a hilarious, comical twist. I am grateful every day for crossing paths with Brock that day in Syracuse.

Sean Snow
5 X Hawaii Ironman Finisher
31 X Ironman Finisher

Concord, New Hampshire
March, 2020

DISCLAIMER:

Now I'm no expert when it comes to racing and training for triathlons.

I suppose you were probably expecting a 'but' followed by some pithy, clever nugget of wisdom that would act as convincing evidence to the contrary; something, in actuality, that would suggest that, despite the opening disclaimer, I really *am* knowledgeable on the subject. Unfortunately, that is not the case here. I am by no means an expert. What I do have is a little experience, some of which has come as the result of making some serious mistakes along the way.

What follows is a chronicling of these mistakes and how they have resulted, somehow, in a fulfilling, though at times painful, journey from triathlon neophyte to being a member of the number one amateur triathlon team in the world.

PROLOGUE

"Fuckfuckfuckfuckfuckfuck.......Fhhuuuckhh!". I couldn't believe how sore, stiff, exhausted, sore, thirsty, cramped, and sore my body could be. In fact, sore doesn't come close to accurately describing the physical state of my every bone, tendon, muscle, and ligament, or the relentlessly excruciating sensations I was experiencing. With every step and every breath I took, I could actually feel each individual muscle tighten up and try to rip itself from all attachment points. Even the tiniest movements were creating unfathomable physical misery that far exceeded my brain's ability to comprehend, and the intensity of the pain was so shockingly unfamiliar that I had no prior experience upon which I could draw to help make any sense of it all. Of course, I had been in pain many times before, even great pain, but what I was experiencing at the 2015 Ironman Lake Placid was on a level that hitherto I had never imagined could exist.

When the race started, I knew that it was going to be a rough day out, and I wasn't foolish or presumptuous enough to think that I would escape without any discomfort, but this was something I simply did not expect, and it hardly made any sense at all. I mean I had trained well for this event, or so I thought, plus I had previously finished a bunch of Ironman 70.3s without any significant physical difficulties that a healthy positive attitude couldn't convert into fun. Hell, I've even stood on the podium in some of them, in my age category, that is.

When I signed up, I figured that I had this whole triathlon business dialled in. The sport, to date, hadn't exactly been a cakewalk, but it was far from daunting. I suppose you could say it was comfortably difficult. Sure, I had never attempted a race of this length before, but it was just a couple of 70.3s strung together back to back, how hard could it be? Dammit, I finished in the top ten at the Ironman 70.3 World Championships, surely I would be capable of managing an Ironman without the need for emergency medical assistance. Everyone I knew at work (none of them triathletes, of course) believed I was a professional, but in Lake Placid, I could barely put one foot in front of the other without feeling like someone was jamming shards of glass into my hamstrings, quads, calves, abs, biceps, pancreas, fingernails, kidneys, and eyelids.

In short, I had never felt this bad in my life, and it was so depressing to realize, once and for all, that I was not superhuman. My colleagues had indeed been mistaken because it was quite evident that nothing I did in this race could be considered as heroic in the least, and this realization made me sad. I felt entirely worthless, inadequate, and impotent, but mostly, I felt angry. The anger was largely with myself, but that didn't mean I was above taking it out on everyone around me, despite the fact that I should have trained more and that my sessions could have been longer, better, smarter. With every agonizing step I took, I asked myself why I had skipped all of those Sunday long runs? Why had I so often reduced their length simply because it was too wet, or too dry, too snowy, too windy, or too sunny? Or simply because it was too, well...Sunday?

I realized that I had been fooling myself, thinking that I was ready for such a staggering endeavour, and I now understood that too many shortcuts had been taken permitting just enough cognitive dissonance to have me believe that I had done all I could to adequately prepare for this monumental task. As I shuffled along, I had so many questions: How could I have let my diet turn to shit every damned night after eight o'clock when I had done so well the rest of the day? What was it about watching CNN in an exhausted state, after a day of training, that would make me believe, despite being university educated, that a full bottle of Shiraz and an entire bag of Twizzlers were adequate, even proper, recovery fuel?

It is truly amazing how small a nugget of positive information needs to be to obfuscate what you know in your heart to be false. Sure, there must have been a paragraph somewhere in an obscure Runner's World magazine article extolling the virtues of antioxidants, and I am pretty certain that I have heard someplace else that red wine contains said antioxidants. It is very easy to wantonly conflate these two bits of information into a theory which basically states that unless I drink red wine in large quantities, I will not be able to finish a race. *Of course,* red wine is good for you, and, while we're at it, Twizzlers are also red. Coincidence? I think not.

Yes I was suffering, and that made me angry because I knew that it was down to my own laziness that I was now hurting so much, and what's more, I was mad because I had always considered myself intelligent. I have a Master's Degree, hanging mockingly on a wall next to my desk back home, that is supposed to designate the fact that I received a top-notch dose of 'higher' education. You would never believe it, however, because, in Lake Placid, my vocabulary had been drastically distilled to simple sentences centred around a single four-letter word: FUCK. I wasn't merely speaking the word so much as it was being exhaled directly from my diaphragm. Thankfully, I didn't possess enough energy to make any of these utterings audible outside of the confines of my own head. Still, every action around me elicited a response that included the word, with four very short phrases reflexively dominating my lexicon: There was "fuck you", or just "fuck off", or "just fuck off", and finally, the ever-popular "go fuck yourself".

An overexcited, happy fan along the side of the road eating a popsicle calls out enthusiastically, "Looking good!".

Response: "fuck off", with the accompanying "asshole" if there was enough energy.

Another fan, trying in some small way to ease my very obvious discomfort, shouts encouragingly, "Almost there!"

Response: "Fuck you". No exclamation point required.

A man with his young son, gawking in admiration at the brave athletes struggling to complete the arduous marathon portion of a race, attempts to commiserate saying, "One more hill!"

Response: "Just fuck off", followed closely by, "Go fuck yourself".

I was not proud of any of this, but I was so completely drained that I was only capable of a singular emotion: Anger. There was no room for love, compassion, and certainly not happiness. Anger was all I had left, and it fuelled me all the way to the finish line.

Even the beloved Ironman volunteers could not escape my ire. These people are selfless, arguably faultless angels who make these competitions what they are, and without them there would be no Ironman events whatsoever. Before the race, I loved these people, and afterward I would soon appreciate them all over again, but during the second half of the run, these fuckers seemed to exist solely as targets for my indignation. When I am so comprehensively exhausted, nauseated, sore, and at risk of cramping up and having my legs seize to the point whereby EMT extraction is damn near imminent, don't dare screw up handing me a cup of warm Coke. I am quite aware that Ironman volunteers are not trained mind readers, but how is it possible that they don't know, through a series of clicks, hand gestures, and grunts, precisely what I require? "No, I don't want a stupid vanilla gel. Why would you ask me that?"

I am a fifty-year-old age grouper in no danger of making it to the Olympics or even qualifying for a slot to Kona, but, for some strange reason, during an ice cup exchange at mile 25, I turned into Dave Scott in the Iron War chiding an innocent seventh-grade volunteer, proudly wearing her Junior High School volleyball uniform, for allowing me to drop the cup she is desperate to carefully place in my quivering, sweaty hand. Before setting out on the run,

I was a calm and determined Dr. Jeckyl. Nearing the end of the race, I would scare the shit out of Mr. Hyde. That is if I had the energy to be violent. As it was, I probably could not have blown out the candles on a toddler's birthday cake. My senses were dull, my mind was irrational, and my intellectual capacity had been radically diluted. I was, indeed, NOT smarter than a fifth-grader.

It wasn't supposed to be this way. I began triathlon to deliver me from a dull, monotonous, mundane life that had been devoid of a measurable goal and lacking in a well-defined athletic purpose. It was supposed to act as an enhancement, improving my life with every race. During the run at Lake Placid, however, I was convinced of the contrary. Triathlon was now trying to kill me, one agonizing step at a time. An experience that was supposed to be overflowing with positivity, now had me drowning in a sea of negative (almost criminal) thoughts. I am normally struck by how positive, friendly, and appealing triathletes tend to be, but in this race, they had, in my mind, all become assholes and/or pricks.

And the signs...the stupid, ridiculous signs people held at the side of the course. Believe me when I say this: you could get a team of Saturday Night Live scriptwriters to create them, but with five kilometres left at the end of an Ironman, they are no longer remotely funny. I get that they are conceived as motivational tools meant to lift up dampened spirits, enabling athletes, for a brief moment, to forget the pain, and to help them find tiny, as yet untapped, reservoirs of energy that might make the finish line seem just a little bit closer. When I saw them after my first lap, I admit that I chuckled, impressed by how clever many of them were, but by the end of the second lap, I wanted to burn them all.

"Smile, you paid to do this", "Run like you stole something", "Oh, hell you've come this far, you might as well finish". These signs received a simple "Fuck off", while "What took you so long?", got an unequivocal "Fuck you" in response because I felt it was more personal. The one that read, "I'm sure it sounded like a good idea four months ago", made me think it was written by some prick who probably used to say stuff like, "I know you are but what am I" when he was younger. I hated all of them, except one. This one spoke to me because it sounded the most true, and I felt as though its creator was enjoying this portion of the event as much as I was. "Worst parade ever". You got that right, brother.

This race, these signs, were turning me into something I wasn't at all proud of, and every step led me deeper and deeper into despair, causing me to wonder aloud what I was trying to prove. The primal part of my brain was telling me to stop. I was not being chased by a cheetah, so what the hell was I doing this for? I distinctly recall vowing never, EVER, to do this again. It was far too stupid.

Then, as I wondered just how unstable a person needed to be to do this more than once, and as my knees simultaneously lost their ability to articulate, causing me to run from the hips like an eight-year-old running home from the park after shitting in his jeans, something strange happened. It wasn't a second wind. I didn't suddenly get a boost of energy, nor did the pain go away or even subside. Somehow, I started to get it. I *was* going to finish. For the first time in five or six kilometres, I actually wanted to finish, not so I could hear the dude tell me over the loudspeaker, "YOU ARE AN IRONMAN?". Fuck that. It wasn't so that I could tell others, or say to myself, "I did it". It wasn't to feel some sort of sense of accomplishment. It just built up out of nothing. It was a feeling I could not describe. I finally understood that the race was *designed* to hurt that much, and the pain was entirely appropriate and, well...good. It still hurt. Of course, it still hurt, but I *needed* it to hurt. I didn't need the finish line, the hugs, or the medal draped around my neck, and I certainly didn't need another T-shirt. It wasn't necessary that I remember what came before or what I would do next. In fact, it didn't matter one iota whether I was a changed person or that I might be, somehow, a better version of the person I had been before the race. None of that stuff mattered at all because, with just a couple of kilometres left, there was *right now*. I didn't want anything else.

The Ironman Lake Placid race had managed to do what nothing else had done for me before: it got me to focus on, understand, and ultimately live in, a singular moment. My form was horrible and I was covered in salt, snot, and regurgitated cola, and my gait had all the elegance of a giraffe trying to stay upright on a frozen pond. I had been effectively stripped of any desire to uphold social grace, as I had been beaten down by a force so much greater than myself, but none of that mattered. Every ounce of fatigue, soreness and utter despondency of the day were all necessary because they permitted me to live exclusively in the moment and forced me to understand that I was on my own. No one was going to help me through it, and that was fine. *Now* was all that was left.

Though I had been searching for so long to find something that would help make me feel whole, up until that point, despite a good deal of success in the sport, I was never quite able to find it. Through all the fatigue and intense physical duress that I experienced in Lake Placid, there was contentment. I hadn't been successful in finding peace, but through the sport of triathlon, it somehow found me.

$$\diagdown \quad \bullet \quad \diagup$$

When you get to my age, you find that when you think back on your early youth, it is difficult to recall actual days or periods of time in their proper context. Chronology doesn't always appear to be accurate. What we actually remember are moments that come back to us because they possess inherent, but not necessarily obvious, meaning. Other people may listen to your recollections and find them mundane, perfunctory, and bland, even if they were present to experience them along with you. Sometimes we do not even truly comprehend, initially, why these particular moments find their way into our memory cache, while others, that appear to be more exciting and interesting, need extra work to bring forward. Some have a much more profound significance, even though we cannot always put our finger on why.

The earliest moment I can remember happened when I was about seven years old and, in some ways, is so clear that it could have happened yesterday.

My mother and I were shopping alone, which on its own was quite novel. It was a rare occasion that my brother and sister were not with us. It must have been a day when I had a doctor's appointment, so my siblings must have been at school. We were in the Zeller's department store at our local shopping mall and, for some reason, we passed through the toy section. This was also rare, as my mother hated distractions. Shopping was an in, find what you need, pay, and get out as quickly as possible chore that was tolerated out of necessity. It was not something she did for pleasure.

From the moment we entered the store, I had been holding her hand, but I let it go to get a better look at the Nerf footballs on display. As I bent down to peruse the balls, she said, "Forget it. Let's go".

Perhaps I was so focused on the footballs, with their colourful, two-toned squishiness, or maybe I so wanted to prolong this uncommon bonding session that I subconsciously chose not to hear her, but either way, her words fell on deaf ears. I didn't hear anything she had said, so fixated was I on the balls, picturing what it would be like to toss one of them around in our front yard.

"Which one's your favourite, Mum?", I asked, without averting my gaze from the magnificent display. "Eh, which one do you like the most?", I repeated. "Personally, I like the light blue one", I continued, entirely unconcerned that she hadn't answered yet. "It reminds me of the colour of the sky".

She did not reply, so, from my crouched position, I looked up to see why, but she wasn't there. In no real panic, and assuming that she had merely moved to the other side of the display, I slowly made my way there, still keeping my eyes focused squarely on those Nerfs.

"Mom?", I called out. Nothing. No reply.

Now, with a tiny hint of gently mounting concern in my tone (just enough to finally take my immediate attention away from the footballs), I called out again, "Mom...Mummy? Where *are* you?".

Still nothing. It was now officially panic time. Not being the most emotionally tough person, it didn't take long for the tears to begin streaming down my cheeks, as the realization that I was most definitely lost, hit me. Though I had been inside the store many times before, I had never had any real reason to pay close attention to the floorplan, having always relied on my mother's tight grip to guide me. Now, however, I was lost. Proper Gilligan's Island lost.

As I began to wallow more and more deeply in my own pity, wandering through the aisles of the toy section, I was noticed by a strange woman. She looked at me quickly, began to go back to mind her own business, did a double-take, and started walking quickly towards me. I guess she knew I was lost because she never asked me why I was alone. In fact, she didn't say a word, but grabbed me aggressively by the wrist, and began to drag me off. Even though I was around seven years old, I knew enough to conclude that this was not normal adult behaviour. She was not wearing a Zeller's uniform, so I deduced that she was not an employee and, therefore, had no 'official' business grabbing me.

I had no idea where she was trying to lead me, but assumed it was to some 'lost child' department at the back of the store, which, somehow, I knew wasn't good. What I needed was to try to stay out in the open where I was sure my mother would be, somewhere. But this woman's grip was so tight and she seemed so intent on dragging me all over the store.

After what felt like a very long time but was probably closer to ten minutes, I began to actively struggle in a futile attempt to free my arm from her G.I. Joe Kung Fu grip. It was no use. She was considerably stronger than me, and my wrist had about the same girth as a garden rake. I started pounding on her forearm, just above the hand that was fused around mine, and by then I was crying loudly, on the verge of becoming hysterical. As I attempted to chop myself free, I kept looking around, desperate for someone to notice that I was being harmed, but the other customers assumed the woman was my mother and that she was merely applying some obviously long overdue discipline. Back then, striking your children wasn't the attention-getter it is today. It ranked at about the same level as smoking with kids in the car with the windows rolled up: Frowned upon now, but normal for the 1970s.

Just as I thought I would need to give up, I noticed, at the far end of the aisle, my mother walking with some serious pace and determination towards us. She reminded me of a cartoon bull getting ready to pounce on a 70 kilogram, quivering matador. Once she got next to us, she put her hand around the woman's wrist and squeezed it. With her free hand, she pointed right in the stranger's face and whispered through clenched teeth, "Let go of my fucking son!".

And that was that. She hadn't even been looking for me because she didn't know that I was lost. She was caught up in whatever she was doing, as was I. We both assumed the other was nearby. Had I not been making a scene, who knows what would have happened. The fact is, she simply stumbled upon her son potentially being abducted. The scene found her, not the other way around and I was delivered from a traumatic experience by the person I loved most in the world.

I guess the point is that if you look too hard for something, it will elude you. But allow things to happen organically and the right thing will come along.

IT'S AT LEAST A LITTLE BIT
ABOUT THE BIKE

*"THE IRRATIONALITY OF A THING IS NO ARGUMENT
AGAINST ITS EXISTENCE, RATHER
A CONDITION OF IT".*
—NIETZSCHE

I must have been about eleven years old when I realized, for real, that life wasn't a hundred percent fair. Maybe it wasn't even fifty percent fair. In fact, on a fairness scale, life gets a pretty shitty grade.

Of course, we learned in school of children all over the Third World (a term I didn't totally get...You mean there's more than one?), who were about my age who didn't have anything to eat. They also had inadequate clothing and shelter, and they never had the opportunity to play Pac Man or Space Invaders. There was no MTV, or any TV, where they were from, and none of this was their fault. These children hadn't forgotten to mow the lawn or make their beds, and it probably wasn't because they threw a snow shovel at their older sister, striking her in the face, just above the nose because she called them a four-eyed loser (I guess that was just me). They simply had the misfortune to have been born someplace where these luxuries did not exist. And, they hadn't asked to be born there either. My mother, in fact, often used their misfortune against my siblings and me all the time by saying stuff like, "Eat your liver and onions. There are poor kids in China who can't afford food like that".

"Lucky them", I used to think. In fact, if I'm honest, I envied those poor Chinese kids. Here I was eating a plate of the most putrid food, made only marginally edible with 750 milligrams of ketchup per mouthful, and the only Chinese food I had ever eaten came from a place in town called Ho Lee Chow and was like taking a bite out of paradise. It was the most delicious thing I had ever eaten and I was sure that it must be what unicorn tastes like.

Chinese food notwithstanding, the notion was that there were people out there who were significantly less fortunate than we were. Our problems were First World. That said, none of it mattered that much to me at the time because I didn't know anyone in China, or Pakistan, or Biafra, and thus, their stories weren't close enough to be relevant. No, it took a painfully personal experience for me to come to my own conclusions as to the lack of fairness in life, and what brought it home was a shiny new bike that arrived, as though from the heavens, on my eleventh birthday. Now, I know you're thinking, "That doesn't seem so bad at all". Allow me to explain.

My birthday is in mid-March, just at the end of what, in Southern Quebec, is usually an extremely bad winter. From early January that year, I had been leaving hints and dropping cut-outs from the advertisements in the newspaper as to what I wanted for my birthday. When it came to schoolwork and homework, I had never had a whole lot of drive. My academic curiosity wasn't great enough to keep me on task outside the bare minimum of what was required, but when it came to the object of my birthday desire, no amount of extra effort was too much.

In this case, that object was a red, knobby-tired, motorcycle-shaped bike with a faux gas tank and a number plate with a giant 3 on the handlebars. It was also equipped with brakes on the grips, as opposed to the crappy 'kick the pedals backwards' kind I was used to with every other bike I had previously owned.

It took three long months of dropping these not so subtle hints before my birthday finally arrived, on a Tuesday, no less, which, unless you are born in the summertime, whereby all days are pretty much the same, is less than ideal. Having your birthday on a Tuesday in March kind of sucks because no one's mom is crazy enough to throw a party on a school-night.

On the day, I woke up as I always did, got dressed and made my way to the living room to prepare the newspapers I would deliver, just like on a regular day. I passed my mom making coffee in the kitchen, and I paused a fraction longer than normal to allow her the opportunity to wish me a happy birthday. I wasn't expecting a big deal to be made at five o'clock in the morning, just a quick well-wishing. She said nothing, however. Not a peep. I didn't even get a "good morning". She just lit a cigarette and sipped her coffee. I shrugged it off and continued to go about my routine.

As I was getting back from completing my route, I came across my dad getting into his car to leave for work. "Hey Dad", I said expecting him to take the bait and get out of the car to tousle my hair and ask me if I felt older. Maybe a wink and a "Happy Birthday, kiddo".

Instead, all I got was a "Yup" as he shut the door and backed out of the driveway, not even looking behind at me to wave goodbye. I was momentarily stunned, thinking that my own parents had forgotten my birthday, and I wondered what kind of people do that until I figured out what I surmised must be going on. Obviously, I assumed, they were merely pretending to be nonplussed by this particular Tuesday so that the surprise, planned for later on, would be that much greater.

School was a blur. Focusing on maths and French and whatever else I had that day was an even more arduous task than usual. All I could think about was getting home to see that bike waiting for me. When the bus dropped me back off at home, I knew enough not to expect the gifts to start flowing right away. Of course, I knew I would have to wait, at least until my dad arrived home from the office, which meant there were going to be three painfully long hours to endure. I even remember doing my homework for a change, in an agonizing effort to pass the time, and still no one had yet wished me a happy birthday. I understood that my older sister and younger brother wouldn't have said anything because, unless it's your own birthday, or Halloween, or Christmas, dates meant very little to us. I did find it a little odd, though, that my Mom hadn't said anything. She was playing one heck of a good game, so I decided to call her bluff and act like this was just a regular Tuesday night.

When I heard my Dad's car finally pulling into the driveway, I breathed a huge sigh of relief because surely this meant the end of the charade was upon us, and we could commence the festivities.

It was not so, however. Nothing about my father's arrival that evening signalled that it was in any way different from the previous Tuesday. He checked the mail, engaged in idle, perfunctory chit chat with my Mom, took off his shirt, tie, and pants and sat down in his underwear, readying himself to eat supper. At this point, I was starting to get concerned. "Jesus", I thought to myself, "these fuckers have forgotten my birthday". I was getting emotional and tears were not far off, but I did everything not to show it. The whole middle child syndrome was being played out right before me, and I steadied myself to issue a stern complaint. I was just about to say something when my mother interjected and announced that we would be eating in the dining room.

Now we were getting somewhere because the dining room was reserved for special occasions, and today, most certainly, qualified. The planets were finally starting to align themselves properly as we all sat at the table while my mom brought in my favourite dish: lasagna with garlic bread. This was a birthday supper if I'd ever seen one. It was delicious and everyone seemed to enjoy it with gusto. We were happy and chatting about our days, laughing and having a good old time, but no one had, as yet, wished me a happy birthday.

Just then, my mom got up to go back into the kitchen and returned with a birthday cake that had eleven candles blazing away on the top. My dad turned off the lights and they all sang "Happy Birthday to Brock". All the anxiety I had been feeling most of the day finally melted away by the warmth of the love of my family. Now, feeling loved, I was truly happy. I made my wish and blew out the candles so thoroughly there was no way it wouldn't come true. That bike was as good as mine.

Unfortunately, there were no large packages anywhere. In fact, I saw no gifts at all, but I had confidence in my parents. They had pulled off quite a good show so far by not letting on, for the entire day, that they knew it was my birthday. I trusted them to deliver at the right moment and I wondered how they were going to present the bike to me. What tricks were up their sleeves? Secretly, I hoped they hadn't simply placed a photograph of the bike, cut out from the catalogue, inside a birthday card, promising that it would come when the weather was better. That had the potential to become a disaster. I mean tons of things could go wrong between now and then. I could do something stupid, or they could just forget. No, it had to be the real thing.

As I thought about where they might have hidden the bike, my mother saved the day by stating that she had forgotten the ice cream, and asked if I would go and retrieve it. That had to be a ruse. You see, at our house, we kept all the large frozen foods in the chest freezer which was downstairs in the garage. The only ice cream we ever had was the giant, plastic bucket of Neopolitan, three flavoured, bargain stuff that stayed in deep freeze for months without being touched, once the chocolate strip was done, that is, and that bucket was in the garage, which was the perfect hiding place for a brand new bike.

Why, you might ask, would my mother ask the birthday boy to fetch the ice cream? It's my special day, after all, shouldn't I be allowed to relax and have someone else take care of such tedious minutiae? Because, I assumed, that was where the bike was, and she wanted me to discover it by 'chance', thus making it seem like so much more of a surprise. At least that was what I hoped was the case. Truth be told, I hate ice cream with cake. I find it makes it all soggy and gross, but, of course, the ice cream was merely the delivery system for the bike.

The way our house was put together, the kitchen was on the ground level. There were three bedrooms upstairs on the top floor with a small communal bathroom. Down a flight from the kitchen was where my bedroom was, along with the garage, the door to which was just to the left of the bottom of the staircase. It was this flight of stairs that I took on my journey to the ice cream and the object of my desire (hopefully). The door to the garage opened to the left. To the right was a vast open section where, in a normal house, the car would be. In our case, it was too full of sporting equipment, unused lawn care machinery, defunct and discarded kitchen appliances, various carcinogenic chemicals, chlorine for the pool, and a whole array of other clutter. To the left was a rarely-used workbench next to the freezer.

When I got to the bottom of the stairs and readied myself to enter the garage, I carefully planned out how I would go about it. I was sure that once inside, to my right would be the big surprise doubling as the ticket to a world of freedom and impending bliss. I decided that I would avoid even looking that way until the business of fetching the ice cream was complete, and only then would I take a measured peek at the other side of the space. It was my clear intention to prolong, and hence savour, the joy I was hoping was waiting for me there.

I opened the door, fighting the burning desire to go right, and veered to my left. I then dutifully opened the freezer and found the bucket of ice cream right away, closed it again, and turned to face the right side of the garage, eyes closed. Then, I slowly counted to ten before gently opening my eyes.

I had dreamt of what this moment would feel like for months, and I had never wanted anything so badly. This was a new bike, something I had never had before. Previously, I needed to rely on my limited ingenuity to build Frankenbikes from spare parts pulled out of the trash of people in the neighbourhood. It wasn't unheard of to ride something that wasn't even entirely a bike. I had used wheelbarrow parts and lawn mower parts, motorcycle bits, and a shitload of duct tape. I had even made bikes produced largely from discarded pieces of wood. What was about to happen would mean an end to all of that. A new bike might actually be more than I could emotionally handle, but I was hoping to get the chance to give it a go.

As I slowly opened my eyes, the entire world paused momentarily as time simply stopped ticking and was in a movielike standstill. There, in the absolute dead centre of the garage, right above the grid covering the sump pump, was my brand new, number three, cherry-red, motorcycle-replica bike. It stood there like a piece of magnificent installation art that glowed under what appeared like the golden light of the sun shining only on that one article.

At that moment, my family came roaring down the stairs, falling over one another as they exploded into the room, in a panic. They assumed some horrible accident had befallen me in my attempt to retrieve the ice cream. I heard none of it as I was in a state of absolute contentment. Apparently I had shrieked as though I had been attacked, and they found me on my knees, prostrate to the utter beauty of what stood before me. I regained my composure and instantly leaped up off the ground to straddle the bike, pretending to ride it at top speed. Attached to the right handlebar grip was a device that turned in my palm and made loud, engine revving noises as I pulled it towards me, and I was just cranking it. Beyond happy, I felt like Evil Knievel. This was Nirvana as I was in absolute harmony with the entire universe, and nothing seemed capable of diminishing the pleasure that coursed through my veins. It was as though I had been submerged in an incredibly comfortable warm gel that suspended me so perfectly that no movement was required to be in sheer comfort. I was back in the womb, no doubt experiencing the perfect state of being.

That is until I wasn't. In my reverie, I could just make out the fact that my father was gesturing with his arms while performing a sweeping motion in the distance, and I could tell that he must be saying something, and saying it quite loudly. The sounds, however, were muffled as though I was hearing him from underwater. Like I was coming to the surface of a deep pool, his voice became clearer and I could tell that he was upset about something. After a few moments, I was snapped out of my trance to hear my father shouting, with severe consternation, "GET OFF OF THAT BIKE!". He said it so loudly and angrily, and slightly in a state of panic, that I figured he assumed that all my jumping around would break the stand holding the bike upright. I guessed he thought I would harm it somehow before I ever had the opportunity to ride it outside.

"Don't worry", I assured him, "I'll be careful. I won't break anything. I'm so happy. Thank you. It's exactly the one I wanted". I was actually gushing.

But he wasn't done. "I SAID GET OFF THE BIKE RIGHT NOW", he continued, his anger getting hotter. "IT BELONGS TO YOUR BROTHER".

I could not believe what he was saying and was absolutely certain that he had to have been joking, so I started to chuckle, playing along with him. Unfortunately, his attitude did not change at all, and he repeated the last bit to make sure I heard and understood him clearly, "It's for your brother", he said more calmly. "You don't need a bike. You built one last summer", he added, completely regaining his composure.

I was crestfallen and hurt beyond belief. The injustice was dripping from his tongue and hung from the ceiling like a sleeping bat. Just as I was preparing myself for a good cry, he continued: "Your gift is over there", and he pointed to the area I hadn't even noticed, just behind the bike. "It will come in very handy, I think".

I descended from the bike to see what they had purchased for me. There was a box with a ribbon around it and a tag that read simply, 'Brock'. There was no 'Happy Birthday', or 'For Our Son on his Birthday', or any of that kind of stuff. It was just a box inside of which sat my birthday gifts: a bicycle pump and tire repair kit.

Well Happy Fucking Birthday to me.

For the first time in my life I learned that things would not always be fair and, more importantly, that stuff rarely turns out the way we expect them to. This lesson could be applied to almost all areas of my life since, but in particular, to triathlon.

BILL AND LANCE

"A JOURNEY OF A THOUSAND MILES BEGINS
WITH A SINGLE STEP".
—LAO TZU

The path I took to finding triathlon was not as direct as it was for most people, at least that's what I suspect. Where I came from, triathlon was not one of the 'go-to' sports, like hockey or football. We did not think about it much, if at all, frankly, because it basically didn't even exist, and very few people had ever heard of it.

I grew up in the province of Quebec, on the South Shore of Montreal, which means that when I was a young boy (until I was about 20 years old, I'm a little embarrassed to say), I wanted to be Guy Lafleur. I did not want to be 'like' Guy Lafleur, I wanted to actually be him. Dave Scott? Who is that? Mark Allen, Scott Tinley, never heard of them, but ask me the entire roster of the 1975 Montreal Canadiens...no problem. Mike Pigg? Never heard of him either. Must have played for the Leafs.

By the time I reached high school, I had at least heard of the Ironman in Hawaii, and the one in Lake Placid would come on TV every year on Wide World of Sports, but the sport itself was still of no consequence to my athletic life.

I guess the first real spark of interest in triathlon came to me at the age of thirty-six while I was driving to Boston from Montreal for the 2004 Boston Marathon. Having done the drive before, I knew I would be in for about five and a half hours of being fed up with NPR and the one U2 'Unforgettable Fire' CD I had in the glove compartment. Based on what I could remember from previous trips, I knew that I could expect to be spending most of my time shouting profanities at the windshield, just to keep from falling asleep. This time, however, I had been smart and made a stop at the Westmount Library to find a book on CD that I hoped would keep me company. After combing the stacks for the better part of a half-hour, I decided upon Bill Bryson's A Walk In The Woods because I figured a good tale about adventure in the natural world was what this long ride needed. It was a bonus that I had some familiarity with certain sections of the Appalachian Trail, about which the book was written, and Bryson has a way of making me laugh, which was something I was looking forward to assuaging me along I-90.

After about an hour listening to local radio, I decided to give Bill his turn. I was so looking forward to it, and I made sure that the tank was full and the coffee was topped up. I didn't know a ton about him, but one line from his book The Lost Continent, always stuck in my mind: "I come from Des Moines", he wrote, "Someone had to". Brilliant. That resonated with me because I grew up in a place few people have ever heard of as well. I reached over to the passenger seat, pulled the CD out of its case and slid it gently into the player, turned the volume up slightly, sunk into my seat, and prepared myself to hear the soothing voice of the author introducing us to his travails along the AT.

The story began: "I want to die at a hundred years old with an American flag on my back and the star of Texas on my helmet, after screaming down an alpine descent on a bicycle at 75 miles per hour".

When I heard those words, the first thing I thought was, "Well that doesn't sound much like Bill Bryson". Actually, that's not entirely accurate; the first thing I thought was more like, "What the fuck is this bullshit?", then the Bryson bit came to me. Same difference. The point is, this car ride was no longer going to be about a funny, overweight, middle-aged dude's journey along the Appalachian Trail, accompanied by an even more out of shape, emotionally troubled, alcoholic, long lost friend. It was about to turn into a cyclist's journey from testicular cancer to winning bike races.

I realized that someone had messed up and placed the wrong CD in the Bryson box. What I did not realize, at that moment, was that someone's tiny, insignificant mistake could piss me off so much. I was expecting something else and my mind would not let me forget that, at least not at first. Have you ever ordered a root beer at McDonald's but they put Coke in it instead? The two beverages look exactly the same, and when you take a sip, you're totally baffled for a moment or two. Your anger subsides, though, because Coke tastes just as good. As I continued to listen, it didn't take very long for me to forget about the Bryson book entirely, and I definitely didn't know at the time that this tiny mistake would change my life. Now, before you put this book down so you can run to the bathroom and throw up, let me explain.

Lance's story did not change my life the same way it did for millions of other people who read it. Thankfully, I do not have cancer. I was not even able, at that time in my life, to relate to the cancer part of the book at all because no one close to me had contracted or died from the disease as of yet. What I did find interesting, despite the title of the book, was that the few bits and pieces that actually spoke about the bike, were fascinating to me.

When I returned from Boston, I started reading everything I could get my hands on about the sport of cycling, and I never fathomed it could be so interesting. I bought magazines, read articles, pamphlets, and any book that remotely had cycling as one of its subjects. I even rented videos and watched cycling-themed movies over and over and over. 'Quicksilver', 'A Sunday in Hell', 'Breaking Away', and my personal favourite, 'American Flyers'. I loved them all. Though I still ran every day, I was turning into quite a velophile, reading all the Tour de France previews, reviews, as well as every other race report I could find, including the really expensive European ones you can't get just anywhere. I even ripped the knobby tires off of my Gary Fisher Tequila, replacing them with slicks and switched out the mountain bike handlebars for drops.

I had become cycling obsessed, and I began to dream of being in a bike race. Now I needed to find a way to make that happen but

I knew nothing about the amateur bike racing scene consisting of Tuesday night crits, Fondos, and sportives. These were not things that made it into the local newspaper and, as far as I knew, simply didn't exist. It was always my assumption that bike racing was for professionals and young people on their way to becoming pros. I was almost forty years old at the time; surely there were no races, I assumed, for people that age, even though, when I thought about it, there was no good reason why there wouldn't be. There were tons of running events that I competed in all the time. Every city in North America has 'old timer' hockey, basketball, and softball leagues. For some reason, it never occurred to me to make much of a search. The only type of bike racing for all ages that I had ever heard of was the middle bit of a *triathlon*.

So that was it. In order to race my bike, I was going to have to become a triathlete, and I began to research just how to make that happen. Once the decision was made, I took to investigating that elusive little sport the way I had with cycling. It was a little harder, however, due to the paucity of resources compared to bike racing. There were very few books about the sport and absolutely zero major movies on the subject. I knew there was so much I would have to learn, but after all, it came down to three basic things that everyone knows how to do: swim, bike, and run. How hard could it be?

- RUN -

Running is something I have always done, though not always competitively. As kids, we ran everywhere and all the time. We ran to baseball practice. We ran when we played hide and seek. I even used to run when I delivered the newspaper in the morning. My first running *race*, however, was part of a duathlon that included a mountain biking section and took place in Victoria, British Columbia. It was a pretty good day, as I recall, and I managed to get away and stay ahead of all the guys in my category. That's right, I beat *both* of them to win my age group and stand on the podium. I was twenty-two, my head swole up and barely fit through the door of the Coquitlam Centre shopping mall, where I came crashing back down to reality, and picked up my trusty paint scraper to chisel dried-up gum off the floor. I wasn't turning pro any time soon, so my job as 'four to midnight' janitor would have to cover my cost of living a little longer while I took two months off from running. In fact, I didn't even look at my sneakers for that period.

Unfortunately, this became my training routine for the next ten or fifteen years: I would run/train like crazy for a couple of months, then let something trivial like a holiday weekend or a sale at Costco get in the way for two or three days. Afterwards, with my routine all out of whack, I would make excuses to stretch those few days into two or three months. I repeated that set, with horrible eating habits thrown in for good measure, over and over, without notable success, for over a decade. Suffice to say, this was not ideal.

One failed marriage, three university degrees, several moves from Quebec to British Columbia to Nova Scotia to British Columbia to Quebec later, and I was ready to enter my next race. Lucky for me, it came right at the end of one of my three-month 'on' periods.

A couple of teachers at the school where I worked, noticing that I ran before preparing to teach high schoolers the importance of physical education each day, asked if I would join them in a really cool relay race on Cape Breton Island in Nova Scotia. It sounded like a great idea, so right after work one Friday afternoon, eight adults with luggage and enough food to last a month, jammed themselves inside a white van that comfortably seated seven (with no luggage), and set off on a fifteen-hour drive from Ste-Anne-de-Bellevue, Quebec to Baddeck, Nova Scotia, and checked into a budget (read shit-hole) motel (notice the 'm'). There, we threw our bags on beds we would never sleep in and went for a 'shake-out' run (whatever that was, I had no clue). With the practice run completed, we did the only logical thing to do the night before a big running race in Nova Scotia: we began drinking until there was just enough time to find our way back to the motel, grab our bags and head over to the start line.

Generally speaking, the race format was pretty straightforward, but required the runners, and their teams, to be logistically well organized. Firstly, it was a relay race, which means there were individual stages run, for the most part, by different runners at a time from each team. There were a couple of crazy people who had no team and simply ran the entire race themselves. The event was called the Cabot Trail Relay Race and consisted of seventeen stages ranging from eight to twenty-one kilometres in length, for a total of 276.3 kilometres. Each stage had a starting line, so it wasn't a true relay with a baton or anything. My team had me do stage four, a twenty kilometre run up Smokey Mountain, which I finished in third place. I was very happy, not because I felt it was such a great accomplishment on its own, but because both guys who beat me had run the Boston Marathon before, which I understood was a huge deal and something reserved for accomplished runners. I mean it was on TV and everything. My team was happy with my performance and rewarded me by having me do the final leg as well, which was an eighteen-kilometre flat stage. I finished fourth.

Once that event was over, I decided to set my sights on trying to qualify for Boston, and began training in earnest, which meant I ran every day. There was nothing scientific about my regimen, as I simply ran as hard as I could every single day at the same pace and on the same three or four routes. I never once did an interval session or tempo run. In fact, if you had told me I should have at the time, I wouldn't have had the foggiest clue what you were talking about. As far as I could tell, the Boston Marathon was a running race, so I ran. My formula only allowed for the weather to dictate the pace and duration of each run. Nice out? Long and hard. Shitty? Long and hard. Snow? Long and hard, but slow. I ran exclusively off-road because I found it took longer to get bored, and if I felt really good, I would go farther.

Cabot Trail was at the end of May, and by October I felt ready to attempt my first marathon. It was my brother, Chris, who actually got me to sign up so he would have someone to run with (and share the driving and accommodation costs), and the race we chose was called Le Marathon des Deux Rives which finished in front of the famous Château Frontenac in Quebec City. Neither of us had any real expectations since it was a first for both of us, and we made a pact to stay together. I told him that if he felt I was going too slow, he should feel free to leave me behind because he had been training for about a year for this, and it was he who had run cross country in high school.

We took off at a steady pace in a giant pack, but I soon felt claustrophobic with so many people around, and the pace was way slower than I was used to, which I figured was probably because the race was at least three times the length of any of my training runs. I asked my brother if he would be against picking up the pace a little. He cautioned me that forty-two kilometres is a long way, but seemed open to the idea. After all, we could always just slow down again.

We took off and I instantly started passing dozens of runners on the right side of the road while my brother went left. It took about a kilometre to get by the whole bunch we were with, and I lost sight of Chris. I assumed he must have picked it up more than I had, and was gone. Instead of feeling angry about having been abandoned, I was actually kind of relieved because now I could go at my own pace without trying to keep up with him.

From that point, the kilometres just flew by and I was enjoying every step. I was having fun passing way more people than had gone by me, until eventually, though I could see people ahead, nobody came by anymore. I was actually starting to think that running was easy, and I couldn't understand why most people hated it so much. What was this mythical 'wall' I heard so many runners talk about? As far as I was concerned, it seemed to be a whole lot of bullshit because this was a piece of cake.

Then we crossed a bridge over the St. Lawrence Seaway and I noticed for the first time that it was windy. Up until that point the breeze had been at my back, so I just assumed I was fast. Now, however, I came to the scary realization that headwinds really suck. Just as I decided that it would be necessary to pitch my body a little forward to make myself a little more aerodynamic, I noticed the thirty-kilometre marker at the side of the road. There was an aid station there, so I took a cup of water (one of the few I had taken all day) and tried to drink it on the run, but damn near drowned myself. Not wanting to need a lifeguard on dry land, I opted to walk while I sipped clumsily from the cup. I knew I was tired, but it wasn't until I began to walk that my body reacted the same way as would that of a heroin addict injecting a whole syringe full of the stuff. Son of a bitch, it felt so good to just walk.

As soon as I threw the empty cup in the general direction of a trash bin and attempted to begin running again, I got my first ever visit from the man with the hammer who, apparently, was intent on beating the shit out of me with it. That's right, I hit the wall, and I hit it hard.

Now I knew what they meant. Previously, I had thought that hitting the wall was nothing more than being really tired, exhausted, even. No big deal. Suck it up, everyone gets *tired*. I've been *tired*. Now I knew that it meant so much more than that. There was simply nothing left in me to give, and though I really wanted to go faster, my body just couldn't. The final eight kilometres weren't much more than an intermittent walk, jog, cramp, wince, and walk again. It was awful and it seemed that the end kept getting further and further away with every agonizing step.

When I finally crossed the finish line, I looked down at my watch which read 2:56: something. "Okay", I wondered, "based on how shitty I feel right now and how much I just walked, that's probably not good". I had no idea what a good marathon time was, and I felt really bad because I was sure that Chris must have been waiting for me to finish for a long time. My next thought was "if I don't find a porta-potty in the next sixty seconds I'm gonna shit myself". My brother was going to have to wait a little longer.

Turns out I qualified for Boston and had to wait another hour for Chris to finish. It seems he had an even worse day than I had.

I ended up running Boston the following year in just under three hours and continued to run it for another five years, until it was no longer a novelty and I started to want something else. That something else came in the form of ultramarathons, which I dabbled in for a few years, having about the same level of success I had found with the marathon distance. By the time I had decided to give triathlon a go, I had raced in marathons and ultras from Maine to Seattle and from Atlantic Canada to the Rocky Mountains.

- Bike -

As far as cycling goes, other than merely as a means of transportation, there was very little out there when I was growing up. None of my friends actually owned a real road bike, or at least not on purpose. If someone happened to have access to a racing bike, it was likely to be at least fifteen or twenty years old and brought over from the 'old country' by a great uncle. It could have been a Mercier with a Campagnolo groupset or a Peugeot with a real fancy checkerboard paint job, but it wouldn't have mattered, because it would still end up being modified by one of us, and covered in spray paint for sure.

There weren't any mountain bikes either. Or BMX bikes. As I recall, bicycles did not have categories back then. They were just bikes. Because we were bored stiff and from a small town, bicycles were nothing more than a collection of parts that were traded like baseball cards, and it was not uncommon for an old, plastic, glittery green banana seat to find itself under the ass end of no fewer than four or five different kids, on four or five completely different bikes, in the space of one summer. It would not have been considered highly out of the ordinary for one of us to show up for an orchard ride on a bike consisting of a 57cm road frame, a regular-sized mountain bike rear wheel with whitewall tires, a banana seat with a high metal seat back, and a go-kart steering-wheel for handlebars. It was equally normal for the front wheel to have been stolen from a defunct baby carriage.

We were not part of youth developmental teams racing in organized criteriums around coned-off sections of city streets, but we did race each other all the time. As a matter of fact, we were always racing. It didn't matter where we were headed, or if we were headed anywhere at all, we always raced to get there (wherever 'there' was). The races themselves weren't really all that different from what I have come to love about professional cycling: there were tactics, alliances, hills, sprints, winners, losers, and the best part was that somebody always lost some skin. I remember one incident in particular that pretty much sums up what a typical ride was like back then for me and my friends.

I am from a town of about 3000 people called Otterburn Park that wasn't quite rural nor was it exactly what you would call suburban. I guess you could call it a sub-suburban, semi-rural, villagey, bucolic type of place. The people in town were working class, which is to say that everyone's dad (and a few moms) had a job. There was no old money and no one was *rich*, but nobody was considered poor either. Other than a couple of farmers who ran the local apple orchards, and the merchants and professionals who owned the various small businesses required to make the town function, most people worked in jobs thirty or so kilometres away, in Montreal.

Otterburn was built at the foot of a mountain of modest elevation, called Mont St. Hilaire, and there were two main sections in town: the Park and the Heights. The Heights, obviously, were at a higher elevation and were newer in architecture than the Park. Though there wasn't much difference in the level of affluence between the residents of the Heights and the Park, it was generally accepted that the Heights were somehow 'nicer'. I lived in the Heights while most of my friends were from down in the Park. Those of us from the Heights knew how and where to obtain bike parts while those from the Park were experts at assembling them. The relationship was symbiotic, for sure.

Of the friends I had in the Park, the Marler brothers were the best at building bicycles as well as the most fearless riding them, usually at speed.

Being at the foot of a mountain, the town was full of wonderfully sloping hills of varying grades which were always a blast, so long as you were going down, that is. Of all the hills on offer, the absolute best for descending was Mountainview because it wasn't just a straight shot down like many of the others. Don't get me wrong, these could be pretty fun as well, but they were more like a ski jump: super fast but not requiring a whole lot of skill or tactics to negotiate, just balls. These were built solely for speed, but the thrill was over so quickly, it was hardly worth the effort it took to ride up in the first place.

Mountainview, though, was a thrill seeker's treat. It was like descending a world cup downhill ski run, but on wheels. There were twists and turns, steeper sections, flatter bits, blind bends, potholes, smooth parts, and sections covered in washout gravel. This was a hill you could sink your teeth into, literally — I've seen it happen. It was as though the people who did the original planning for the town wanted a steep road that was made specifically for racing bikes, and merely having an expensive, fancy one did not guarantee success on Mountainview. It was a good thing too, because none of us had one. On this hill, you couldn't just bomb down willy-nilly without thinking. There needed to be a strategy, and a game plan to execute it, because it required skill, and you had to be ready to react to whatever might be going on around you. Mountainview would expose your weaknesses in a hurry and spit you out the back, right on your ass.

On the day in question, there were four of us: me, my best friend Puke (or P.J. to most people and Patrick to his parents), and the Marler brothers, Kennie and Kevin. Puke and I each had our own bikes. Mine was a burgundy 'girls' bike frame with BMX wheels and regular drop handlebars. Puke was riding a red 'Road King' frame with the original black and white banana seat and Easy Rider handlebars. The Marlers were riding tandem on a forest green VeloSport ten-speed road bike that Kevin had permanently borrowed from some French kid in the next town (this kind of 'borrowing' happened all the time). The drop bars were turned up to look like ram horns and allowed for a much more upright position. Kevin was piloting the bike itself, while Kennie sat atop the handlebars with feet on either side of the forks.

We were all innocently riding along shooting the breeze until we reached the top of Mountainview street, at which point we readied ourselves for a race. There was no official agreement that this would actually *be* a race, but, as always, it ended up as one nonetheless.

Everything we did was a race or competition, just one with no actual prize other than the knowledge that you had won. Who could get to the stop sign first? Who could chug a bottle of cream soda the fastest without throwing up? Who could hold his head underwater the longest without passing out? Who would be the first to touch a real boob? Who could fit the most jawbreakers in his mouth at once? (actually, that wasn't really a contest because Kennie always won that particular challenge. But if he wasn't there, it was a contest). Whatever we were doing, we morphed it into some sort of race. There was rarely any gloating or sore losing. We never argued, or engaged in trash talk. It was simply always, and utterly purely, a race.

As we approached the top of the hill in front of the municipal pool, all conversation ceased while we entered race mode. We did not pause to lay down any ground rules or set up a handicapping system; we just got to the top and took off full gas. Being a tandem, the Marlers were slow off the line, but as soon as their extra weight hit the fall line, they were gone. There was no real hope or expectation that they would be caught, as the two of them basically disappeared down the road. Before Puke and I could gather much forward momentum, we came to the unspoken understanding that first place was spoken for and that we were now a two-man race for second.

We were neck and neck, and moving friggin fast as we approached the first bend in the road, and, just as we were leaning in to take the turn, we heard a howling, primordial scream from down the hill. It wasn't your typical "woohoo" type of catcall. No, this was Bates Motel, knife in the shower type of shrieking, accompanied by the foulest language you could imagine. Puke and I knew, instantly, that the Marlers had surely crashed, and done so violently, and we figured one of them must be dead, or close to it. What was strange, though, was that from where we were, out of sight of the accident, we could only hear one voice doing all the hollering: Kevin's. Kennie was silent, so we assumed he was the one who was dead or unconscious.

The race that had been going on between me and Puke was now over, but we didn't slow down at all. Now, we were travelling at panic speed, which is probably faster than racing speed, and way less controlled. Part of me wanted to get to the bottom of the hill as quickly as possible to assess the damage. Another wanted me to dismount, leave my bike in the ditch, and run home.

When we finally made the last right turn, where the hill flattened out, what we saw was part carnage, part yard sale, part escape from a mental institution, and part Apocalypse Now. Kevin was screaming because he was in so much pain all over, and because, for some reason, he was pissed off at Kennie. With all the yelling, my attention was directed almost exclusively at Kevin. It would have been difficult to notice much else. He was bloodied everywhere: elbows, knees, hands, face...especially the face. His shirt and shorts were torn and he was missing a shoe. But, at least he was upright and walking around, mostly in circles, and just madder than hell.

Kevin, and what was left of his bike, were on the right side of the road, almost in the ditch of the Mc Veigh's front yard. Across the street, some fifteen metres away, lay Kennie in a heap of mangled flesh and bone. His body resembled a fallen, leafless branch. Or several branches, I guess. Several broken branches on their way to the shredder. His arms were everywhere all at once, and his right leg looked like it had an extra joint halfway up his shin that bent in the opposite direction to his knee, like a Flamingo. He was a motionless, silent, mess. We determined then and there that he was fucked.

What had happened was that as they began to hit the final turn, the front wheel started to slip on some loose gravel and Kennie had jammed his right foot into the spokes. This resulted in the bike coming to an abrupt halt, forcing the two boys over the handlebars and into the pavement, without losing any of the kinetic energy that, seconds before, had belonged to the bicycle.

Because he was concussed and unconscious, Kennie lay silent. Kevin, being neither, was far from quiet, and dropped a series of F-Bombs all over the place, seemingly unconcerned that his brother might have, in fact, been killed. He resembled a crazy person, and the more he raged, the more Puke and I noticed something not quite right with his face. Sure, it was covered in blood and gravel, but there was more going on there that just looked wrong. At first, we couldn't figure out what it was, and if Kevin hadn't been so enraged, we may never have figured it out.

Every time he started in on Kennie, calling him a "fuckin stupid fuckin retarded fuck faced dumb motherfuckin fuck head", Puke and I noticed that the 'fff' sound was off. It tended to lilt towards more of a 'ssshhh'. This strange sound caused us to focus our attention on his mouth. We stared at it for a few moments, seeing something sort of odd, but still undefined.

Puke figured it out a nanosecond before I did. Suddenly, it all made sense. In addition to the various burns, lacerations, contusions, and lesions on his face, there stood the answer in plain view.

"His fuckin lip is gone", Puke exclaimed, then turned to face Kevin. "Your fuckin bottom lip isn't there anymore. You only got one lip". Puke was right, Kevin looked like a reverse Bugs Bunny, appearing to have bucked bottom teeth.

It took us about fifteen or twenty minutes, but we eventually found his severed lip. It was on the other side of the road to where the rest of the remains of the accident were. In other words, it was on the Kennie side of the road. Puke found it close to Kennie in the gavel, like a dirty gummy worm. Weird.

Anyway, that was the kind of cycling we did as kids. We didn't have a clue who Greg Lemond or Bernard Hinault were, but it was always an adventure.

- SWIM -

Swimming wasn't a whole lot different from cycling for us, which is to say that, apart from the lessons we took when we were really young, there wasn't anything that I would call 'organized' for us to join. There was no local swim squad to race for or anything like that. The only reasons we had to swim fast were because the water was cold, someone was chasing us, or we were in a hurry.

Most of us were introduced to the world of swimming by way of lessons whereby we would earn some sort of government qualification for having achieved a randomly selected level of proficiency in various swim related tasks, such as treading water and performing surface dives. Really handy stuff, but not exactly solid Summer Olympics preparation. For instance, you earned the Orange badge for Level 1 if, when you were placed in the water, either under your own power or, as was the case for me, were thrown in by one of your parents, you somehow managed to avoid sinking to the bottom and proceed to die. It wasn't exactly necessary that you possess the skill or talent of Mark Spitz to get the orange badge.

Another feature of swimming lessons in Otterburn was that they took place outdoors. There was no indoor pool in our community with safe, clean water that was regulated and maintained at a perfect 80 degrees Fahrenheit. No, we took our lessons outside, about 45 seconds after the ice finished melting off the surface. It wasn't uncommon to hear the geese returning home from Florida during the first lesson in June, and it didn't matter what your skin colour was before entering the pool because by the time the session was over, we were all a shaking, shivering, goose skinned, indigo blue, resembling characters from the movie Avatar.

When I say 'swimming lessons', I'm sure that you, most likely, picture an indoor Aquatic Centre made of beautiful stone with tons of blue-tinted glass and latte-drinking moms and dads sitting in the stands of the multiplex athletic facility. You might even imagine a ten-lane, fifty-metre swimming basin with a diving centre, a fountain, and no less than three slides. Adjacent to the pool are vast rooms with tennis and squash courts, and a weight training area with the title, 'Flex Plex', above the frosted-glass, sliding doors. Oh, and a cafè and smoothie bar. That's what I picture, anyway, because that's basically where I bring *my* son for his lessons...in January. Unfortunately, that is not what we had in Otterburn Park in the 1970s.

First off, we were not made to take swimming lessons because we had a burning desire to learn the elementary backstroke properly. At eight or nine years old, the difference between the various strokes meant nothing to us. What we cared about was how big a splash we could make when jumping in, preferably from somewhere high up. There wasn't a whole lot of, "Hey Mom, check out the catch on my breaststroke. Isn't my propulsion astonishing? And my take out feels spot on". No, we cared about no more than four swim related tasks or accomplishments at that age: 1. How long can I hold my breath underwater? 2. How many people can I drench when I perform a can opener off the high diving board? 3. Can I make it all the way over there and back? (and it doesn't matter where 'there' is. It is a totally arbitrary location unique to any aquatic situation). 4. What is the highest thing I can jump off?

That's it. We didn't give a shit about whip-kick or Cardiopulmonary Resuscitation.

Second, I was not learning how to swim because my parents felt that it was a monumentally important skill-set to acquire. That was nothing more than a lucky ancillary benefit. The primary reason for the lessons was to provide my mother with a comfortable transition from a life of daytime freedom during the school year, to having three kids at home all day, all summer long. My lessons would start right as school was finishing, near the end of June, which gave her an hour or so of downtime before having to say, "Go play outside", fifty or sixty times a day.

I am pretty sure that extreme cold affects the human body in many ways by inhibiting the brain's capacity to acknowledge what is happening in real-time, in an attempt to save the soul from unbearable memories that might possibly haunt us in the future. I say that because I took swimming lessons, and life-saving lessons, for eight to ten years, but, since they took place before eight o'clock in the morning and in water that required only one digit before the degrees Celsius symbol, I can remember no more than a couple of major things about them.

I recall having to be peeled off of the inside of the Frost fence by two lifeguards in my desperate attempt to escape the frigid temperature. To this day, lacking any significant body fat, I am repulsed by the idea of cold water touching my body, and I still can't stand, and can easily be thrown into a fit of rage, when I get splashed. It doesn't matter how warm the water might be, as soon as it makes contact with the air on its journey to my skin, it has cooled down to a temperature far below that of my body and, thus, is still shocking.

The second thing I remember is that there was a shallow trough that all bathers were required to walk through on their way from the locker room to the pool deck area (unless, of course, you didn't want to; you could simply hop over it). It was about five inches deep and was filled with a caustic, antiseptic fluid that was so strong it was the colour of a beer bottle and was about as clear as black coffee. When you placed your foot in the bath, it would completely disappear from sight, and the smell was so strong it would not only clear your nasal passages, but it actually improved your sense of hearing as well. It was a mixture of Vicks Vaporub and a strong gin and tonic.

Most people, fearing their feet might possibly melt off in the chemical bath, would simply step over it and make their way directly to the pool. I *never* skipped an opportunity to gently place both feet in there and lounge for a few glorious seconds in what I considered to be the most luxurious feature of the municipal pool experience.

The foot bath, as it was officially called, was exactly that: a bath. Compared to the pool that awaited me on the other side like an ice fishing pond, it felt warm and thoroughly inviting. Both the pool and the foot bath were 'solar' heated, and it did not take a Ph.D. in thermodynamics to understand that a one by two metre, eight-centimetre deep puddle is much less of a drain on the core temperature of a typical sixty-pound nine-year-old than a 25 X 25 metre, four to fifteen-foot deep block of liquid ice, especially when that heat source, though large, is 150 000 000 kilometres away. I loved that warm little basin of carcinogens.

Other than the lessons, most of the swimming we did as kids revolved around jumping off of stuff or into things we were not supposed to, but that was, when I think about it now, an excellent incubator for my future interest in two-thirds of triathlon. In addition to 'swimming', there was always a running (or more accurately, a running away) component as well. By 'running away' I mean from the police or angry adults, which was an excellent exercise for improving cardiovascular capacity, as well as learning how to cope with stressful situations.

'Pool hopping' was actually a simple summer evening activity performed by bored suburban teenagers unlucky enough not to have pools in their own backyards. The concept was not complex, really: you get three to seven people together, wait until after dark, and late enough for most homeowners to be tucked into their couches watching TV, run around the neighbourhood, and jump into the swimming pools of people you don't know, hoping not to get caught.

That's the theory, anyhow. It sounds like a stupid and shitty thing to do, but we never meant any harm. We were always sober and never engaged in any sort of vandalism at all. In fact, as far as teenage pranks go, it was pretty tame. We tried to be as quiet as possible. If there was a solar blanket on the surface of the water, we never tore or removed it. We would simply push back the area we needed, returning it when we were done. We never stole a towel, the patio furniture remained undisturbed, and while we were on-site, we didn't even whisper. We would discreetly slide into the pool and silently climb back out when we were done, ready to move on to the next house. Even if we knew for sure that the family was not home, we would still never linger too long.

Sometimes, however, despite being as stealth as possible, we would be in the middle of the pool when a light would come on and the homeowner would exit the house with a flashlight and a baseball bat and mention, not exactly in passing, that the police had been notified of our trespassing and that we were not welcome back. It was at this time that we would scatter and take off running, all in different directions because it was way too conspicuous to be a pack of soggy teenagers running down the street if and when the cops drove by.

It took me eight years from the time I drove to Boston to the time I signed up for my first triathlon. Yes, a journey starts with a single step, but most people don't wait eight years to take a second one. I guess, in the end, it really doesn't matter. I took it didn't I?

GIVE IT A TRI

"THE END OF A MELODY IS NOT ITS GOAL; BUT,
NONETHELESS, HAD THE MELODY NOT REACHED ITS
END, IT WOULD NOT HAVE REACHED ITS GOAL".
—NIETZSCHE

Knowing you want to do something and actually getting around to doing it, are two very different things. After thinking about it for so long, I finally signed up for the most convenient, and shortest, triathlon I could find: The Amica 19.7 New London Triathlon. My running had been going as well as ever, I had been biking both indoors and outdoors for several years, and I had bought a wetsuit. I figured that qualified me as ready. I mean, come on, I actually owned a wetsuit.

I was not particularly nervous about the race at all. People kept asking me if I was worried that I'd be able to do it, and frankly, I was a little insulted by the concern. In the past ten years or so, I had competed in no less than fifteen marathons, six of which were in Boston, with only one taking me more than three hours to complete. I had even suffered through several ultramarathons that took more than ten hours of continuous running to finish, and there were two Tacx trainers in my basement that had been demolished from overuse, as well as two cracked steel frame bikes, acting as testaments to the hours upon hours that I had spent cycling. I had even, not three weeks before the race, cycled from my home on the South Shore of Montreal to Lake Placid, New York, whereby I got off my bike, changed clothes, and played 36 holes of golf (albeit not that well). I then stayed up all night with a bunch of coworkers and left at 5:00 AM the next day to ride home again. That's a 400 kilometre round trip mostly through upstate New York.

Sure, I hadn't actually done any lap swimming in sixteen years, but, as I said before, I bought a wetsuit and wore it for eighteen minutes while I was in the store. How much more ready could I be for a little piddly half-mile swim, fifteen-mile bike, and 3.1-mile run? Am I worried? Please. I had already planned my bike route from the race in New London back to where I was staying in Killingworth, Connecticut, fifty kilometres away.

As we drove into the expansive parking lot, I had my first experience with the pre-race triathlon community that I didn't quite understand at the time, and, if I'm honest, still really don't fully comprehend now. There were scores of racers riding their bikes hard, fully kitted up, doing lap after lap of the parking lot and surrounding streets. I wondered what they were doing this for. Were they trying to top off their weekly training mileage before the start? Not knowing any better, or, frankly, anything at all, I put on my entire racing kit, which consisted of a pair of royal blue, cotton/spandex blended cycling shorts, a Hudson High School Physical Education cotton T-shirt, no socks, original Bell cycling helmet (which more resembled something you would don to scale El Capitan than something aerodynamic for cycling), and a pair of black OAKILY sunglasses. That's right, OAKILY. I bought them off a really trustworthy vendor on Canal Street in Manhattan. He had loads of them, right next to a suitcase full of ROLLEX wrist watches.

With that done, I headed for transition in a shocking state of self-consciousness, trying desperately to appear as though I had the faintest idea what I was doing. I had my bike, cycling shoes and helmet with me, and I was wearing the rest: running shoes, cycling/running kit, and number belt (which was also a novelty to me and took twenty minutes to figure out). There were people with bags and buckets and Rubbermaid bins, and I wouldn't have been surprised to see someone show up pushing a Costco shopping cart. What did these people know that I, obviously, had not read about in the race manual? I mean, what did they have in there? I overheard a couple of them discussing what nutrition they were going to use. First of all, I assumed by 'nutrition' they meant food and drink, and, second, I was baffled by the term 'use'. What were they going to 'use' it for? You 'use' a pen, or a hammer, or a remote control. You 'eat' food. At least that's what I do with it. Maybe they planned on rubbing it all over their bodies.

It seemed everyone was spending so much time in transition doing so many important-looking things. If it wasn't for the fact that the race organizers wouldn't let me in because one end of my drop handlebars didn't have a cap on it (I'm still waiting on an explanation of that rule), I would have been done in around forty-three seconds. Why did every second person have their own pump with them? My bike came with tires already filled with air, and they certainly hadn't lost any significant amount walking it from the car to my slot in the corral. They were tweaking wires, testing brakes, changing gears with the rear wheel in the air, and looking at every single component. I could only name five components on my bike, two of which were the wheels, and would have had absolutely no idea how to adjust or repair any one of them. For that matter, I wouldn't even know if any of them were 'off' in the first place. How can you know if something needs fixing if you don't know what it does when it's working fine?

The longer I stood there watching, the more inadequate I felt. I was now beginning to have serious second thoughts regarding my borderline cocky demeanour of the previous day. Sure, I could run an eighty-kilometre race, entirely unsupported, above 10 000 feet of elevation in Montana, terrifyingly named, Devil's Backbone, but the transition zone at a sprint triathlon, that shouldn't take me much more than an hour and a half to complete, had me feeling like I had shown up to a gunfight brandishing a dull, plastic butter knife. Everything seemed so alien to me that I was surprised by just how much it all surprised me, if that makes any sense. I had raced so many times before and participated in a wide array of sporting events, but everything I was experiencing was so new and so vastly different from anything I had seen before or anticipated. For example, I watched the guy next to me who was wearing a full-body professional-looking triathlon-specific kit, covered in company logos, indicating to even the most casual observer (me), that he knew precisely what he was doing, let all the air out of a very full-sounding tire, only to, without the slightest hesitation, attach his yellow Joe Blow floor pump to the valve, and pump it back up again. I was unaware that tire air had a 'best before' date. As I watched in a state of innocent incredulity, I felt the same way I had years ago when a friend of mine and I drove across the Northern United States and witnessed something so totally incongruent with reality.

On that occasion, we had been driving for a couple of days and it was getting late, the sky was pitch black, and we were exhausted. We had left Sault Ste-Marie that morning and tried to stop somewhere in Minnesota, but every motel along the highway was full. We decided, instead, to push on through the night. Around ten o'clock, the heavens opened up, causing us to drive no faster than thirty km/hr due to the exceedingly limited visibility. The rain was so thick and the drops so large, it seemed as though the road surface was moving in all directions. Finally, it got so bad that we were forced to pull over, and when we got out of the car to see what was causing the illusion on the road surface, we were stunned by what we witnessed. It turned out that it was no illusion and that the ground was, indeed, moving. It was alive and covered with thousands of frogs. This was not normal and it scared the shit out of us because there was something ominous that we both vaguely remembered about the signs of the apocalypse (Exodus 8:2). It felt like we were definitely somewhere we did not belong, and someone or something was trying to get us to leave.

Now, in transition, I was having the same feelings.

Once I got that scene behind me, I noticed something else

that also gave me a moment of pause. Many other triathletes, it seemed, were already wearing their wetsuits and were walking towards the beach to do a 'warmup'. I had never been much of a warmup type of guy, always figuring I would need every ounce of energy I possessed just to get through the event, but when in Rome... I guessed it was time to grab my brand new wetsuit, put it on for the second time ever, and go for my first real swim in over a decade, so I skipped back to the car to retrieve it. I was so excited to actually have the opportunity to get it wet for the first time, as it represented one of the final pieces to my triathlon puzzle. I ran, I cycled, now I got to put on a real wetsuit, like everybody else, and smoothly glide through the water. I couldn't wait. I was about to get to feel what it was like to be a real triathlete.

It was a bit of a struggle, but I pulled it on, only up to my waist because that's what everyone else was doing, and walked to the beach with my girlfriend, Anne and my son, Owen. I couldn't help but feel a bit like a gladiator, brimming with personal pride. With my wetsuit on and my bathing cap and goggles dangling from the fingers of one hand, I looked like all the other competitors, and *they* were all real triathletes. I suddenly felt like I belonged to an exclusive clan, making me one of the cool kids at long last. As we approached the water, I felt as though I was headed into battle. Sure, I was older than most first-timers, but *they* didn't know I had never done this before. I mean, how could they? I looked just like them. It was now time to finally become a triathlete; the moment had come to find the "will to strive, to seek, to find, and not to yield". These words of Tennyson were dancing around my brain as I pulled my light blue swim cap on (with the race logo on the side — how cool was that), and affixed my goggles. I was the king leaving the comfort of his castle to go off to battle, and as Anne zipped up the back of my wetsuit, I indeed, felt like a God.

Then, suddenly, I didn't. The second the zipper hit its upward limit at my neck, and the little velcro flap was fastened tightly, all thoughts of heroism died in an instant. I should have tied it all the way up in the shop when I purchased it, because now was not a good time to feel just how constricting it was for the first time. I felt like Houdini in a straight jacket, only he knew how to escape. I was stuck, couldn't breathe, and my skin turned to alabaster as I began to sweat profusely. There was nothing I could say to my girlfriend because I had been talking up this day for years, and my son looked at me with awe. I was his warrior, his hero...and I was fucking dying. Hiding these feelings as best as I could, I kissed them both and headed into the water where I figured everything would feel the way it is supposed to; the way it appeared absolutely everyone else was feeling. It was impossible that any of them could have felt the way I did at that moment, because, if they had, there was no way any of them would have signed up for a second race.

I began walking out into the ocean (Long Island Sound — that's the ocean, right...the water was salty) and every step I took felt less and less natural. The sensations that were hitting my legs were so entirely unfamiliar. Every other time in my life that I had waded into the water, I could actually feel its wetness touching my skin, but this time wasn't like that at all. I could see the water surrounding my legs, but my sensory receptors couldn't feel a thing, kind of like when you've been to the dentist and tried eating again before the Novocaine wears off. My mind was having such a hard time processing the lack of data from one of my senses that didn't match the data it was getting from another. Imagine ordering a Vanilla ice cream cone. The teenager scoops out what looks exactly like every other vanilla scoop you've ever seen. Unbeknownst to you, however, he has scooped up 'two-week-old halibut' flavour instead. When you lick it, your mind will hurt itself trying to comprehend what just happened.

I decided that my body would just have to get used to this new feeling and that it was time to simply dive into the water headfirst. The instant my head and body were submerged, my brain was inundated with so much information, none of which was pleasant, that it very nearly shut my whole body down. First, the water was shockingly cold and it, quite literally, took my breath away, causing me to panic like an eight-year-old getting the wind knocked out of him for the first time. The body requires oxygen to survive, a fact we are born knowing, instinctively. Somehow, we already know how to breathe when we come out of the womb, even though we've never done it before. No oxygen = no life, period. The water temperature also caused my muscular system to seize up. The whole thing cramped AND I couldn't breathe. Not exactly Oreos and milk.

Second, though I was not moving, the water was moving me, which was another very unusual sensation. I had no control at all. I was completely at the mercy of a giant force, easily capable of having its way with me, and yet, due to the rubber, I couldn't actually feel the water touching my body (at least not right away), and it was difficult, due to the suit's buoyancy, to just stand up. The wetsuit was intent on staying on top of the water and was fighting every effort I gave to merely plant my feet on the bottom. Add to all of this the fact that the water all around me, and for as far as I could see, both above and below the surface, was teeming with jellyfish. There were so many of them that you had to find a path through them, just like you would in a forest or a maze.

I tried so hard to gain my composure, but I couldn't, which, on its own, caused me further anxiety. There had never been a time in my life when I could not at least mask my nervousness in order to move forward and get things done. Now, I had absolutely no control over anything, and that terrified me. There was no breathing exercise I could employ to calm me down. How can you perform breathing exercises when you can't breathe? I kept trying to convince myself that this was bullshit and that it was just something novel, so I tried to make myself believe that I could just suck it up and get over it. No one else appeared to be having any trouble at all, so I decided to attempt to swim to the first buoy and back. That, I figured, was all the warming up I would require.

I took about five front crawl strokes with no change in my level of anxiety and switched immediately to breaststroke. I was still screwed, so I turned, headed for shore, flipped over onto my back, and basically let the waves bring me to the beach. When I hit the sand, I crawled up it like Tom Hanks in Castaway. Anne and Owen were standing there waiting for me, looking so proud. They had no idea.

"How'd it go?", Anne asked, expecting me to downplay how excited I was and how cool the wetsuit felt. My mouth said, "It's a little tight. Might be a bit too small", while my brain was secretly sobbing, and screaming, "I'm fucked. There is NO way I can do this. My triathlon career is over before the gun has even gone off. I know I'm a pussy, but I'm okay with that. Just get me the fuck away from the water".

There were still around fifteen or twenty minutes before the anthem would be played, heralding the start of the race. For every other event I have done, this would be my *alone* time: kiss the girlfriend and son, now piss off and leave me to my thoughts. This time, however, I clung to them like I used to do to my mother on vaccination day. I was procrastinating, hoping that if I waited long enough, they'd cancel the race and I wouldn't have to go back into the water. Basically, I was volunteering to shovel the driveway so I could avoid studying for my grade eleven chemistry exam. As the minutes ticked on, I became more and more agitated and started talking gibberish about anything other than the race.

"Did you lock the car?", I asked Anne in desperation, "Maybe I should go check".

"It's locked", Anne replied a little confused. "You want me to zip up your wetsuit?"

"NOT YET!", I snapped back, a little too quickly and loudly not to be awkward. I ran the risk of letting my fear show, so I backed off a bit, "Sorry, no thanks. Not just yet. I might actually leave the top Velcro thingy unattached. It scratches my neck", I lied. "Hey Owen, is that a Rolling Rock bottle cap? You should start a collection. Hold on, I'll go get it for you". Now he too was looking at me like I was an idiot. Neither of them had ever seen me act this way before a race. Mind you, they had never been anywhere near me this close to the start before, so they probably assumed that I must always act this irrationally. Without knowing how to respond, he looked over at Anne and asked if they could go ride the roller coaster. God how I wished I could go with them.

At this point, all the racers were making their way en masse towards the inflatable archway at the starting line, while I stood in place letting them all pass in a last-ditch effort to delay the start of the race, hoping that the extra time would allow me to get over this anxiety. I had been *nervous* hundreds of times, but I have never, as far as I know, experienced clinical anxiety before. I'd been *anxious*, but what I was going through this time was way different. It seemed as though my mind and body were shutting down, one system at a time. I had no idea what was going on, but have since looked up the definition of anxiety to see if, in fact, that is what was happening.

A few of the symptoms are 1. Feeling of overwhelming fear... check. 2. Fear of going crazy or losing control...check. 3. Feeling you are in grave danger...check. 4. Feeling you might pass out...check. 5. A surge of doom and gloom...check. 6. An urgency to escape... definitely check. 7. Dizziness...check. 8. Heart palpitations...check. 9. Shortness of breath, 10. Trembling, 11. Sweating, 12. Chest pressure, 13. Turning pale, 14. Feeling detached from reality, 15. Weak in the knees, 16. Burning skin, 17. Pins and needles, 18. Hot and cold flashes, 19. Numbness and tingling sensations...check, check, check, fucking check. I had every single symptom, plus I couldn't stop peeing, whatever that meant. The closer I got to the rest of the competitors, the worse I felt and the tighter my wetsuit seemed, causing me to inch it open a little every couple of seconds in an attempt to alleviate the pressure inside. Often at events like these, you hear very inspirational people saying stuff like, "follow your heart", or, "trust your gut", or "go with your instincts". Well, my instincts, gut, and heart were screaming at me to take the fucking rubber straight jacket off, sprint to the car, and drive fast and far away.

I know there was music playing, people wishing one another a good race whilst doing a lot of high fiving, but it was all a blur to me. I didn't actually acknowledge any of it. None of that stuff was registering in my frontal lobe. Physically, I was standing around with the others, but mentally, I had checked out. The guy directly behind me put his hand on my shoulder, causing me to jump like a dog being awakened from a deep sleep.

"Yo, Dude. Your suit is open at the back. Want me to zip it up?", he asked.

The very loud, angry voice in my head was shouting, "Yo Dude. If you touch that zipper, I'm gonna rip your fucking arm off and beat you to death with the wet end!". Controlling that voice, I managed to kindly, and in a low, soft voice lie to him: "No thanks. The zipper's broken. I'll be fine. Thanks".

I still had no idea what I was going to do once the horn sounded, and I was desperately searching for a believable excuse to abandon. I had wanted to be a triathlete for so long, but it appeared that it just wasn't in me. It wasn't going to happen. I thought about yanking the shit out of the zipper hoping it would fall off, preventing me from starting. Maybe, I could 'lose' my goggles, or perhaps I could start a fight with somebody. My mind raced, desperately trying to find a way out when I heard a loud horn and the crowd of people in front of me began to melt into the water. The sound snapped me out of the mental fog, and two words made their way from the deepest recesses of my memory to my lips and I whispered them to myself: "Bob Ayotte".

I didn't know why my mind went there. I hadn't thought of him in over twenty-five years; I didn't even know that I still remembered who he was. He had never been in my immediate circle of friends, but I certainly knew who he was.

When he was in grade nine or ten, Bob had found out, just after the Christmas Holidays, that his family was going to be moving to the States, and that he would, obviously, be changing schools. He had always been a bit of a free-spirit, who had absolutely no problem expressing himself. In fact, his lack of verbal filter had landed him in trouble with the school administration from time to time. It was this very feature that made him attractive to many of the rest of us. He was the guy who wasn't afraid to say most of the things we were all thinking so often.

The day his parents told him they would be leaving our little corner of the world behind, Bob decided he wanted to say 'goodbye' to our school in a memorable fashion. Being a time long before the advent of Facebook and Twitter, he knew that once he was gone, it wouldn't take long for him to be forgotten, and he was desperate for the gap between departure to distant memory to become as wide as possible, and, thus, he hatched an extremely bold plan, revealing it to only a select few people.

The cafeteria in our high school was about the size of a typical hockey rink. It was sunken, and at either end there was a staircase of five steps that were approximately ten feet wide. On either side of the staircase was a thick, black, square, iron railing that continued for the entire length of the pathway leading from the cafeteria to the gyms in one direction, and the locker bays to the other. Between the two staircases, there was an aisle that ran the entire length of the cafeteria and separated the seating areas to either side, where hundreds of students ate their lunches.

Bob's bold plan was to wait for the entire school to be comfortably eating in the caf, duck behind the lockers in the South Bay, take off all of his clothes, place a paper bag over his head, with eye holes cut out enabling him to see, and streak the length of the cafeteria. When he made it to the other end he would climb the stairs on the North side, turn left towards the Ross Gymnasium, where he would put on his gym clothes and figure out what to do next. He didn't much care what came next because he knew that the worst that could happen was that he would get suspended. He was moving anyway, and, therefore, didn't give a shit about getting in trouble. We all knew what his plan was, but not when, or even if, he would go through with it, and for quite some time, we ate our lunches wondering if today would be the day. At first, we could feel the anticipation, but, eventually, it died, and we started to believe that it was never going to happen.

Then, a couple of weeks after letting a few of his friends know of the plan, we were tucking into our PB & J sandwiches, talking about math class and hockey practice and whatever we had watched on TV the night before, when we heard the beginnings of a roar. My group of friends always ate at the last table closest to the North end stairway (it was the closest to the gym). The roar started way behind us at the South end, and it grew louder by the second. We turned to each other, nodding knowingly. It was on.

Today was going to be the day. We craned our necks behind us to get a better look, and, sure enough, there was Bob jogging down the aisle, heading towards us and waving at the crowd of diners on both sides. His legs were striding along with the grace of a gently trotting gazelle, his arms waved majestically to his many adoring fans, and his wang was dangling and bouncing off his upper thighs, as though in slow motion. The crowd went wild. We were enjoying the show immensely, secretly wishing we possessed his kind of courage, and it looked as though Bob was enjoying himself at least as much.

Everything was going perfectly to plan except for one tiny, overlooked detail. It seemed the paper bag he had placed over his head wasn't perfectly tailored for the job, so, though he cut holes for his eyes, as he moved his head from side to side to look at the students he was running past, the bag didn't totally move with his head. By the time he reached us at the North end stairway, the bag had changed positions enough that the eye holes were far off to one side, effectively rendering him temporarily blind. Now, it seemed, he had a problem on his hands and he needed to make a very quick decision: should he stop running and fix the bag, or soldier on relying on muscle memory and tiny glimpses to see where the stairs started?

He chose the latter but decided to pick up his speed so that he could leap from the cafeteria floor to the top of the stairs all in one shot. When he reached our table, he was going at a pretty good clip but was veering a little too far left. We tried to bark instructions at him so he could right himself, but he thought we were just cheering him on. He recognized our voices and turned his head to the left to acknowledge us, but the bag stayed right and the turning of his head brought his whole body even further left. When he figured he was close enough to the stairs, he leaped at full speed, trying to make it to the top. Unfortunately, he was way too far from the bottom step at take-off, and too far left. He was airborne for less than a second when GONG!!!! He came to an instant and abrupt halt.

He had crashed into the railing on the left-hand side of the stairs hard...with his scrotum. The room, full of hundreds of excited students, fell instantly, eerily silent. Even Bob made no sound. He was in far too much pain. The only noise that could be heard, came from the reverberations of the thick, metal railing that was still vibrating from the force of the impact, like a 2.5-inch square tuning fork.

Being entirely stunned into silence, we were collectively paralyzed by the sight of what had just occurred, and no one responded initially to his very obvious need for first aid. By the time the lunch monitors awoke from their momentary catatonia, Bob had lifted his wounded, exposed, and badly bruised testicles off the ground and headed for the gym lockers, where he was met by Mr. Crowe, the Principal.

Bob moved away sometime later and will always be remembered as a legend.

Though I was nowhere near the front, neither was I, unfortunately, close enough to the back of the bunch to allow me to bail. In fact, it became terrifyingly evident that I was being given no choice about starting the race at all. The crowd of people swept me up and, literally, pushed me into the water. I was still spazzing out, but as I got waist-deep in the ice-cold, jellyfish infested water, I again thought of Bob and said to myself, "I guess sometimes you just gotta bash your testes against a railing".

I'd like to say that once I dove in and began swimming, a warm calm enveloped my body and I had the zen-like focus of Mr. Miyagi, but that wasn't quite the case. In fact, my anxiety was heightened by the initial proximity of all the other swimmers. I felt so out of control because I could not move to my left or right, as there was always someone, if not a whole school of someones, right there. The panic returned with a vengeance and I, once again, could not breathe. Mercifully, my swimming was so bad that I kept veering right, and as I was being passed by so many people, a gap opened up and I swam headfirst into the first buoy. I was in such a state of hysteria that I grabbed on to that son of a bitch as Gloria Stuart did to that door floating around the North Atlantic in Titanic. The only positive notion running through my head was that, with all the people in the water around me, there had to be somebody who would be able to save me when I started to drown (and it sure felt like it would be only a matter of seconds before that began to occur).

When I saw a gap of at least ten feet between random swimmers, I let go of the buoy and started thrashing again, hoping I would be able to gain some semblance of composure. It never happened, though, and I made a bee-line for the next buoy, which appeared to be four or five kilometres away...minimum. Luckily there was a kayaker keeping the crowd from going too far off-course, about halfway. I grabbed the front of the kayak and told the teenager paddling it that if he said I wasn't allowed to hang on, I would be forced to tip him over and use his drowning body as a step to get in the kayak myself and paddle it to safety. The scariest part of that encounter was that, though he chuckled and said, "that's what I'm here for. You can hang on as long as you like", I was deadly serious. There was no doubt in my mind that I could have beaten him over the head with the paddle and used him as a personal floatation device. "I just can't move you forward at all", he apologized. Useless prick.

I told myself that once my breathing got under control, I would let go and continue with the race. The funny thing was that I was enjoying the best form of my life to that point, so I wasn't panting because I was tired or out of shape. I was hyperventilating due to panic. Finally, I let go and began thrashing my way towards the next buoy, but after no more than ten strokes, I was forced to switch over to breaststroke again, which I also found too difficult. Once again, I made the immediate alteration to a sort of backstroke/float and scull technique.

As I approached the next buoy and reached for it, I couldn't help asking myself what was going on. I *knew* how to swim, in fact, I had always been pretty good at it. I had never been afraid of the water, even open water. We used to jump off the train bridge back home, fully clothed, into the Richelieu River because a train was coming...for kicks. I could remember sneaking into the Ste-Dominique quarry with my friends to jump off of the cliffs fifty or sixty feet up, always forgetting to lock my legs at the ankles to avoid having my nuts slap against my buttocks. We swam all the time. Why, now, was I so damned terrified? It just didn't make any sense. Unfortunately, these thoughts did nothing to allay the terror I was presently feeling.

I maintained the pattern of stopping at every buoy and every kayak for pretty much the entire time in the water. The rest was basically spent on my back wondering why I had forgotten how to swim, and how I was going to explain to my co-workers that, although I'd been chirping about becoming a triathlete for eight years, bought a bike, a wetsuit, goggles, and spent a ton of money on the entry fee, I was giving it all up because I could not complete the swim portion of the shortest race available.

The distress did not begin to subside until I was near the final buoy and I could actually touch the bottom with my fully extended toe. I was amazed that, although the water had become shallow enough to walk in, almost everyone else continued swimming until they were less than waist-deep. To me, perhaps because of how much I had struggled for the previous 750 metres, this was the stupidest thing I had ever seen. The only thing that was more ridiculous, was that these people actually seemed to genuinely be enjoying this.

As soon as I was waist-deep, the disquiet I had been experiencing, melted away. Although I still questioned how I would ever be able to do this again, I felt the kind of freedom and elation that hostages must experience when liberated from prolonged, torturous captivity. My breathing normalized again, and I was so happy to be done with the 'swim'. If you had told me there was another lap, but I could get out of doing it by punching my own mother in the face, I would have gone full Mike Tyson on her. There was no way I would have been able to get back in the water.

Once we ran out of the ocean, there was an area where volunteers were stripping the wetsuits off of our soaked bodies. I did not need these people because my wetsuit was unzipped before the start and, doubting I would ever wear it again, was off my body before I was even on dry-land. Officially I finished that portion of the race in the longest 19 minutes 37 seconds of my life. High school math class never felt that long. Monday afternoon staff meetings didn't feel that long. My time was good enough for 210th out of 321 participants, which was, to me, a complete miracle because it meant that there were over 100 people who were even slower. Unbelievable. Did they do the course twice? I concluded that they must have simply shown up late for the start.

Once out of the water, I sprinted at top speed into transition, completely stunned that everyone else was not doing the same. Ben Johnson, doped to the gills, would not have been able to beat me from the water's edge to my bike.

Ever since it was invented, the bicycle has been a symbol of freedom, a notion that was never felt more fully than it did for me that day. My bike represented emancipation from the shackles of the sea and my wetsuit. I decided not to tarnish that freedom by coasting, so as soon as my feet touched the pedals, I was hammering all out and didn't stop until I was back in transition again. Every pedal stroke took me further and further from the terror I had endured that morning. I had always loved riding my bike, but this was true ecstasy, and it didn't matter at all that I passed dozens of riders with not a single one going by me. That wasn't why I was riding. I rode to feel the rapture of not being in the water any longer, and there was absolutely zero fatigue.

I had been enjoying the ride so much that I was taken completely by surprise when it was over, and I totally forgot where to rack my bike. I actually had to take off my helmet to see the number sticker so I would know where to go.

By the time the five-kilometre run started, I had miraculously forgotten about the swim. All things considered, it had been a spectacular day, despite the first part. I had wanted to be a triathlete for a long time, and now I was one, sort of. No one could ever take that away from me. Apart from those first twenty minutes, I loved absolutely everything about the event.

As far as results went, I finished sixth in my age group, and 28th overall in a time of 1:25:36, which made me quite happy. Now, I had to learn how to swim again because it was time to move up to the Olympic distance.

- Olympic -

When I returned home from Connecticut, I wasted about twenty minutes before registering for my first Olympic distance race. At that stage, I still viewed anyone who did races longer than that as full-on professionals, figuring only a pro would have the time required to dedicate enough hours and energy to train for such lengths. Those people were gods to me. I had even spotted a few of them in their natural habitat in the New London race, with their Ironman Lake Placid T-shirts and Ironman Canada finisher's jackets. They even had stickers on their vehicles, and some were so high up in the pantheon of triathlon royalty, that they had tattoos on their calves. These highly trained athletes were to triathlon what Tom Brady is to football, and I didn't consider myself as being worthy of their company. At least that's what I thought.

I did, however, feel that I was ready to give Olympic distance a go. The run, after all, is just a 10k, and I couldn't remember the last time I had done less than that, other than the race in Connecticut, that is. This didn't sound so tough, and the forty-kilometre bike ride shouldn't be a problem either, as most training rides, if you could call them that, were about that distance. I was convinced I was ready to tackle the National Capital Triathlon in Ottawa, sort of. The swim leg of the race still scared me, and this one would be even longer than the last. Just because I had received a finisher's medal for my participation in a sprint triathlon, I was still reluctant to call what I had done *racing*. Racing means going fast and I really only did that for two-thirds of the event.

It's about a six-hour drive from Killingworth, Connecticut to where we live near Montreal, and I spent five hours and nine minutes thinking and rethinking about the swim debacle. The whole thing still didn't make any sense. Dammit, I knew how to swim, and I had never been afraid of the water before, so I concluded that it was because the last swim 'workout' I had done, prior to the race, had been fifteen or so years before the race, when I was a graduate student at Acadia University.

When I thought about it, I was surprised that it had already been that long ago, and just as shocked that I hadn't thought of my time there in that long, especially considering that it was at Acadia where I had met a real triathlete for the first time. In fact, it was that chance meeting that had me swimming laps in a 25-metre pool in the first place.

It was quite early in my first year at the university and I was out for a run before going to class. Wolfville, Nova Scotia is right on the Bay of Fundy, in a lazy, rural setting. I had been running all around the area since the first morning after arriving in town, and I found it strange that in such a beautiful, rolling setting, I came across no more than four motor vehicles, one of which was a tractor, and not a single other runner. This is a college town, surely I couldn't be the only person to enjoy running at the entire university. The closest I ever came to seeing a like-minded human being was this odd cyclist I encountered every single time I had been out. He seemed strange for two reasons: 1. He was riding what I now know is a TT bike, which to my pre-triathlon eyes was as normal as seeing someone riding a swing-set or a coat hanger. It did not look remotely natural at all, and he completed that picture of oddity by wearing an aero helmet. I never even wore a helmet on a bike, unless I was on my mountain bike going very fast down a, well, mountain. What he was wearing looked positively stupid. 2. Every time he passed me, he would look back towards me and stare. I assumed he thought I was as strange to him as he was to me. We were, after all, the only two people out getting any kind of purposeful exercise. It was still pretty creepy, though.

One day, as he paused and looked back, almost going off the road, he did a U-turn and pedalled back in my direction, causing me to instinctively clench my fist in preparation to defend myself from being raped or murdered. He didn't appear to be super menacing, and I heard no banjos off in the hills, so, though I was a far cry from feeling at ease, I was fairly certain that I would be able to win the fight, if it came down to one, that is.

It turned out his name was George and he was the cross country running coach at Acadia. He stopped right next to me and asked if I would like to join the team, which sounded like a great idea, and over the course of the next couple of months, we became pretty good friends. He even loaned me one of his road bikes so we could do a little cross-training. We rode mostly during the afternoons before practice, and on weekends. George also thought it would be good for me to start swimming from time to time, to supplement my training. It was during one of these Wolfville pool sessions that I wore a Speedo for the first time since I was about ten years old, and it felt surprisingly good. It was also the first time I ever did a swim workout, and where I learned how to execute a flip turn. It is also the last place I ever performed one because every time I tried it, I would throw up a little bit in my mouth. My body doesn't do well upside down, it seems.

George had pictures of when he had done the Hawaii Ironman, and he was the first person to tell me about that legendary race and how he had met his heroes, Mark Allen and Dave Scott. It was in his kitchen, over a bowl of curry, that I first learned of the Iron War, which was all very fascinating, and I was quite interested, but it was nothing that someone like me would ever have the opportunity to try. Once I left Wolfville in May that year, I pretty much forgot all about George and triathlon altogether.

So, that was it: the reason I had such a hard time in Connecticut was that it had been way too long since I had a proper swim. It was time to crack on and start doing some pool work, only now, since my horrible experience in my last outing, I was terrified of swimming around other people. That race had spooked me and I was afraid that I would panic again and totally embarrass myself if

I went to a public pool. There wouldn't be a lane slow enough for me, so I was forced to come up with an alternate plan. There were three weeks between getting back from Connecticut and the start of the Ottawa race, which meant I had three weeks to train my swimming enough to avoid seizing up again in terror. I concocted a plan that seemed not only fool-proof but ingenious, at least at the time.

Being a teacher, I had the summers off and, thus, had the entire day, every day, to squeeze in my running, biking, and swimming, and still find enough time to be a decent dad and boyfriend. When I applied for my first teaching position, the principal conducting the interview asked me what my top three reasons for wanting to become a teacher were. "The first two are July and August", I replied. "And the third is...Wait, what was the question?". Not seeing the humour, she was not impressed at all and said so. Fortunately for me, it was early December and the teacher whose position I would be filling, had quit in a huff, leaving the school desperate for an immediate replacement. She was out of options and hired me on the spot. Ever since I have enjoyed the summer off.

Three weeks was all I had. My swim training consisted of two components, neither of which I would recommend to an up and coming triathlete, and one of which was kind of stupid and potentially dangerous.

The first was to squeeze into my wetsuit and wear it pretty much all the time that I wasn't biking, running, or going to the grocery store. I would have worn it to my son's soccer practices, but Anne wouldn't let me. The concept was really rather simple, I just did everything I would have done anyway, only dressed like a

Navy Seal. I mowed the lawn, built a deck, played hide and seek, all in my black, rubber suit, in the scorching summer heat. Sometimes it got dangerously hot, but I figured that if I could stand it in the backyard, I'd be able to stand it in the water. There was no way I was going to be unfamiliar with how it fit for the next race. Sure, there were several close calls when I almost fainted playing street hockey in front of the house, but it was nothing a couple of litres of Gatorade couldn't fix.

The second component was way less dangerous but, most likely, equally as ineffective. In our backyard, we have a twenty-four foot, round, above-ground swimming pool, and since I was refusing to swim in any twenty-five-metre pools where other people might be, it was going to have to be where my swim training magic would hopefully happen. I was going to attempt to exorcise my open water demons in a four and a half foot deep, circular, suburban, family pond, which I knew, before starting, would be like training to climb Everest by going on a hiking trip to Florida.

What made this decision even more bizarre is that I live less than a kilometre from the Richelieu River, where I spent most of my childhood summers frolicking in the gentle currents while paddling at the Otterburn Boating Club. I could have practiced in open water every day if I wanted to, but the truth is, it never even occurred to me to try.

My plan was remarkably so simple that it needed just two modifications to take it from outright stupid to merely functionally idiotic. The inaugural iteration had me squeeze into my wetsuit, which was, more than likely, already on my body, put on my goggles and swim cap, jump into the pool, find the side and throw my feet over the edge. This permitted me to assume a prone swimming position with the rest of my body face down in the water. Once tightly 'hooked' to the pool's edge, I would commence the standard front crawl stroke, minus, of course, the bit with the kicking, which I figured was okay, because I had read somewhere that triathletes hardly do any kicking anyway, preferring to save their legs for the bike and run.

The first time I attempted this method, I lasted about twenty minutes before the pain on the tops of my feet became unbearable and I began to bleed. The solution I came up with, which was as unrefined as the initial method itself, was to place a towel over the edge to act as a cushion. It worked only marginally better than before, the biggest problem being that the more powerful was my catch and pull, the higher the likelihood that the towel would slide off the side of the pool and into the water.

After a few days of struggling with this particular exercise in frustration and futility, I figured it was time for some sort of modification. Now, instead of draping my feet over the edge, I would just swim back and forth a shitload of times which had some obvious drawbacks, not least of which was trying to avoid the urge to push off the side at the 'turn'. Every time I forget to not push, I would rap my head off the opposite wall in a matter of seconds, without having taken a single stroke. Even without the push, it would take no more than three strokes before I hit the other side. The biggest problem with this technique, however, was that it literally made me sick. I'm not big on spinning and somersaults and the like. Rides at amusement parks render me involuntarily bulimic, so all the back and forth made me want to Huey in about two minutes.

The final adjustment actually came to me while watching the Tour de France on TV. Well, it didn't so much 'come to me' as I stole the idea from a commercial that aired during one of the final stages. It was an advertisement for an Endless Pool, which has the swimmer swim against a current created by a powerful jet throwing water directly at his or her head. I couldn't afford one of these contraptions, but my pool, as do all of them, had a jet. It was small, almost powerless, and poorly angled, but it did send a steady stream of water/air bubbles in a direction away from the pool wall. "Perfect", I thought. "I'll just do that".

I would love to say that it worked like a charm, but it didn't. It did do a much better job than the previous attempts, so it would have to do. The biggest obstacle was that the flow was nowhere near powerful enough, so when I would draw the water back with my right hand, my left hand would jam against the wall next to the water outlet. Basically, it was doable so long as I didn't try to surge, which really wasn't much of an issue because it wasn't like I was doing intervals or anything fancy like that.

I spent an hour every day in my endless backyard pool, and by the time the first week of August was almost over, I felt as ready as ever to hit the open water, which is to say that I was marginally less terrified than the last time.

In the final couple of weeks before the Ottawa race, I did one other thing to make an attempt at lessening my swim fears: I convinced my brother Chris to sign up and join me in the race, which, in the spirit of full disclosure, was quite selfish on my part. When I asked him to come along, I made it sound as though I was doing him a favour by introducing him to such a fantastic sport, even sweetening the pot by offering to lend him a reasonably new bike to train and race on. It took a little convincing, but, in the end, he was actually kind of keen.

"It'll be great", I suggested. "The swim's a little intimidating at first, but you get over it real quick. It's not like you've never been in the water before".

It was a little underhanded, I admit, but I really did think he would like it, and I hoped it would be something we could do together more and more in the future. As we have grown older and had jobs and families, there have been fewer and fewer things we can share, so he accepted and I secretly hoped that this race would be slightly less uncomfortable knowing I had someone to go through it with. After all, misery loves company, and so does terror. I also knew that as scared as I had been the first time, I knew I was a better swimmer than Chris, so as long as he experienced a fraction of the anxiety I had, I should be able to beat him out of the water. He was borrowing one of my bikes only a couple of weeks before the event, thus limiting his training time, and in the only running race we had done together, I had finished ahead of him. By bringing him to this race, I was pretty much assured of finishing no worse than second last, which is kind of like being the smartest kid in summer school, but I needed the incentive.

Race day finally came and the weather was perfect. The sun was out, but it wasn't too hot or humid. The air was fresh and there was just a slight tickle of wind. For some reason, I awoke confident, being really only worried about one thing: I had also felt super confident the morning of the Connecticut race, and that didn't turn out so well, at least not the first bit.

The overall distance of the event was nothing to be intimidated by, as I did that in half of a typical training day, and as far as the swim was concerned, I was no longer uncomfortable in my wetsuit. I wouldn't go so far as to say that it felt like a natural extension of my body, but who actually thinks it is supposed to be? Wetsuits, despite what their manufacturers try to tell us, are not built for comfort. My cycling shorts didn't exactly couch my package in a world of velvety luxury either, and my running shoes didn't quite have the same feel as a pair of slippers. No, comfort was not an issue.

My goal for the day was not complex: I wanted to make it through the swim without holding onto any buoys and without resorting to the backstroke. If it was necessary for navigational purposes to do a little breaststroke or even doggy paddle, that would be fine, just no panic floating and no threatening the kayakers. I was confident that my bike and run would be fine.

I arrived early and met up with my brother in the parking lot. He appeared to be a little nervous, so I tried to act like the seasoned veteran that I clearly wasn't, feeling it was my duty to take him under my wing as Tom Skerritt did to Maverick in Top Gun.

"What's up?", I asked. "Don't feel too nervous. The entire race is only fifty-one and a half clicks. You probably biked that far yesterday", I said, trying to allay his apprehension.

"Nah, it's not that", he informed me, with a tinge of pique in his voice. "I rented a wetsuit yesterday, but I only tried it on this morning, and it's way too small".

He was quite concerned, and I could see some of what I had felt with my first wetsuit experience coming through. "It's probably not too small", I said, trying to exude enough confidence for the both of us. "They're supposed to be really tight. It's kinda hard to breathe at first, but ya oughta get used to it in no time", I clearly lied. I tried to lighten the mood with a little humour and told him to take it out of his purse and try it on so I could see it for myself.

He was right, it was way more than a little tight. There was no way it would have fit Yoda. I did my best to try to ease the pressure by telling him that the water probably wasn't that cold anyway and that it might actually be better this way because your first triathlon should not be the first time you try on a wetsuit. I confided that I had made that mistake and that I almost withdrew from my first race because of it. What I didn't say was that I was a little pissed off because I had just lost a significant piece of my competitive advantage over him, as I was counting on him having a similar first race experience to me. He is way braver than I am, so I didn't expect him to quit, but I was hoping he'd feel some serious discomfort. It was now up to my limited experience, which consisted of a grand total of one sprint triathlon and three weeks of backyard 'swimming', to get me out of the water ahead of him. That may not sound like much, but compared to the zero amount of water time Chris had done in well over fifteen years, my swimming experience seemed quite formidable, and it gave me a little essential self-assuredness.

As we walked to the beach to do our warmup, I acted as a tour guide/older sibling/Councillor to my brother. With all the advice I was giving him, all the answers to his questions, all the pointing to the little tricks and ticks people were performing in their pre-race rituals, I was trying to make him feel more at ease, as well as a little overwhelmed all at once. I was yinning and yanging all over the place trying to make him feel better about the coming experience, but introducing a kernel of anxiety at the same time. I wanted him to feel a little of what I had in my first go, but I also thought that the more I overloaded him with information, the more he would keep his mind off of what could potentially be a terrifying experience.

I brought him to the race so that I could have someone to beat, but I was actually feeling a little sorry for him. My own level of anxiety was on the rise with every step we took in the direction of the water. I could only imagine what demons he was battling right then, which made me want to give him the warm understanding hug that I didn't get in Connecticut. I kept looking at him to monitor his demeanour so as to allow me to recognize, and, thus, circumvent, a potential meltdown. The thing is, he didn't seem scared, or remotely nervous at all. To him, this was going to be a wee swim before going on a bike ride. Here I was dying a thousand deaths inside for the both of us, and this little prick was as cool as a cucumber.

Watching him during the warmup resulted in mixed emotions. On the one hand, I felt sorry for him because not only was his jammer way too baggy and falling off, and his freestyle stroke made me look like the guy from Total Immersion. On the other hand, he was smiling and enthusiastic and was actually looking forward to the race as a 'fun' experience. At that same point in *my* first race experience, I was contemplating leaving my girlfriend and son in the parking lot while I drove home, crying.

Once the gun went off, I was able to put these things aside to focus on not hanging on to any foreign, floating objects. The warmup had gone well and I hadn't felt the same anxious feelings as the last time. I positioned myself way to the outside of all the other competitors, enabling me to be as close as possible to the shore and away from everything and everyone else, and giving me my own water to thrash about in. After all, I did not really care how fast or slow I was, only that I beat Chris, while not panicking.

To my surprise, the strategy seemed to be working...for about 75 metres. Then, out of nowhere, and for no apparent reason, a very dark, internal panic enveloped my entire body. It came on rather slowly at first, and I attempted to fight it off, trying to think of anything else, but nothing worked. I began to hyperventilate, my body stiffened, I was nauseated, and my sight blurred. I was officially terrified. I tried breaststroke, but for some reason, that made everything worse, and it didn't help that the buoys floating on the water for course marking and safety, were an entire field of swimmers away from me, making my initial decision to stay close to shore seem a little misguided. I flipped onto my back, totally demoralized, and began my best attempt at the backstroke. I felt like such a loser and stayed on my back until the turnaround. Every time I would feel a little better and attempt to flip back onto my front side, the panic would return with a vengeance, kind of like when you drink too much and get the bed spins whenever you close your eyes.

I decided, again, once and for all, that triathlon just wasn't for me. Perhaps I should look into duathlons, or just stick to running. Or lawn bowling. What pissed me off more than anything was knowing that Chris was definitely going to beat me in the one area I thought had been a sure win for me. He was always better in school than I was, winning scholarships, awards, praise, and good-paying jobs. Fuck me, he got a brand new bike on my eleventh birthday. For once I thought I had the better of him. Once again, all I could focus on was getting out of the water. Maybe, if I was lucky, I could catch him on the bike or run, but even if I did, I still wasn't a proper triathlete, and that was what I wanted so badly.

When I made the turn at the halfway point of the swim, I didn't even bother to try to flip onto my stomach until the first buoy on the way in, but when I did, I looked around and saw three people in front of me on their backs, and another two doing the breaststroke. I could also see the finish archway off in the distance, which allowed me to realize that I was more than halfway through the swim and that I was not the only loser out there. With this epiphanic chunk of knowledge floating around inside my head, I decided to try swimming freestyle again. Perhaps it was common to have swim anxiety, and maybe I wasn't a total failure after all. Could it be that we all have this problem from time to time? My mind cleared itself of all negative thoughts, and I swam all the way to the end without the slightest discomfort.

When I got to shore, I was so happy that I no longer gave a shit that Chris was going to beat me. All I cared about was that it appeared as though I had overcome my fears and that I could actually swim again.

The bike route was boring in its simplicity. It consisted of an out and back on a paved park road, closed to the public that we had to complete four times. As I had done in Connecticut, I just put my head down and pedalled as hard as I could in a desperate attempt to catch up to my brother. I knew he was ahead of me, and I tried looking for him on several occasions, hoping to catch a glimpse of him going in the opposite direction, but I never saw him once. "Jesus", I thought to myself. "He must be just nailing it". Though I was a little pissed, I was actually starting to root for him. I mean, if he was so far ahead that I couldn't even see him, he might be able to win his age category. Sucks for me, but good on him.

The run was also an out and back that we covered twice, and it was here that I started to really feel as though I was in my true element. I was sure I would see Chris coming home for the win as I headed out for one of my laps. I went out, never saw him. I came back, again, no Chris. I went out again and never saw him. I didn't understand what was going on. How fast could he be? I assumed he was either going for the overall win, or he was dead. I knew I was going pretty well, and there wasn't much out on the course to cause any accidents, so I assumed he was standing on the podium, waiting for me to finish.

I made the turn for the final time and headed for the last 2.5 kilometres feeling fresh and happy with most of the day's performance. I was reflecting on how I could try to harness the latter portion of the swim and apply it to the whole thing, when I finally saw my brother heading out to the turnaround. "Cocky bastard", was all I was thinking. He must have finished and was now 'cooling down' by doing an extra lap, rubbing his great finish in our faces. The thing was, however, although he was just cooling down, he really did not look particularly fresh or as happy as he should have after such a great performance. I shrugged it off and ran towards the finish line. Once across, with my medal around my neck, I walked over to where Anne and Owen would be waiting to meet up.

To my surprise, my parents were there as well. They hadn't mentioned that they were going to be at the race.

"What are you guys doing here?", I asked my dad.

He seemed quite happy to be there and replied, "Chris told us he was in a race this weekend, so we thought we'd come out to see".

I had also told them that week about the race, but got no reaction. I looked at my father standing close to the path the runners were still racing on, with just a little bit of 'pissed off' in my expression. He said, "Chris is doing really well. He's almost finished".

I must have been much more fatigued than I actually felt, because my mind was unable to compute properly what was being said. As far as I knew, Chris must have been finished ten to fifteen minutes before I did, and was now just shaking out the lactic acid.

"What do you mean?", I inquired. "You're saying he's not done yet?".

My father answered with an undue amount of pride in his eyes, "No. He's on his last lap. Looks super strong".

I stared at his ear because he was craning his head to see down the path, then I looked down at the ground, stunned. There were two completely different emotions battling each other inside my head: On the one hand, I was quite happy that I had actually achieved my goal of beating Chris (a goal I had actually started to feel guilty about throughout the race, but no longer did). On the other hand, I was pretty pissed off that my dad hardly noticed that I had finished... ten minutes ago. In the same race. How about an 'attaboy', or a 'good job'? Some acknowledgement of what I had just accomplished would have been nice.

"Yeah, he looks good", I said, trying unsuccessfully to mask my sarcasm, and walked to the finish line to see him in. I really was happy for him when he crossed the line, but it did feel a little like he got another new bike on my birthday.

My results for the race were pretty good: Swim (1.5k): 32:56 (60th place). Bike (40k), 1:09:32. Run (10k), 41:46. Good enough for fourth in my age group and 15th overall.

- NEXT STOP ½ IRONMAN -

One summer, two triathlons. So far so good. I was very happy with my overall results to date, and I was encouraged by the improvement in my ability to swim more than 100 metres freestyle without flatlining. Something had finally clicked (at least I thought it had) in my head, allowing me to ignore the ridiculous, unfounded swim anxiety. I was riding the high of my little triathlon wave and was desperate to keep riding it before the weather brought it all to an end for the year. Also, I wanted to go bigger, so I went in search of a half ironman distance race and was lucky enough to find one very close by.

There was a multiple distance triathlon festival of sorts happening in September in Montreal, forty minutes from my front door, called L'Esprit de Montreal. I signed up instantly, without even looking at the course map or reading any information about the event beforehand, but once I did, I could not have been happier. It was the perfect match for what I needed to make the leap to the longer distance. The entire course would be closed and traffic-free, in Parc Jean Drapeau on Île Notre Dame, right in the heart of the city. Basically, it was an urban race in a setting ironically free from motorized traffic. I say 'ironically' because the bike portion of the race was to consist of twenty-one laps of the Formula One race track, the Circuit Gilles Villeneuve. The great thing about this circuit is that, though the province of Quebec is notorious for having roads that are so poorly maintained that they resemble the remains of a blown-out mine-field, the race track itself is kept in pristine condition using taxpayer dollars. You could lose a Volkswagen in one of the several potholes on the road leading to the place, but would be very hard-pressed to find the smallest crack in the Tarmac of the track itself.

The swim was to be held in the Olympic Basin, which was man-made for the rowing and canoeing events at the 1976 Summer Olympic Games, and is ostensibly a current-free, 2000 metre long, 100 metre wide, three-metre deep, swimming pool. Adding to the comfort it provided, there are underwater cables, normally acting as anchors for lane markers used in summertime rowing events, that line the length of the course, making it unnecessary to look up during the swim. Any feature that would diminish the likelihood of a panic attack was welcome, including the fact that growing up as a provincial level canoeist, we used to have the provincial championships in the very same basin. I had been in the water dozens of times in my youth and knew what to sight along the sides of the course to know how much distance was left to cover. This was set up to feel like a truly 'home' race, and I could not have designed a more fitting course for my first long-distance race myself. The parcours was to half ironman distance racing what putt-putt is to golf. The only thing missing was a windmill on the run. There was a tunnel, though.

I woke up race morning in my own bed, feeling confident about what lay ahead and thinking that if I couldn't get rid of my open water swim anxiety 'once and for all' here, then I was doomed and might as well go shopping for a badminton racquet or a bowling ball. There was no traffic on the way to the race site, and just as we turned into the parking area, 'Eye of the Tiger' came on the radio, which I considered an outstanding omen. When we parked the car, I took my bike down from the roof rack and checked the tire pressure. Perfect. All my gear was surgically organized and where it should be. There remained one last task: place the bidons, chilled to perfection overnight in the fridge in my own kitchen, into the cages on the bike frame.

"Aaahh fuck!", I exclaimed in frustration.

"What's up", Anne asked, while giving me a bit of the stink eye for my choice of language with Owen right next to me.

"Forgot my fuc...I, uh, left my water bottles full of Gatorade in the fridge".

Luckily, the athlete's village was between the parking lot and transition, so I was able to buy two bottles and enough electrolyte powder for the race. It's amazing how much we obsess about being extremely organized so as not to forget anything, yet there seems to be something that gets overlooked every time. I had bought two brand new bidons specifically for this race the day before, and the moment I looked in the back of the car at the empty shopping bag where they should have been, I was reminded of my burned-out grade nine French teacher, Mr. Gelinas.

Mr. Gelinas appeared to be perpetually frazzled and completely absent-minded, constantly needing to be reminded of where we were in our lessons. One morning, in particular, stands out, and it was this incident that came to me race morning, causing me to chuckle and improve my mood.

It was the first period of the day, and we were all in our seats, waiting for the final bell to ring, signifying the start of class. Ring it did, but Mr. Gelinas was nowhere to be seen. No worries, he was often thirty seconds to a minute and a half late, which was unprofessional for sure, but for him, entirely normal behaviour. A minute passed, then two minutes. We sat and waited. Five minutes came and went, and still, we waited. After fifteen minutes had gone by, we finally heard heavy-footed running coming from the hall, heading in our direction.

Mr. Gelinas exploded into the classroom with a stunned look on his face as though he was being chased, sweating profusely and breathing heavily. His hands and wrists were covered in purple ink, obviously from a losing battle with the photostat machine. His briefcase was open, and his shirt was buttoned all wrong. He stared at his desk, leaning on both palms as he tried to regain his breath and composure, searching desperately for some sort of clue on the desk pad in front of him that would remind him of where he was physically in addition to what he was supposed to cover during the lesson.

Just then, something jogged his memory, and he stood up bolt straight in shock.

"Uh, what's the matter, sir", Pascal Charbonneau timidly asked.

Mr. Gelinas replied very softly and almost inaudibly, as though he was revealing a secret that would put us all in grave danger, "I forgot my car".

We assumed that he meant that he had forgotten to lock his car, or forgot to turn the lights off in his car, or, perhaps, that he forgot something *in* his car. But, no, that wasn't it at all. He had forgotten his car altogether...at home.

With that said, he calmly got up from his seat, walked slowly toward the door, and left to go home and fetch his car. While he was gone, we were too stunned to misbehave and we kept asking one another, "How the fuck did he get here, then?".

Looking into the back of my car for water bottles that were back home, I felt like Mr. Gelinas on race morning. I just hoped that this particular brain fart would replace the panic I usually felt in the water on race day.

With that problem behind me, I set my sights on the swim, and when the gun went off, I looked for one of the underwater cables. They were difficult to locate at first, which was a welcome distraction from the crowds of swimmers, but once I found one, I lasered in on it and only lifted my head to breathe. That cable was my lifeline and it kept my mind at peace, allowing only a minor touch of panic to trickle in at the turnaround, and it only happened because I had suddenly noticed that I hadn't had a panic attack yet. This thought, of course, made me anxious. It was like being told NOT to think of a pink elephant. Of course, the first thing that comes to mind is a giant fuchsia pachyderm. Luckily, I was able to quickly recover, and when I saw the end of the basin approaching, I was surprised at how fresh I felt. I guess panicking uses a great deal of energy. I was so happy and I wore a giant, ear to ear, 'Hey Kool-Aid' smile as I exited the water.

My demons were finally dead, and I was so elated that I remember almost nothing of the bike or run, other than that it was really cool to take the turns super tight on my bike with the tires touching the red and white banks, allowing me to pretend I was Michael Schumacher.

When I looked at my results after finishing the run, I was quite surprised at how well I'd done (4:31:41, 5th in my age group and 18/224 overall).

By this time, I knew that there was a World Championships for Ironman 70.3 and that it would be in Las Vegas the following year. I wondered if my time was good enough to grant me access. I had qualified for the Boston Marathon before, so I assumed that the methods and requirements would be similar, in other words, they would be based on a time standard. Once I looked into it, I realized that things were different for Ironman branded events. The only way I could punch my ticket to the Worlds was to win my age group at an Ironman 70.3 race. If I were to finish in the top three, there would still be a pretty good chance, though no guarantee, as it was contingent on the size of the field in my age category. If that were the case, I would have to rely on what they called a 'roll-down', which requires a Doctorate in advanced mathematical statistics to fully comprehend.

The more research I did, the more I came to understand that I needed two things: 1. I needed to find an Ironman 70.3 race reasonably close to where I lived, and 2. I needed one of those fancy triathlon bikes that all the cool racers had. I set out on a mission to find both, and by the end of September, it was mission complete.

The search for a race wasn't very difficult, but not quite as simple as I thought it would be. I live in the province of Quebec, and I grew up skiing several times every winter at Mont Tremblant, where there just happens to be an annual Ironman 70.3 race. I assumed it would be an easy slam dunk to register for that one. It was the most convenient, logical option, which I figured would be a piece of cake to get into due to the fact that, to me, it didn't seem to be particularly exotic. The way I looked at it, they would be begging for participants.

Turns out I was wrong. Super wrong. It is one of the most popular events on the Ironman calendar, selling out mere hours after registration opens. It was the only race in the 70.3 series I had ever heard of, but I had always assumed that was because it was the only one in Quebec, not because people from all over the world wanted to race it.

I continued my search and came across an event in Syracuse, New York, which is only about a four to five-hour drive from home. Other than that, the next closest race was much further away and was a qualifier for the 2014 season, and I was looking to get into the 2013 World Champs. Though it seemed to be a bit of a no brainer, I was a little hesitant to sign up for anything happening in Syracuse because I had been there only one time before, and the place hadn't exactly left a stellar impression on me.

A few years prior to my first foray into triathlon, I had signed up for an ultramarathon event there called 'The Green Lakes Endurance Race', that offered two options: 100km and 50km. Anne, myself, and our eldest son, Felix, who was thirteen at the time, made the trip down to upstate New York, after having made a reservation at the Carrier Circle Super 8 Motel, in East Syracuse. Now, everybody knows that the Super 8 isn't exactly the Four Seasons, and bathrobes, massages, and complimentary spa treatments should not be expected, but what we encountered was way beyond anything I had anticipated. The overall feeling we got just moments after opening the door to our guest room could be summed up with the simple phrase: 'Snots on the wall'.

I could have handled the fact that every piece of furniture, as well as the bathtub and the sink and the carpet and the telephone and the top of the television, were scorched with cigarette burns. The fact that the carpet was on the wrong side of filthy was manageable. A strange, curly, dark hair on one of the towels (sorry, THE towel) could easily be removed with a pair of rubber gloves and some tweezers. What could not be ignored, however, was a line of boogers on the wall next to one of the beds, in an obvious pattern that had been carefully designed and maintained over time to look like a medium-sized penis. This was a level of filth that we were absolutely incapable of ignoring.

It took all of twenty minutes to look around the guest-room, the lobby, and the room where they hid the pool under three centimetres of algae and moss (indoor pool, by the way), to decide that we were going to have to relocate to alternate accommodations.

After driving around for about an hour, we settled on the Econolodge closer to downtown. You know that your original choice is vastly sub-par when you *upgrade* to the Syracuse Econolodge, where the reception area is behind a thick layer of bulletproof plexiglass. Our new room did not possess the charm that a booger wall offers, but that night (the night before the race)

Felix had eaten a whole bag of Cheetos and downed a litre of iced tea that he only partially digested, and painted the wall next to his bed in semi-fluorescent, faux-cheese scented, vomit.

The race itself did not make any of this more romantic at all. I had registered for the 100km, and it started out just fine. The course consisted of several loops of a lake and open meadow that attracted and incubated the heat from the sun like a magnet and was, therefore, dubbed, 'The Serengeti'. After completing a few laps, however, the wheels came off all at once, and I was forced to abandon a race for the first time in my life. I hated myself for it, but at least it allowed us to check out of the motel and leave Syracuse behind a day earlier than expected.

I wasn't exactly thrilled about the location, but I signed up for my first Ironman branded race there nonetheless. The name Ironman represented everything that triathlon meant to me and I am quite sure there isn't a triathlete in the world for whom it does not resonate. With my name officially on the start list, it was time to begin training in earnest.

The next task I had before me was to find, and purchase, a triathlon bike that I could afford on a teacher's salary. Upon setting out to complete this assignment, I found out two things almost immediately:

1. Real triathletes (as well as cyclists) do not call them 'triathlon bikes'. In fact, when you use that term, you can actually hear the bike shop employees laughing at you when they ask each other loudly and mockingly, "Hey, Jim. This gentleman is looking for *triathlon* bikes. Do we even have any *triathlon* bikes?". I guess calling a TT bike a 'triathlon' bike is like referring to a video game as

a *computer* game. Apparently, what I was really looking for was a TT bike.

2. TT bikes are super expensive, as in more expensive than the car I drive.

After visiting several bike shops and realizing there was no way I was going to be able to afford any of the bikes I saw, and not really knowing exactly how to go about purchasing a second-hand bike off the internet, I started to do a little research. The first step I took in this regard was to obtain a copy of <u>Triathlon Canada</u> magazine and flip to the equipment review section. As luck would have it, that month they reviewed a Giant Trinity Composite 2, which they said was an extremely fast bike, especially for the money. The modest price tag of $1500 took me quite by surprise because that was a sum I was prepared to pay, and was considerably less than anything I had seen so far.

There was a Giant factory store near to where I worked, so I popped in and saw the bike hanging on the far wall, and I stared at it lovingly until the salesperson sauntered over. Desperate not to look like a total novice, I confidently asked if he had any in my size, as though I had a clue what my size was.

"Your size in what?", he asked, painfully holding back the urge to roll his eyes, and pointed at the bike I was looking at on the wall, "This bike?".

"Yah", I replied, trying to save a little face, "I ride a Felt, so I'm not sure if the sizing's the same".

I had absolutely no idea what size my Felt F7.5 was, and was terrified that would be his next question. The last thing I wanted was to have to point to my hips and tell him that it was about that high. Instead of asking about the size of my present bike, he just said, "It's cuz this one's for women. The men's section is over there where the walls aren't painted lavender and dusty pink", and he gestured towards the bikes on the other side of the store, that came in colours like red, black, orange, grey.

"Oh", I said, sheepishly, "do you have any over there that might fit?".

"So you want a TT bike?", he asked, pretty sure I didn't have a clue what he was talking about.

"No", I said. "I'm looking for a *triathlon* bike, like this one", I pointed at the bike I had been ogling. "Only for men. I'm five foot ten".

Now, in reality, I am five nine, that is if I perch myself up on my toes a little. I really don't know why I lied, and I regretted it instantly, knowing that an inch or two might actually make a difference in the sizing. If I was buying running shoes, I wouldn't tell the guy I am a size thirteen when I know I'm a ten.

He turned his head towards the workshop area, sufficiently annoyed that he had already wasted seven minutes on me, and yelled, "Nate, you've got a customer out here".

I immediately assumed 'Nate' was the newest member of the staff and was, therefore, assigned all the loser customers, a category to which I fit into snugly. I was actually a little relieved because, being the low guy on the totem, he might feel as nervous as I did at the moment.

It turns out that 'Nate' was one of my former students, whom I knew as Nathaniel. I breathed a huge sigh of relief and confessed instantly that I didn't have the foggiest clue what I was doing. I explained to him that I had just taken up triathlon racing and was looking for an entry-level triathlon bike.

"TT", he said, to which I replied, "That's what the other guy said. What the fuck does that mean? Sounds like a tiny insect."

Nate chuckled and said, "Sir, it stands for time trial. No drafting. That's basically what the bike portion of a triathlon is: a Time Trial. TT".

Ahh. Nate brought me to the men's section and showed me the Trinity I had seen in the magazine, only this one was fire engine red.

"It's a really good bike for the money", he assured me. "It's not top of the line or anything, but it'll do the job. And the best part", he added, "is that it looks exactly the same as the much more expensive model, if you squint a bit". I figured it was like having your favourite basketball team draft a player named Harry Bird; not quite the 'real deal', but close enough for me.

"Cool", I said. "Size me up and you have a sale".

VIVA LAS VEGAS

I'm not sure if there is an 'official' age at which going out for Halloween becomes socially unacceptable, but I definitely remember the last time my friends and I dressed up in costumes and wandered the neighbourhood in search of a week-long sugar high.

I was fourteen years old, which I believe is about the upper limit, not because it is childish to continue wearing costumes or eating piles of candy; there are adults who do both of those things every year at my school's annual Staff Halloween Party (my costume last year: gym teacher). It has more to do with the fact that at the age of fifteen, adolescent boys acquire the necessary courage to tell balding, middle-aged, fat guys who fashion themselves as comedians by saying stuff like 'trick' when confronted with the customary 'trick or treat', to "shut the fuck up there Chuckles, and hand over the Snickers bar".

I can't be certain when I stopped believing in Santa Claus, but there is absolutely no question that Saturday, October 31st, 1981 was the last Halloween for which I was an active participant because half the houses that my friends and I visited told us we should be ashamed of ourselves. They seemed to feel that my pal, Mark Halliday's costume was too ridiculous, and not child-ish enough. In other words, it wasn't costumey, lacking a playful aura of crude amateurism most of the other outfits had. It more resembled the work of an expert Hollywood horror flick make-up artist. Only someone far too old to be out for Halloween, they felt, could create such a hideous looking get up, and we were sternly told that what we were doing was unfair because it ostensibly amounted to taking candy from the children who deserved it. No innocent, trick-or-treat-aged child would tarnish the spectacle of Halloween the way Mark was, apparently, doing. One woman even called it disgusting.

Saturday night, one week before Halloween that year, started out in typical fashion, with a few of us just hanging about, bored and not really knowing what to do with ourselves. It's not as though we were doing nothing; there was the typical, mindless, teenage-boy chatter centring around girls, football, school, girls, our parents, teachers, and girls. We certainly weren't attempting to solve the world's problems and there was nothing 'heavy' being discussed. It was mainly sports and boobs. We were simply walking the streets of our little piece of rural suburbia, turning left when we felt like it, or right, heading down any street with no direction, and talking about nothing major, when Mark turned into a random driveway, sauntered up to the front of the house, without a care in the world, and rang the doorbell.

As soon as he turned into the driveway, we knew from experience what was about to go down. We didn't need Mark sprinting from the front door towards us, yelling like a maniac, to know that he had just started a wicked game of Nicky, Nicky, Nine Door, which was the very sort of activity that semi-bored adolescent boys, living in rural-suburbia in the 1980s, did on a rare idle Friday or Saturday evening. We were too young and too scared of our fathers to drink, and too naive, shy, or immature to actually try to have sex (at least not with another person; the alone kind some of us did all the time...or so I'm told). So, we played Nicky, Nicky, Nine Door, or Ring and Run. Same thing.

Once Mark ran past us and we took off down the street and through a couple of backyards, we eventually slowed to a walk, giving the adrenaline an opportunity to replenish itself. After a couple of minutes of rest, someone else would repeat the whole ringing and running sequence, with the new house chosen in exactly the same haphazard fashion as all the others. We never *targeted* any in particular, and it was never a case of picking on someone we didn't like or anything. There was no malicious intent, we were just playing a reasonably innocuous, innocent, and virtually harmless game. And the game, like most childish pursuits, was made more fun because it *wasn't* organized. There were few rules or specific order of turns taken. If you felt like ringing a bell, you rang one. We didn't need to draw straws, and it wasn't a game of truth or dare. Sometimes, in an effort to liven things up a bit, one of the 'ringers' would count to five or ten after ringing, before bolting, thus heavily increasing the chances of being caught.

But, we never got caught. The worst that might happen was that some forty or fifty-year-old man in his undershirt, would run after us down his driveway, yelling, "You little bastards, come back here!" (which is ridiculous. Have you EVER known anyone who actually 'came back here'?), but they always ran out of steam before getting more than a hundred feet from the front yard. And, no one ever called the police either.

There were two reasons, really, why no one ever alerted the cops: First, it was no big deal and everybody knew it (most 'victims' had done the same when they were younger). Second, there was only one patrol car in town, and that one was busy ticketing out of towners for speeding. If you weren't from around Otterburn, and were just passing through, there was a better than even chance you wouldn't make it without first getting your very own speeding ticket.

Otterburn was a predominantly residential hamlet hemmed in by two Provincial routes. One was at the northern border, and the other ran parallel to it at the southern border. In between the two were about three square kilometres of houses and a mishmash of poorly organized streets, avenues, crescents, and cul de sacs. Being built on the side of a modest-sized mountain (Mont St. Hilaire), it was chock full of hills that sloped north to south. The road at the top of the hills was called Ozias Leduc Street, named for a famous painter no one has ever heard of, who lived there in the first half of the 20th century. Everyone called it the 'Top Road'. The one at the bottom of the hills was officially named Chemin des Patriotes, in memory of the Patriot Revolution of 1837, and it skirted the Richelieu River. We preferred to call it the 'River Road' instead. The eastern and western borders were separated by no more than a couple of kilometres, and it was at one of these borders, usually along the river, that the speed traps were set up.

Though the town is situated in a very picturesque part of the province, sandwiched, as it was, between a mountain and a meandering river, it was not a destination for anyone other than the 2000 or so residents who called it home. It was simply a place you drove through on your way to someplace else. Most people wouldn't have even noticed it at all if it wasn't for the speeding ticket in their glove compartment.

All this is to say that, if anyone had called the cops on us, they would have been too busy to respond (and when I say 'they', I mean 'he'). We never did any damage anyway.

After we hit five or six houses that night, interest in the endeavour fizzled so we stopped playing as spontaneously as we had begun. No one said, "fuck it guys. I'm out. Let's do something else", or anything like that. We simply didn't ring any more doorbells. At this point, the end of the game had brought us close to the Top Road where the only commercial enterprises were situated. There were two convenience stores, side by side, a veterinarian, a bank, a bike shop, an ice cream parlour, a takeaway pizza joint, and the only sit-down restaurant in town that served crepes, exclusively. The Top Road was the only avenue in town with a sidewalk, and it was only along one side.

All of the businesses were on the sidewalk side and none of these occupied a building higher than a typical bungalow. Each was quaintly decorated in a sort of Hollywood Main Street, Rock-wellian fashion, and the buildings themselves were all stand-alone structures lined up next to one another, like houses on a residential street. The only real gap was between the bank and the PizzaPro take away place, which had been, for as long as I can remember, a vacant lot with one large tree surrounded on all sides by thigh-high, yellow, weedy grass, and was home to thousands of grasshoppers. The grasshopper field, as we dubbed it, had been that way until very close to the night in question, when the town council, and the Chamber of Commerce, decided to permit the construction of a three-storey, multi-office complex that would house several different businesses, from accountants' and dentists' offices to the office of the local branch of a major real estate agency. The building was something that would put Otterburn on the regional map, as it were, as something more than merely a place to go to get a speeding ticket. Construction had begun in the summer and with every passing week, you could see obvious progress.

After all our ringing and running, we figured we needed to get some calories in, and we made our way to the Top Road to hit one of the convenience stores for snacks. On our way, we passed in front of the construction site and gawked at it before moving on. The building itself was far from finished. It was still in a very rough state and sat about fifteen to twenty metres back from the sidewalk, to allow for future parking space. There was a snow fence around the site to keep people off of the potentially dangerous grounds. It was a muddy, rutted mess of dirt and rocks, without a grasshop-per in sight, and there were stray boards here and there with a few abandoned-looking tractors, bulldozers, backhoes and other smaller machinery. The project was months away from completion, but the main structure was up, a foundation had been poured and the walls were all in place. Not all four sides had been covered in bricks yet, and where the doors and windows would one day be, were, for the time being, only gaping openings. It was sooooo cool, and we really wanted to get closer so we could see more.

A quick look left and right to ensure the coast was clear, and, boom, we were over the fence in seconds. We had no intention of causing any trouble or doing any damage, we simply wanted to get a closer look. First, we approached the opening where the front doors would someday be, but we didn't go inside. It was so dark in there. We were excited and apprehensive at the same time because anyone could have seen us and assumed we were up to no good. Someone suggested we go around the back so we could explore with less risk of getting caught.

Once around back, we all experienced one of those uncommon, spontaneous, group epiphanies, as we saw something so amazing, so otherworldly, so secret and so rare that we could scarcely control our collective emotions. It was like a bolt of lightning had come from the heavens and shone a spotlight in an otherwise world of darkness, on a hidden pot of gold. It was 'like' that, only so much better. There, right before us, on an angle from the ground to a future window, way up high on the top floor, stood an abandoned ladder, left there to tempt us.

In their haste to begin the weekend, the workers had inadvertently neglected to remove it from the site, or, at the very least, to lock it to something on the ground. Other than the four of us, there was no one else around. It was dark. The building was the object of our desire, and the instrument to realize this desire was presented to us, quite literally, from on high. We hadn't intended on trespassing, but now that we had, it seemed as though the stars had lined up so perfectly, that it started to feel like it was our duty to get a better look at the structure before us. As it stood, up until that point, we hadn't broken any laws, *really*. All we had done was stumble upon an abandoned construction site. No big deal. That was nothing we couldn't talk our way out of. Going any further than that was way more than we intended to do, but, Jesus Christ, a ladder left out for the whole weekend that offered entry, not regular ground floor entry, but top floor entry, to the tallest building our little town had ever seen? That was too much. No game of Ring and Run could compare to this. This was like being at-bat in the bottom of the ninth, bases loaded, down by three, and the pitcher decides to start tossing underhand.

We all stared at the ladder, each of us fighting an inner battle. We weren't delinquents, but we wanted to climb it so badly. At some point, the gene that is ingrained in the DNA of every human male that feels it is better to ask for forgiveness rather than permission, kicked in. None of us was particularly religious, but we had been through enough Sunday School to understand all of the "Thou shall not" stuff found in the bible, but you leave a ladder mounted to a brand new building, leading to an opening through which we could potentially witness a kaleidoscope of adventure and mystery, and I dare say, "we shall, Lord. We most certainly fucking shall".

There was actually never any doubt that we would climb the ladder. The only real question was who was going to go first. We each wanted to see what was up there, but I was nervous because whoever went first would be a real criminal. The rest of us would be mere accessories.

As it was, I needn't have worried because Mark had already grabbed the first few rungs and shouted, "Shotty first!", announcing his desire to pioneer this mission.

And up he went. Up we all went. Nobody stayed at the bottom to secure the ladder or act as a lookout. Fuck that, we climbed up, up, up, being periodically kicked in the head by the guy above us, which we were willing to endure because there was no way we wanted to get separated from the bunch, when suddenly, we came to a halt. Mark had reached the top and craned his head over the edge and into the opening in the wall, supporting his upper body with his forearms.

"It's fuckin dark in here", he complained. "I can't see a thing".

From below, I gave a muted shout: "Of course it's dark. It's night time, genius".

"Just go", Kevin added. "Your eyes will adjust once you're inside".

"I don't know about this, guys. I mean, it's black. I can't even see the floor", Mark added with a tinge of actual fear in his voice. This hesitation was quite uncharacteristic of Mark, who was seldom frightened by anything. Kevin, being next in the conga line we had on the ladder, was getting impatient, and said, "Come on, man. Just hop over or get outta the way. I'll go". As he said that, he placed his right hand on Mark's ass and heaved him upwards over the threshold of the window sill.

It took a second or two, but the three of us remaining on the ladder were startled by what we heard issuing from inside. Actually, we were shocked by what we didn't hear. For several very long, pregnant seconds, we heard absolutely nothing. No toolbox being knocked over clumsily. No tripping over loose boards or cans of nails. There was no, "This is so cool. Come check it out", and, quite oddly, no foot landing on the concrete floor. The only sound we heard came after a long, and eerily silent, pause...and it was horrifying. We were scared shitless for we heard what sounded like a 150-pound sack of apples coming to a dull and thudding halt after having been dropped from an airplane. When we heard the sound, the three of us remaining on the ladder descended in record time.

The building, it turned out, was even further from being finished than we had initially thought. In fact, it wasn't really even a building yet. Though the structure was three storeys tall, it wasn't three *floors* tall because it only had one floor...the one on the ground.

Mark lay there motionless and, most likely, dead. We assumed he was dead, but we didn't know for sure. We were teenage boys, which means two things: 1. We aren't old or smart enough to have any kind of real medical knowledge beyond the limited stuff we were able to glean from watching television. 2. We did what any terrified teenager does when scared. We bolted out of there and sprinted home. Panic is a very powerful emotion that, for a brief period, trumps all possibility of rational thought. Fight or flight.

Fortunately, we didn't get too far before the chemicals coursing through the capillaries in our brains slowed down, allowing for the return of semi-reasonable thought, and making us think we should go back to the accident site. After all, we had left a really good friend for dead in a very scary place.

What if he isn't dead, I thought aloud. What if he needed help? Fuck me, he fell three floors to the concrete ground. If he wasn't dead, it meant that it was a miracle, and he would be in definite need of severe medical intervention...soon.

When we arrived back at the building, we went inside, this time through the front entrance.

"Kevin", I said solemnly.

"Yeah", he replied, scared shitless.

"Where are you?"

"I'm up against the wall"

"Where the fuck is Mark?", I pleaded.

"I don't know", Kevin said incredulously. "I think he's gone".

"What do you mean, gone?", I continued, getting more freaked out by the second.

"I mean not fucking here. I've searched the whole floor. He's not here".

We had no idea what to do, so we went home. We figured if Mark had made it out alive, there wasn't much we could do except wait for the phone call that was sure to come the next day from his parents. There was no way we were going to escape catching shit for this one, and we knew we deserved it. So, we just walked home wondering how anyone could have survived such a fall and waited for the other shoe to drop.

Turns out, Mark came-to and simply walked home. The phone call came the next day explaining what happened. We caught shit...big shit. Mark had somehow survived, but with the following injuries: two broken collar bones, left broken radius, broken right hand, broken right radius and ulna, two broken thumbs, six cracked ribs, broken cheekbones, broken jaw, extensive bruising to the face and forehead, shoulders, arms, multiple lacerations and scrapes, mostly to the face, and a cracked vertebra. Legs were fine. He spent most of the week in the hospital recovering as best as he could from all of his injuries.

The rest of us had, in the meantime, decided to go out for Halloween and prepare costumes for the evening. I decided to create something different that year, and went out as a Campbell's Soup can, full Andy Warhol style. It was made of Bristol board, and the artwork was painstakingly completed in red, black, and gold permanent marker. The lid of the can was a big, circular piece of cardboard with a head-sized hole in the centre, and covered in aluminum foil.

Mark, to our surprise, showed up, only he was sans costume. This was understandable seeing as how he had fallen into a building a week ago, so I gave him my lid to wear on his head. His body was covered in casts and bandages, and no horror flick make-up artist could have possibly replicated the gruesome way his face looked naturally. He had a little trouble holding his loot bag, but the 'costume' was perfection. Even though some thought it was over the top, we knew it was brilliant.

Mark taught us all a great lesson that Halloween season: it's okay to jump headfirst into the unknown. The adventure is usually worth it, even if it is painful at first. Sure, you might bust up your face a little bit, but at least there will be a great story to tell.

It was with this same innocently ignorant sense of adventure that I prepared for my first Ironman 70.3 in Syracuse, New York.

- Get Ready For The Big Time -

The race in Syracuse represented the dark building into which I was diving headfirst. It was a scary proposition, as I was sure there would be times when I would be in pain, either physically or mentally. There was no guarantee that I would be able to finish, and my goals may or may not get met. In fact, when I registered I had no clue what the 70.3 stood for. I mean I knew it was a half ironman, but that number seemed so random to me. Yes, I had done three triathlons by then, one of which was the same distance that Syracuse would be, but none of these had the word 'Ironman' attached to them, none were qualifiers for the world championships, and none were particularly special or well-known, other than locally. They were the 'Greater Greensboro Turkey Trot' of the triathlon world. Fun, yes, but small potatoes.

Syracuse, a small to medium-sized, dingy industrial city in upstate New York, that very few people would ever have known about if there wasn't a famous university there, boasting a population just a little larger than Buffalo, ironically, represented the 'big time' to me. The last race I had done was in Montreal, a major city with a population of 1.7 million, and was considered amateur hour by comparison. That seems strange because Montreal is a world-class city by any standard. It hosted the Olympics, yet Syracuse, home to the Erie Canal Museum, seemed of much greater importance in the triathlon world, and was more exotic, to boot. At least it was to me.

Though merely registering for the race required a huge leap of faith, I still needed to be as prepared as could be. It has been said that the definition of insanity is performing the same actions over and over, expecting a different result. This is a very true statement, and one I use on my students all the time, but it's not much different from "if it ain't broke, don't fix it". So far, other than my lack of swimming prowess, I had been doing quite well, even improving, doing the exact same type of training, and in similar amounts, that I had been doing for years. Why would I change that now? Sure, by mixing things up, I might have shown some gains here or there, but the way I saw it, I could also mess things up. A few years ago I dabbled in golf. My first summer I did quite well, shooting a 95 in my first round and eventually going as low as 79. Over the winter I read every golf magazine I could find and went to the indoor golf dome to put into practice what I had read. By the time the following summer came around, my swing was so screwed up from all the potential 'improvements', I barely broke 100 the whole season. I did, however, break two drivers and a three-iron out of frustration, which I fully understand is childish and stupid, but also very satisfying.

Training for Syracuse began the day after the Esprit Triathlon was in the books and consisted of absolutely nothing particularly methodical (and if it did, it was not on purpose). There wasn't even a plan per se, and there was no schedule written down. There was no periodization. No peaks and troughs. No specific diet. There were no differing intensity zones, and certainly no training 'blocks'. There was just one large block which started in September and finished two days before the race in June, at which time I would 'taper' by driving five hours from my house to Syracuse. Perfect plan.

Training for the run was nothing more than going outside

and, well, running. Sometimes I ran further, sometimes shorter distances. The average was about fifteen kilometres every day, and 95% of these 'sessions' were done on trails, snow or no snow. The intensity and pace of the effort were dictated by three variables: 1. The weather. If it was shitty out, I would wear more clothing which made me slower. 2. Trail conditions. If it was muddy or snowy, the poor footing would lessen the pace. 3. Sometimes I felt crappy, so I wouldn't be able to go as fast as usual. That's it. I took exactly zero days off during the entire 'block', and every run was done first thing in the morning, right after waking up and downing a cup of coffee. The only time I would stop during a run, and it happened on pretty much every session, was to poop. This was actually one of the main reasons for choosing to do all of my runs in the woods. That, and there were no cars, but mainly it was so that I could shit in peace. Each session lasted between an hour and an hour and a half.

You probably won't find this plan in any magazines or training books. I no longer use it myself, but I really do believe that there must be something to it because it had always worked before. Some days my legs or feet or ankles or hips or knees were sore (sometimes all at once), but I never got 'injured'. Nothing was serious enough to get me to not go running. These were good times.

Bike training was different, however. I had considerably less experience in that field, and other than the three triathlons I had done before, I had never previously raced my bike (officially), and therefore, I constantly questioned my methods. I didn't change them, but I did question them. I knew that my running plan was not what the experts or other runners recommended, but I usually finished at the pointy end when I raced, so what other people were doing never bothered me much.

Being entirely clueless when it came to cycling, I decided to take a similar approach which was, more or less, to go hard all the time. The only real difference between my approach to cycling from my running was that when winter came, I rode indoors and for less time than outdoors, at least initially. This changed when I discovered the brilliant idea of turning on the TV or reading a book while riding. Before that, the indoor sessions closely resembled torture sessions, not so much because they were physically more difficult, but because they were mind-numbing. Other than the venue, my rides were the same as my runs: go hard until I ran out of time, which meant that two hours outside and an hour to an hour and a half inside was pretty much all I had. If I knew I was more pressed for time, I would increase the intensity. It was that simple. I just always went hard.

Swimming was a very different story. Running was something that I already did on a regular basis, unmethodical though it was, and biking was just running with a contraption underneath me. With either of these, my technique was not a limiting factor, and whenever I felt that I needed to take a breath, I just did. There was no urgency to wait for my head to get out of a giant bucket of water to get enough air. With either of these activities, if, for some reason that had never happened yet, I felt exhausted during a training session, I had the option of just stopping and walking home. This is not so simple in the middle of a lake or even a pool. I was definitely out of my element when it came to swim training and that made me quite nervous.

Because I was quite apprehensive about how to properly train to swim well, I put it off for as long as I could, lying to myself that I needed to establish a solid cardiovascular foundation before entering the pool. My last race had been in September, and Syracuse was scheduled for late June, so as far as I was concerned, it would have been a waste of time to start any earlier than the second week of March, so that's exactly what I did. I waited until the March Break 'Reading Week' was over at school, drove to the John Abbott College athletics complex, and sauntered in with all the confidence of a Tijuana prostitute going to the clinic for a chlamydia test.

After parking the car, I walked right past the information desk at least three or four times, stopping by the basketball courts pretending I was on a scouting mission. I read several pamphlets they had on nutrition, sleep patterns, safe sexual behaviour, and others. I read through the course requirements for almost every program on offer at the College until I finally conjured up the courage to ask about joining the pool, praying to every deity I could think of, that the student behind the counter would not utter the words, "open swim starts in five minutes. You can begin today". Thankfully, once I paid the ridiculously low fee, the earliest I would be able to begin was in two days' time. I had exactly forty-eight hours to overcome the anxiety that had been welling up since the beginning of March when the need to get in the pool became imminent.

When the day arrived, I was completely lost. Nothing about the natatorium felt natural or remotely comfortable at all. I had the same feeling as if a Navy Commander had asked me if I had ever flown an F-18 before, then thrown me the keys (or whatever they use to start those things), and told me to have at it, my country was depending on me. I was entirely out of my element.

There were strange pieces of equipment everywhere, such as kayaks stacked up against a wall, a box of toast-shaped floaty boards in one corner, yoga block thingies in the shape of an eight along one wall, a bin filled with miniature flippers that appeared to have been built for tiny, Lilliputian scuba divers, another filled with flat, plastic, multi-coloured brick-laying trowels that people were using on their hands. And what the fuck was going on with the clocks with all the multi-coloured arrows? Why do they need so many of them? This was definitely a total fish out of water experience.

When I walked in, desperate to appear as though I had a clue of what I was doing, the first thing I noticed was that half of the pool was in chaos with children playing on foam pool toys, throwing beach balls, splashing and thrashing about, and calling out the name of ancient Italian seafarers from centuries past. It resembled the pool of an all-inclusive vacation resort in the Dominican Republic. That part of the pool looked like something I could navigate my way through.

The other half had lane markers running lengthwise and what looked like Himilayan prayer flags strung widthwise across an area near each end, hanging over the water. There were swimmers in three separate lanes, travelling at different speeds, all of which were faster than I could handle, and every single one of them, it seemed very obvious, had a specific purpose for doing precisely what they were doing. I had no idea what MY purpose was, or even that we were supposed to have one. Some were stopping periodically at the near end, but nobody 'rested' at the far end.

Everything seemed orchestrated like the movements of a Swiss watch and each individual swimmer, it appeared, was playing at least a supporting role in this pantomime. As far as I could tell, this looked like the Olympics, and I was about to upset the entire homeostasis of this living organism, which scared me shitless. Unlike in a triathlon, where there is a mass of humanity taking off all at once and resembling the patternless fall of concrete poured out of a cement truck, this was a synchronized, precise assembly line of expert swimmers. Figuring out where, and more importantly, when, to 'jump' in was more complex than attempting to skip double Dutch the day after learning to walk.

Approaching the near side of the pool deck, where it seemed that people began their workouts, I noticed a couple more things. The first was that all the turmoil I had felt the night before, trying to figure out whether I had made the right decision to purchase a Speedo jammer, had been unnecessary. I had laid awake most of the night wondering if the guy at the Sports Experts store was selling me the only one they keep on the shelves, next to the squash rackets and sunglasses, to dust off for that one sucker who would stroll in one day and settle a five-year-old bet between him and the other sales staff. "Hey Deano, yo, bro, check this out. Some old dude just bought the speedo. It doesn't even have a barcode on it". "Yo, no way! That thing was there when I started working here, six years ago. Far out. It's definitely pre barcode". Thankfully, I had made the right move. Almost everyone was wearing one, and those who weren't were sporting the standard 1983 regular length banana hammock.

Something else that struck me as strange was that there were piles of equipment at the near end of each lane that people were periodically putting to use in mysterious ways. They were stuffing the figure-eight shaped foam blocks between their legs and heading off again. Some were holding the toast-shaped boards way out in front of them, and kicking like a kid being dragged out of Toys R Us, up and down the length of the pool, over and over again. These people, I assumed, were *swimmer* swimmers and not triathletes because I was now a triathlete, and I don't think I had kicked my legs once in a race yet, except when I was on my back floating my way to shore. There were water bottles of varying sizes and colours, and everyone was sucking on them like they had been stranded in the desert for days. Wasn't there enough water in the pool? I don't think I had ever been thirsty while submerged in water. I guess I was going to have to learn about that also. Many of the faster, more serious-looking swimmers had pieces of paper soaked and stuck to the toast-shaped boards with actual *workouts* written on them. "Holy shit", I thought, "you mean I can't just go swimming?".

There were people swimming using only one arm, some using no arms. They *had* two arms, they, evidently, just didn't always need them. There were others who had snorkels going up the front of their faces, resembling rhinos, and every single one of them was capable of breathing on both sides. I tried that once in the Ottawa race, and I swallowed four litres of water and the top portion of an acorn. After almost choking to death, my coordination became all wonky and I flipped over like a kayaker doing an Eskimo roll as I attempted to self-perform the Heimlich maneuver.

Speaking of rolling, everyone was doing somersaults at the wall like Michael Phelps and heading back the opposite way, effortlessly. I hadn't even jumped into the water yet, and I was scared, fighting the urge to sprint out of there crying. If we were all fingers, I was the little piggy going wee wee wee wee wee all the way home. In fact, my uneasiness started even before venturing out of the locker room. While changing into my swimsuit, a soaking wet, supercut, perfect swimmer body guy came past me and into where the toilets and urinals were, still wearing his cap and goggles. This was more intriguing than college calculus to me. "What could he possibly be doing", I wondered, "taking a piss?". But that couldn't be the reason because when he finished, he hurried back to the pool. He actually got out of the pool to take a leak. I had never done that before and I realized that there was so much to learn.

It was odd to me that nobody just swam. I mean, when it comes to running, people do workouts with intervals and sweet spots and fartleks and tempos, high-intensity sessions, low-intensity intervals, of course. But, there are also people out there, like me, who just run. None of the runs I had ever been on had any specific goal, other than to get into better shape. I never called a run anything other than a run. It was never a 'workout', 'session', 'effort', or 'routine'. I went for runs. "Going for a run. Be back in an hour or so". I've said that hundreds of times. Nobody in the non-playground section of the pool was just "going for a swim". Everything was a 'session', and everything had a specific purpose. Every stroke had its own pace and place. And drills, holy cow, what was with all the drills? I ran cross country for Acadia University and I've been running for 25-30 years, and I've never done a running drill. Sometimes the coach would try to get us to do specific workouts, but never a drill, certainly not one requiring extraneous equipment.

Every time one of the swimmers I witnessed would stop at the equipment/water bottle end of the pool (AKA the shallow end), after having completed a portion of an interval or effort, they would immediately throw their attention over to the clock. Every single time. They would stare at it until it was time to take off again. The clock was like something they needed approval or recognition from, like your mom on the Motel 6 pool deck during a summer road trip: "Mom...mom...mom...mom...mom...MOMMMM!!!!!!! Check this out. No hands!".

I finally found the courage to get in the water and start swimming. The first several workouts, if you can call them that, were in the yellow lane marked SLOW, and all I did was thrash about going back and forth, kicking as hard as I could. So hard, in fact, that I was exhausted before I had completed fifty metres. What I attempted to do those first few times was desperately try to emulate the style of the smoothest-looking people, seeing if I could sustain my effort for forty-five minutes. I never counted my lengths because I didn't want to know how far I wasn't going, and I always tried to time pushing off from the wall when there would be the least likelihood that I would be in close proximity to another human being. The last thing I wanted was to be a burden on those going faster than I was, and *everyone* was going faster than I was. I had no desire to get in the way of a real swimmer and throw off their specifically tailored workout.

Sometimes I would get the timing wrong and I would catch up to people, which actually made me so happy, and was so out of the ordinary, that I would simply stop in the water and wait for them to take the lead again. What else was I supposed to do? On one occasion, the ex-hockey player in me tried to pick a fight with the guy behind me. Fucker kept tapping my feet. Length after length, I would get to about the middle and he would start tapping. Finally, I'd had enough and I stopped abruptly and turned violently towards him. I got right up in his grille, close enough that our goggles were touching.

"Dude. What's with the feet? Fucking pass me, asshole!", I barked.

He apologized and I timed it so we wouldn't be near each other for the rest of the session. When I headed to the locker room afterwards, I noticed an information card entitled 'Swimming Etiquette' taped to the wall directly above the urinal. As I took a leak, I read it, as you do. On it were described a few important points, one of which was that you should 'politely and gently tap the feet of the swimmer ahead of you, indicating your desire to pass at the next turn'. OOPS.

After a couple of weeks, I managed to work my way out of the yellow lane. If you can grab your ass with both hands, I don't think you're permitted to spend more than two weeks there, so I made the brave move to the blue, MEDIUM, lane where I stayed for another few weeks. I followed the same process that had worked for me in the yellow one, just trying to fit in and not be the slowest. Whenever I would stop for a breath, I would always look at the clock, with its multi-coloured arrows, for some clue as to what I should do next. I didn't know what I was looking for, but that's what everyone else was doing, so I merely followed the crowd. It's a good thing they weren't all hitting the crack pipe after each lap.

Eventually, I worked my way out of the blue lane as well. I had been feeling pretty comfortable for a few sessions when a fit sixtyish guy came over and gave me shit. At first, I thought he was complimenting me on my speed or form, but it turns out he was accusing me of being a 'hot dog', artificially increasing the pace of the lane. I apologized, feeling pretty good about myself, and moved over to the green FAST lane, where I was humbled in about twenty strokes. I had a very hard time trying to keep up, at least at first. I kept at it, though, and after a while, I noticed a couple of regulars who I could just about keep up with, so I tagged along with them. They each took turns leading the effort, switching off fartlek style when they needed a break. I never led, and they didn't seem to mind. I just went when they went and rested when they did, and when they stared at the clock, so did I. I even nodded my head in the affirmative, as though I understood completely when they would say stuff like, "Blue at the top" or "fifty on a minute". It was difficult to keep up, and even more difficult to pretend I wasn't breathing hard. Without knowing it, these guys made me faster and more confident than ever, and I never even thought to learn their names.

With about a week to go before the big race in Syracuse, I felt that the pool had been great and that I had improved so much, but it was time to get some open water swimming in. Of course, because I was a little nervous about heading out into a wide-open lake, I put it off until the last day before leaving for Syracuse. Unfortunately, the day I chose was a violent, freezing cold, windy, raining sideways kind of day. The conditions were just awful, and, if I'm honest, quite dangerous, especially since I was all by myself. Looking out at the dark, grey choppy water, I said to myself, "Hey, I'm a swimmer now. It's raining, so what. I'm going to get wet anyway, right? It's not windy underwater. Fuck it". I walked down the beach and waded in, fully kitted up in my wetsuit, goggles, and cap. I dove in and took about 100 strokes getting a little less than about forty metres out, turned around and sprinted back to the car absolutely shell-shocked. It was the most terrifying experience ever. I was way more scared than I had been in Connecticut, and I was shaking and having flashbacks as I drove away.

What a mistake. How was I ever going to find the courage to go out into open water again? I was scheduled to race in a couple of days, and now I had developed PTSD. As I drove home, freezing cold, with the heater on full blast, I kept repeating the following mantra to myself, out loud: *You dumb bastard, you dumb bastard.*

- Syracuse -

When the weekend of the Syracuse race finally arrived, I felt physically ready. Running was good. New bike was shined up and primed to roll, and though I had zero open water confidence, I knew I was a much better and faster swimmer than I was in my last race. For the whole five hour drive I was feeling pretty confident and I was looking forward to competing against the big boys and girls. When Anne asked me if I felt ready for the race on Sunday, I had the urge to say "Bring it on". I didn't say it, but the feeling was there.

Then we turned onto Apulia Road heading for the venue, and the first thing I saw was what looked like a professional athlete, fully kitted up with helmet number, bike number, full hydration package, and going hard on his state of the art road machine towards us. I tried not to let it get to me, and I told Anne, "must be a pro just seeing if his bike is tuned properly". Then we saw another athlete looking even more professional than the first guy, and his kit was covered in sponsor logos. Right behind him was another and another. The road was ugly with triathletes hammering out what looked like a difficult bike workout. There were so many of them, I was starting to think I had missed the section in the Athlete's Guide about the MANDATORY SATURDAY SUPER FUCKING HARD BIKE WORKOUT. "Is this really what they do in the big time?", I thought to myself, starting to feel entirely inadequate. I had left my biking stuff back at the Hilton Garden Inn in East Syracuse. I looked at Anne, and she immediately asked if we were about to drive back to get my helmet and shoes. "Let's just park and see what's going on. It's still early, so we'll have time to go back if we need to", I said with absolutely no confidence that it was the right thing to do.

As we got closer to Jamesville Beach Park, we noticed that scores of runners had joined the cyclists in what, again, looked like quite intense training sessions. They were checking their watches and altering their tempos. If this was merely an intimidation tactic, it was having better than the desired effect because I was beginning to get nauseated, dizzy even. I hadn't been planning on, nor was I prepared to do, a final training session, let alone two, like these people were apparently doing, but they looked so confident. Everyone appeared as though this was just another day in the office, each having the same attitude pasted on their faces that said both, "this is how a real triathlete does it", and "that's right, I'm in way better shape than you. See you at the finish line, loser".

My heart was racing, and though I was sitting in the passenger seat giving it everything I had to avoid throwing up in my lap, my pulse rate was way higher than these people who were doing intervals in the scorching heat, the day before the race. I was starting to think that everything I had heard about 'tapering' was a load of crap that real athletes tell us to trick us into not training enough just so they could be sure to kick our asses on Sunday. Bastards.

When we had been in the hotel room before leaving that morning, I was rushing Anne and Owen in a nervous tizzy. "Let's go. Hurry up, I wanna get there early to get the lay of the land", I urged. The earlier we got there, I figured, the less nervous I would be because I would have more time to come to terms with all the stress of a new venture. Now that we were there, I was even more of a mess. Everybody appeared to be doing *something* that I had never even thought of, and there was zero percent body fat anywhere. At the other races I had done, there were more than a few slightly larger people who you could tell had been sort of bullied by office co-workers into competing, or who were there just for the fun of it. The people I saw in Syracuse, so far, were there for anything but fun. They all meant serious business, and it seemed that I had not read the memo they had all received.

Though all of these observations were causing me a great deal of stress, so long as I was still in the car, I seemed capable of managing and compartmentalizing it. The KIA was womblike, keeping me safe from all the dangers lurking out there that were ready to pounce and mock me for being so naive as to think I could do this.

When we finally parked the car and I opened the door, I was initially struck by the heat of the air, the searing brightness of the sun, and the matrix of the unknown that smothered me like a hot, itchy blanket. It was all so overwhelming. There were athletes all over the place, in various stages of unpacking and preparing their equipment. Everything they did was so purposeful and bee-like. There was a very specific reason for absolutely every action they took and every move they made. They all appeared to be both highly tuned uber-athletes and expert bike mechanics. There was zero hesitation in any of their movements as nobody looked around with questioning eyes. Each person was intently focused on the singular task at hand, which they performed adroitly and totally, before moving on to the next extremely logical item on their well-engineered subliminal 'to do' lists.

By contrast, the back of my car looked like a cross between a daycare centre and a yard sale. If you took a quick peek, you would have assumed I was off to the flea market to sell a bunch of random crap, as there was absolutely no rhyme or reason to where anything was. There were no special itemized or labelled Rubbermaid containers for swim, bike, and run gear, no 'nutrition' buckets or washing stations.

The guy next to me had a Park Tool work stand set up in the bed of his F-150 pickup truck and was giving his very expensive Argon-18 a complete tune-up with the apparent proficiency of a master bike mechanic. And he was shirtless, showing off his entirely ripped, lean, super body. He looked at me and, with utter confidence, asked, "Yo, Dude, you running a disc or an 80 mill tomorrow?".

I looked to my left and right in hopes that he was talking to someone else because I had absolutely no idea what the hell he was getting at. As far as my set-up was concerned, I was merely secretly hoping that I didn't get a flat the next day because, though I could replace an innertube, it would take me the better part of forty-five minutes to complete the job. Plus, I hadn't brought a spare anyway. Once I realized he was talking to me, and that I needed to say something quick that would hide the fact that I was a total noob, I turned the tables back on him and gave my best effort at sounding like the kind of cocky prick I hate with a passion, and said, "Dude, conditions call for the 80. Disc is a bad move. Come on, Bud, you gotta know this shit. Last-minute decisions won't cut it".

He lowered his chin, looking at his feet like a chastised puppy and softly replied, "Yo, you're right. S'pose ta be a bit breezy. Thanks, Dude".

I dodged a bullet there. I had absolutely no idea what he was talking about, but I got away with it. It was now time to make my way over to the registration tent, but first, I had to figure out whether or not I should bring my bike with me then, or wait for later. I had read that it needed to be in transition on Saturday, but many of the cars in the parking lot still had bikes attached to them, and there were scores of people still out on the road playing peloton. I decided to leave mine on the roof and come back for it later.

Registration was, pretty much, uneventful, except that I was a little surprised by the sheer number of documents they made me pretend to read before signing. Also, for some reason, and this still happens now after having done this for years, my mind went completely blank when it comes to contact information. What's my girlfriend's phone number? No idea. I was hoping that nothing serious happened to me on the course because if they were to call Anne's number to inform her that I was in the hospital bleeding my way through a coma, they would end up ordering an extra-large pizza. The only phone number that I could remember off the top of my head was from 1985, for Jerry's Pizzeria in Lennoxville, Quebec. The only other number I could remember with ease was my bank account PIN number, and I didn't feel comfortable giving that out to just anyone. There's only about $67 in there, but better safe than sorry.

Once everything was signed and my chip was tested, I gathered my swag bag and was directed, without any choice to do otherwise, to the merchandise tent where I was encouraged to spend about seven thousand dollars. These Ironman people aren't stupid because I bought one of almost everything. Who doesn't need an official Ironman barbecue cover? As far as I was concerned, you cannot go through life properly without one, especially since it matches the oven mitts that I had already picked out. And a set of Ironman cufflinks, even though I am a Phys. Ed. teacher and only own two dress shirts, both from Gap.

When we finally made it out of there, the first booth I saw was from a local bike shop having a blowout sale on a bunch of crap they were unable to sell at their brick and mortar location. The sign said that everything had to go, so I helped them out a little by buying an aero helmet, two bidons, some energy chews, and about forty-two gels (I had no idea about fuelling).

Inside the swag bag we received from Ironman was an issue of Triathlete Magazine, which I only read on the morning of the race while taking a dump. In it was an article stating that you should NEVER try or use anything new on race day and that all equipment and nutrition should be familiar. I wondered whether I would be okay. Let's see, a new bike that I had ridden in the bike shop parking lot once, new tri-suit, new helmet, new sunglasses, different gels. There was very little about the race that wasn't going to be completely brand new and foreign to me.

With shopping completed, I went through the manilla envelope we were given at registration containing my bib number, timing chip, and about a hundred stickers, all with my number on them. Oh, and three giant plastic bags (one red, one blue, and one green). The envelope made me a bit giddy at first, because of all the stickers. Who doesn't love stickers? What to do with them was a bit of a mystery, however, and the fact that they were labelled only compounded how dumb I felt. *Helmet sticker.* Okay...front of the helmet, side of the helmet, anywhere I want on the helmet. I didn't know. *Bike sticker* and *stem sticker*. Why does my bike need two stickers? I actually started to think that by 'stem' they meant something other than what I thought it was, and if it was something else, I was sure that I didn't have one. Do people really remove the entire cockpit of their bikes on race day creating the need for separate identification? Because I wasn't sure where they all went, I figured I would wait until after the MANDATORY race briefing to affix them. Surely the precise location of these stickers would be one of the headline items at the meeting.

There were to be several times at which the MANDATORY race briefing would take place, thus making it not only convenient for people arriving throughout the day, but also to ensure that everyone attended so they could receive the vital information being offered. Being mandatory, I was anal about getting there early, so that I was sure not to miss the part where they take attendance, and so that I could get a good seat. There isn't much to do at the race 'village' at Ironman 70.3 Syracuse, so Anne and Owen stayed with me.

The meeting took place outside under a giant permanent awning. Being open on all sides, I chose a seat near the edge so that my family could be near me without officially taking up any of the seats I assumed would be reserved for the folks racing the next day. The athlete's guide made it sound as though the setting would be very formal and that it would be open only to those competing in the event. I took a seat at one of the picnic tables and waited for the person to come around taking attendance, which no one did. There were about as many people under the age of ten, and quite obviously not participants, as there were athletes under the awning.

I soon realized that my definition of 'mandatory', was quite different from that of the race organizers. For me, it means that you have to be there and, furthermore, that failure to do so will result in some sort of punishment or penalty. Apparently, however, it means that you can come if you have nothing better to do. Though it seemed like it didn't matter at all whether I attended or not, there were things I needed clarity about, so I stuck around.

The meeting followed your standard format of information session via a lecture of sorts followed by a question and answer period. It became obvious in no time that the information portion of this meeting was intended exclusively for athletes who haven't mastered the fine art of reading, because everything the presenter said came directly out of the athlete's guide, which was on the event website. For those athletes who arrived by horse and buggy and had no access to the internet, there were hard copies of it everywhere in the ironman village, in addition to having the major points (course maps, rules and regulations, feed zones, mile markers, flow of transition, etc.) on large posters that were placed in obvious and well-travelled areas throughout the venue.

Once the lecture was over, without any of the questions I thought were important having been addressed, people began raising their hands to ask about the very stuff that had just been, very clearly, covered, that only the person in first place would need to know.

"Do we make a right or left on Apulia coming out of transition?".

Dude, you're 67 years old and your boobs are bigger than the blonde on WKRP in Cincinnati, just follow the person in front of you. Failing that, how about you just follow the fucking signs. What concerned me more was that most of the people asking these absurd questions, that even a total virgin like myself had already figured out, had done the race before and were on a first-name basis with the Ironman guy who had given the lecture.

"Listen, Clarence. It'll be the same set up as last year".

"Oh, okay. Thanks, Phil".

What made it even more strange was that there was nobody rolling their eyes upon hearing such stupidity. It was then that I realized that triathletes must be the nicest type of athletes on earth. They are cheerleaders with bikes and bathing caps. I grew up playing a lot of hockey and if you asked the coach what the starting line-up was right after he had just announced it, you'd likely get a punch right in the temple.

The questions *I* had weren't answered, and after hearing what everybody else was concerned with, and having seen most people looking like they had everything totally dialled in, I was too shy to ask, for fear of appearing as though I was ill-prepared or that I hadn't done my homework. I still didn't know what items, apart from the bike, needed to be left in transition overnight. Do our shoes and helmet stay with the bike? What about nutrition and water bottles? How was I supposed to dress in the morning? Did I show up in full kit, wetsuit and all, or do we change clothes once onsite? When should I eat breakfast and what should I eat? What is the normal time to go to bed, and what time should I set my alarm for? Transition opens at 5:00, do I need to be there at that time? Earlier? Will there be traffic in the morning? These were the things I needed to know about.

Being an Ironman event, and assuming everyone, other than myself and a few obvious other newbies, had vast experience, it was my understanding that there must be a standard formula or code we were expected to follow for all of these matters. My ego was way too fragile to withstand potential pointing and laughing if I showed up race morning in a pair of jeans with my tri suit underneath while everyone else donned their wetsuits right out of the car. My nerves were stretched to their breaking point as it was, I needed someone to ease the tension I was feeling. I would have listened and done whatever they told me, even if they had said I was supposed to show up to transition at 2 AM in a pink onesie.

Once the meeting broke up, we walked back to the car to fetch my bike, which needed to be stickered up and brought to transition. It was almost noon, so I figured I would need to rush. Luckily one of the cars in the row behind ours had a bike still on the roof rack with the stickers already attached, so I now knew where they went. With that done, it was time to head over to transition, which was about halfway between the parking lot and the beach where the swim start would be. As we walked, I noticed that almost nobody going in the same direction we were had their bike with them. Instead, they were in their wetsuits with caps and goggles on. I overheard two ladies: "So, going for a last-minute swim workout?", one asked a total stranger dressed the same.

"Nope, just a final test to feel-out what the turnaround is like", she replied. "I did the last workout this morning, but the buoys weren't out yet".

A wave of inadequacy washed over me, and what little confidence I was feeling for having conquered the bike sticker paradox fell to the gravel beneath my feet. Practice swim? Two practice swims? I swam two times the past week and I thought that might have been too much because my shoulders were always killing me for a couple of days afterwards. If I did a swim workout the afternoon before the race (or TWO workouts), I would surely drown before reaching the first buoy in the next day's race.

As we continued to walk, Anne and Owen tried to engage me in conversation, but I heard nothing they were saying. I was too busy thinking about all the things I was doing wrong, as well as the myriad of stuff I had probably neglected to do altogether in my 'preparation' for this race. I decided to just focus on the things I could control for now and try not to worry about what everybody else was doing, which was a task that was super hard, especially when I saw how crowded the swim course looked, and how few bikes were racked in transition. There were no more than twenty or so of us in there, along with perhaps another fifty or sixty bikes that had already been left. I knew from the race website that this would mean there were another 1900 triathletes still out there getting faster somewhere. All that was left was just us rookies who didn't know any better. I felt I should get to know these people because I would be with them at the back of the race all of the following day.

According to much of the literature on the sport of triathlon, most experts believe that transition is of utmost importance and is considered to be the fourth discipline of any triathlon. Precious minutes could be gained or lost there and, thus, the whole notion of the term 'transition' possessed a certain gravitas which, now that I was there, I somehow did not feel. I found my spot and racked my bike, then I looked at it for about a minute, standing there all lonely, hanging pathetically by the chin of its seat, wondering what else I should be doing. I drew a blank. There was absolutely nothing I could think of that needed to be done. I walked around to the front end of the bike and pretended to adjust the brake levers and gear shifters. They looked fine.

The fact is, if there had been something wrong with them, I would have had no idea how to diagnose the problem, nor would I have been capable of remedying it. I shrugged my shoulders, squeezed my tires, and took a controlled look around to see what the others were up to while trying to pretend I was looking for something, or someone, in particular.

Everybody else in transition was spinning pedals, changing gears, and checking various components that I wasn't sure I even had on my bike. A few were letting the air hiss from their tires, which, just as it had done in Connecticut, baffled me. There had never been a good reason for me to ever let the air out of anything, be it a bike tire, car tire, basketball, pool floaties, or anything else. In fact, air leaving my tires has always been something to be avoided, and a sign of something wrong. Tires with no air = bad.

Considering I had now completed three triathlons and that I had read every publication about the sport (or at least looked at all the pretty pictures), there was only one thing that I knew, with absolute certainty about triathlon, and that was that I knew absolutely nothing. It all seemed to be totally enigmatic. Every person I saw and every action I witnessed, brought home the fact that I was entirely out of my element, and made me want to leave the venue and rush back to the hotel where I could pull a pillow over my head and hide from all of it.

After leaving the transition zone and meeting up with Anne and Owen by the beach, I fought the urge to just say, "let's go. We gotta get outta here". There had to be things that needed to get done, but I couldn't think of what they might be. Registration was complete, my bike was checked in, the race briefing had been attended, shopping was taken care of, I even had a good look at the swim course, which appeared to be seventeen or eighteen kilometres long. I had eaten a snack. What was left? Why were there still so many people here?

The decision was made to just leave, but it made me feel so

guilty. Surely there was something glaringly obvious and important that was being regretfully neglected. As we pulled away along Apulia Road, we actually had to slow down several times to slalom our way around all the runners and cyclists. Now I had never done a race of this magnitude before, but it was just a race after all, and it started the next morning at first light. Were these workouts really going to help? Shouldn't these people try to get some rest? These were questions I asked myself in a pitiful attempt to feel better about my decision to leave.

Once back at the hotel, there was very little, beyond the television, to keep my mind off of what was going to happen the next day. The stress level was high and was exacerbated by the boredom of the room. It was like trying to concentrate at work, knowing you have an appointment for a root-canal afterwards. I tried going to the pool area and soaking in the hot tub, which felt good but did nothing to relax me. By three o'clock, I was stir-crazy and made the decision to go to the grocery store to purchase a bottle of wine, convincing myself that the antioxidants it contained were good for me and the alcohol would help me to relax, and allow me to sleep much easier. I was only planning on having a glass or two with the pasta we had ordered from a local pizza place.

Buying the wine ended up being exactly what I needed. It was a distraction, which is really all I truly required, but it also came in very handy later on that night. I hadn't really worked out what time I should turn out the lights and shut off the television. If I shut everything down too early, I would run the risk of tossing and turning because I wasn't tired enough to sleep. If I waited too long, I might not get enough. As it happened, the decision was made for me by Mr. Shiraz. The lights went out when the bottle was empty. Or, at least I think that's when they went out. I recall finishing the bottle. The next thing I remember was getting up at around 12:30 to take a leak and stubbing my toe hard on the mini-fridge that I hadn't seen because all the lights were off.

So, I drank a whole bottle of wine, but I had read that it is very important to hydrate adequately the night before a race. The wine I drank was in liquid form, so I convinced myself all would be okay. After going to the bathroom, I noticed that I was starving, so I ate two bowls of Raisin Bran and a Pop-Tart, then went back to bed where I stayed awake the rest of the night, feeling stupid. By three o'clock, after laying for a few hours with the TV on mute, my internal alarm went off, exactly twenty minutes before the actual alarm on my watch. I have been blessed with one of those subconscious mechanisms that will not allow me to sleep in if there is something important to be awake for (usually it means that I never get to sleep at all), but on this occasion, it wasn't any internal signal that was triggered by circadian rhythms or barometric pressure. This time it came from a much lower part of my anatomy. The Raisin Bran, half of a pizza, two plates of baked ziti, a bottle of wine and a pair of Pop-Tarts, had completed the process of digestion in my gut and had reached the end of their journey. I needed to poop, like NOW!

Once I was done in the bathroom and wiping the sweat from my brow, I could concentrate on preparing breakfast, starting the fuelling process for the long day ahead, and getting ready to drive over to the race site. Our hotel was about a thirty-minute journey from Jamesville Beach Park, where the transition was set to open at 5:00 AM, so we left at four o'clock, just to be on the safe side.

It was dark out and the only people on the road had M-Dot stickers on their cars and, thus, it could be assumed were headed for the same destination as we were. This brought me a great deal of relief as Anne drove while I intermittently switched back and forth between sipping on an extra-large Dunkin Donuts coffee and a bottle of red Gatorade. The convoy of triathletes on the highway reassured me that we were headed in the proper direction, as well as letting me know that we had left at the correct time.

That warm, fuzzy feeling died a rapid, bloody death the second we made a left turn onto Apulia road as, though there were still several miles to the entrance to the park, we were met with parked, bumper to bumper traffic. What I saw before me was a sea of glowing red brake lights attached to cars that were sitting completely stationary in front of us. We moved so slowly that I had plenty of time to remove my seatbelt, exit the vehicle, empty my distended bladder on the front lawn of an unsuspecting Syracuse resident, and return to the car less than a first down away from where I had left it. The pace of traffic was so slow, in fact, that I was able to complete this task three more times before we finally arrived.

Prior to leaving the hotel, I had been concerned with what time transition would open. Now, sitting in the car doing permanent damage to my prostate by attempting to hold in several litres of a combination of Americano and electrolyte beverage, I became more troubled with worrying about what time it would be closing. With every passing minute, my angst was amplified exponentially because I was sure we would never make it in time, and I began to do the mental math in a desperate attempt to determine if it would be better for me to leave the car and finish the journey on foot. Panicking was making me even more edgy by the second. I began to fidget and search for something to occupy my thoughts. In my sleep-deprived, agitated state, all I could come up with was to keep pounding back the coffee and Gatorade, which, of course, blew my bladder up like a birthday balloon, making me even more uncomfortable and fidgety. After having pissed on most of the front yards along Apulia, I finally finished my coffee and was able to relieve myself in the empty cup.

We eventually made it to the parking lot just before six o'clock. I grabbed my three bidons filled with the same red Gatorade that I had been drinking all morning, and the rest of my stuff, and rushed off to transition, which was a five-minute walk from the car. Everything that I could think of that I would possibly need for the day fit neatly into a plastic grocery bag. The only thing too big for the bag was the enormous mass of inadequacy I felt as I watched what others were carrying to transition. Some athletes, in fact, had so much payload that they required the aid of their loved ones, significant others and children, to help them haul the expedition worthy quantity of goods and equipment they had brought along. These pseudo-sherpas were being bogged down, literally, by so much cumbersome paraphernalia, that they had trouble making it all the way without rest stops, resembling the long trek from Everest base camp to the summit, with transition being the top of the mountain. It would have come as no surprise to hear the name Tenzing called out. Where I had a plastic bag, they had full seventy-litre backpacks, hockey bags, rucksacks, and even wheeled airport-style luggage. I swear I saw one guy with a shopping cart filled with two large, white, twenty-litre chlorine buckets overflowing with stuff.

Watching all of this, I made a mental checklist and deftly ticked off all the items I was sure would be required, and cross-referenced them with what I had in my grocery bag. I had in my possession three bidons of Gatorade, all of which would be mounted on my bike (one in the cage on the down tube, which I would soon notice was beginning to come loose, and two behind my seat). For 'food' I had fifteen gels (I haphazardly figured that I would require one before the swim, one before the bike, one every twenty kilometres on the bike along with one just before dismounting, one in transition before the run, then one every five kilometres on the run. There were three spares in case I dropped any along the way). There was one packet of Cliff Blocks because they looked good at the bike shop the previous day. I had never tried them before, but they appeared to be nothing more than giant gumdrops my grandfather used to buy at Marks and Spencer. There was one small carton of chocolate milk (these were my pre-vegan days, and I had heard a well-known triathlete wax poetic about the nutritional benefits the beverage would offer. I figured if it was good enough for Rinny, it was good enough for me). Next to the chocolate milk, I had two granola bars and a package containing two unfrosted, strawberry Pop-Tarts. There was also a can of Pepsi to chug before the run. I love sugary, fizzy drinks before running, and the extra caffeine would be a boost.

Aside from 'nutrition' (and I hesitate to actually call it that for two reasons: 1. Nothing that I brought with me to consume during the race could be construed as remotely nutritious. 2. It is a triathlete's term that I have come to hate without really knowing why. Why don't we just call it food? Is it because it sounds more scientific? It exists in the same realm for me as the word 'utilize' which is bandied about by people unsuccessfully trying to sound more intelligent than they actually are. What's wrong with the word 'use'? We do not 'applicate' sunblock to our skin, we apply it. We don't utilize the toilet paper. We use it. Simple.). I had one pair of cycling shoes, one pair of sunglasses, and one race belt with bib number attached. Everything else that I deemed necessary was on my body. I wore my tri-suit (for the first time), my helmet (also for the first time), timing chip, and my running shoes. My swim cap and goggles were safely tucked inside the chest of my wetsuit which covered the tri-suit.

I was looking forward to getting into transition, not just so that I could liberate myself from the plastic bag, the handle of which had cut off the blood supply to most of my hand and was macheteing its way through my fingers, but also so I could witness what mysterious trinkets and gadgets were hidden in the various vessels the other athletes had transported with them.

Have you ever been in the departure lounge at the gate of an airport and watched people waiting to board the plane with a 'carry-on' bag that no reasonable person could fit inside the trunk of the average American made sedan from the 1970s? The people who drag these body bag-sized pieces of luggage are also the ones who attempt to take advantage of the loophole in the rule that allows them to port, in addition to the body bag, a purse or computer bag. This supplemental bag is usually large enough to house the entire control room used for a NASA shuttle launch. Since when do purses come with two shoulder straps and a waist belt for load management and the words THE NORTH FACE embroidered in twenty centimetre high letters across the back? When I see these folks waiting to board, I always feel my blood pressure rise because they always seem to get on the plane just ahead of me, making me wait, with fifty people behind me, watching 'Joe Carry-On' attempt to wedge his expedition 'purse' into the overhead compartment. He inevitably will end up sitting next to me and attempt to raise the armrest that is intended to separate us, causing me to steal a line I once heard used on a flight to London, "Not gonna happen, Dude. That's a *we* decision".

Transition, it turns out, was not much different.

The first thing I did, when I arrived at my bike, was place the shopping bag on the ground and pretend to pore over the bike, looking for imperfections. I wiped off the dew that had accumulated overnight, constantly peering out of the corner of my eye to see what the experts around me were doing. Everything appeared to be so orchestrated and ritualistic as though I was witnessing an elevated level of OCD performed on a mass scale. These people were all laying out large towels directly under their bikes and placing small pieces of carpet between their bikes and that of their neighbour, like a welcome mat. Next, it was time to make sure there wasn't a single PSI of air in their tires so they could pump them chock full of the fresh stuff. This process took no less than seven to ten minutes. Following that was the performance of what looked like a full-blown chemistry experiment, as they concocted the ideal electrolyte to glucose mixture ratios in each of their onboard hydration systems, tasting every ten or so seconds, like

Gordon Ramsay. With that done, they laid out the day's equipment and clothing choices with the meticulousness of a Marine in Boot Camp: cycling shoes clipped to pedals with elastic bands tied to them and the bike frame to ensure they would stay perfectly level, running shoes with socks already opened up and stuffed inside each shoe, helmet laid on top of aero bars with sunglasses opened and placed inside the up-turned helmet. They had all of their nutrition, displayed in the exact order they planned to ingest it, next to the shoes, running belt and hat. Gels were neatly taped to the top tube of the bike. With that done, they would check to make sure all of their components worked and that the bike was in the perfect gear to start the ride.

I was in total awe of what looked like a high school marching band during half-time of a Friday night playoff game. It did not appear that they needed to think of what was to be done either. Every task was completed like a routine that had been practiced for hours and performed by rote. Watching all of this, I realized there was much I still needed to learn. My technique, being way simpler, skipped many steps, and took less than two minutes: Take water bottles out of the plastic bag and place them in bottle cages. Take seven gels and place them in the little pouchy thing attached to the top tube with duct tape because I had purchased it the day before and couldn't figure out how to affix it correctly. Leave everything else in the plastic bag. Done. I read that it is important to spend as little time in transition as possible. They probably meant *during* the race. Oh well, what's the difference?

When I was finished, there were many people still checking their brake lines, fiddling with computers and wiping off tires.

There were even athletes sitting in folding beach chairs drinking electrolyte concoctions, munching on energy bars, and having good old conversations with each other. It resembled a Sunday afternoon summer cookout. I would not have been surprised to see one of them break out a Hibachi and a volleyball net. This was all very entertaining, but my bowels were urging me to exit transition and find a honey bucket as soon as possible.

On my way out, I made a mental list of items I had seen some of the other athletes with that I might think about bringing for my next race: floor mat, towel, teddy bear (I assume for good luck), six-pack of Red Bull, Tupperware bowls (plural) of food with cutlery, folding chair, headlamp, flip flops, sweatshirt and sweatpants (matching, of course), pump, multiple three-litre jugs of water, and a toolbox (not a mini toolkit but a full tackle-box with a handle and all).

I didn't know what most of it was for, but these people seemed to believe it was all necessary, crucial even. At the very least, I would need to get a sturdier shopping bag for next time...and maybe a popcorn machine and an ironing-board.

From transition, I headed directly for the porta-potty farm that existed in a parking lot the size of a football field, on the way to the swim start. On Saturday, these plastic, personal outhouses had been closed and zip-tied to avoid being prematurely filled with piles of smouldering human excrement. When I left my bike and gear on race morning, I really needed to empty my bowels pretty badly, and I gave myself a five to ten-minute window for that to get done before an unfortunate accident would ensue. Based on what I remembered from the day before, having seen hundreds of these cabins, I assumed my ten-minute window was plenty wide enough.

As I approached the parking lot I saw masses of people resembling the crowd you would likely see at a free outdoor Dave Matthews concert, only here everyone was wearing suits of black rubber. I didn't understand why everybody had decided to congregate in a parking lot, standing on asphalt, when they could wait for the start of the race on the beach. What I found even more bizarre was that they were all waiting around in the most organized fashion. There were dozens of single and semi-double file lines stretching all the way up to about twelve feet from the toilet doors. I couldn't help but wonder why they would gather in such a fashion, but I had to put these thoughts aside because my window was rapidly closing.

I put my head down and briskly walked straight towards the closest toilet and was about to enter when I noticed two things simultaneously: 1. They were all occupied, every single one. That's right, all 150 thousand of them. Not a single vacancy. 2. These folks were waiting at least 100 people deep in line at each toilet.

My window was instantly shattered. It was evident that this wait required more than a mere window; I was going to need a giant, multi-panel patio door to endure this line-up. Somehow, I was going to have to figure out how to ignore the fact that my abdomen had become entirely distended with three or four kilograms of fully processed raisin bran and Pop-Tarts, and head back to the end of the line, desperately trying to formulate an escape plan. Maybe I could run into the water, drop trou (or in this case, wetsuit), and liberate a school of brown eels. I suppose I could run into the forest and unload in front of a family enjoying an early morning pre-race breakfast. I could discreetly fish a plastic bag out of one of the garbage bins nearby, duck behind a porta-potty, and go in the bag. I could attempt to beat the shit out of twenty or thirty people waiting in line and cut to the front. All of these options raced through my mind in seconds, but I decided to hope for the best, go to the back of the line and pray that most of the people ahead of me just had to piss. If worse came to worst, I could just poop in my wetsuit and hope it flushed out during the swim. At least that would keep my mind off of drowning.

Once at the back, the bonding began. Have you ever noticed that when you are forced into relatively close quarters with a group of strangers, it is impossible to avoid the creation of a pseudo-congregation, a brother/sisterhood, as it were? Most of the time it happens when something has gone wrong. It doesn't have to be anything life-threatening, like a train wreck or hostage situation. In fact, it is usually something a little more innocuous, though annoying, like, say, a delay on your flight from Denver to Toronto, forcing you and your plane-mates to be stuck together for six hours going nowhere. It is made all the more strange because had nothing gone wrong, you would have still have been together for five hours on the flight without really being able to move, but you may not have uttered a word to anyone. The delay forces a reason to commiserate and communicate with one another.

The same sort of thing happened while waiting in the bathroom line in Syracuse. All the criteria were present: 1. A long wait, 2. Closed quarters, 3. Strangers with a clear and present, common crisis. This artificial congregation of otherwise entirely unlikely friends is what Kurt Vonnegut called a *Granfalloon*. The best thing about my particular granfalloon was that they were able to distract me, temporarily at least, from the uncomfortable cramping sensation coming from my overloaded intestinal area, allowing me to ease up the vice-like grip my butt cheeks were performing under my tri-suit. This was no easy feat because I really needed to go, and it is a testament to the power of fear that is hard-wired into our DNA to perform a number of vital functions from fighting tigers, fleeing from tigers, and distracting us from otherwise uncomfortable situations, sometimes involving tigers.

While waiting in that line, terrified that I might soil myself at any moment, I listened to and watched tiny vignettes of information being offered by those around me.

The first thing I noticed was that everybody seemed to know each other, as though they were part of the sisterhood of travelling triathletes. There were hugs and handshakes, even the odd, overly excited high-five. Some even knew each other's names, making me, apparently, the only stranger, and causing them to talk around me as though I was as inanimate as a traffic cone. There was no way I dared to open my mouth for fear of finding the one topic these people would find offensive. In other words, I didn't want to be the guy trying too hard to fit into a group of jokesters, and ultimately offend everyone: "Two guys from Pittsburgh are fucking a seagull....What, no bird jokes?".

Even the topic of their conversation, triathlon, made me nervous because it seemed that *their* triathlon reality was grossly different from mine. They spoke of their training, which, compared to what I had done, sounded so scientific and methodical. I would need a B.Sc. to figure it out. They talked about zones and intervals, wattages and cadences, heart rates and training logs. If I had kept a training log, at that time, there would only be three different entries repeated many times: Went for a run — 65 minutes, went for a ride — 2 hours, swum — 45 minutes. That's about it. These folks mentioned where they were in their periodization, and had coaches (plural), who designed twelve-week training blocks with low carb days and brick workouts.

Really? Coaches? What for? I didn't know such a thing existed. If you're not training for the Olympics or doing a sport for which you are being paid, why do you need a coach? For a minute I wondered whether I had stumbled upon the 'Professional' bathroom line. I could see no reason to pay someone to show me how to run or ride my bike. Sure, my swim stroke could use a little healthy technical advice, but I wasn't going to pay anyone for it unless there was prize money on the line. My immediate goal was to finish the race, preferably without stopping at all along the way. Who can't do that without a coach? Yes, ultimately I would love to do well enough to qualify for Vegas, but I didn't expect that would happen, and it didn't seem worth paying a coach to marginally improve my chances.

Looking at the kits these people were wearing, I surmised that they must have had sponsorship deals because they were covered in advertisements for all sorts of products, some triathlon related, some not so much. They looked like human-sized NASCARs. Apparently everyone within a twenty-yard radius of me had been part of the group of athletes I had seen yesterday still training the day before the race.

"So, what'd you get done yesterday, Sue?", one of them asked another, warming up her upper body with military-style callisthenics.

"Not much. Didn't want to blow my taper", was her matter of fact reply. She actually used those exact words, for real. She said it just loud and proud enough to force everyone around her to take notice and cross-reference it with what we had done. It was designed to intimidate, and, speaking for myself, it was working. "I just biked the course", she continued.

"Wait, what?", I said to myself, almost audibly. "You mean you biked 90k the day before a 90k race?". Now, sure, I was a complete Ironman neophyte, and, yes, my big pre-race workout consisted of a few kilometres of worrying followed by a lengthy soak in the hot tub at the hotel, but 90k seemed a little excessive, especially when she added that she had completed a 'shake-out' swim as well, whatever that was. What was she trying to 'shake' out, and, furthermore, what was she shaking it out of?

After tripping on my chin listening to this, it became quite evident that she wasn't the outlier, but that I was. None of those around our little congregation seemed to think that what Sue had done was over the top in any way at all. If anything, it appeared as though she was the slacker in the group, and must have been recovering from an injury or something. Why else would she be taking it so easy on such a crucial training day? Why indeed?

After the subject of their training had been exhausted, they briefly tackled the matter of how their tri-club needed a new executive, because the president was retiring that summer. I must have looked like a puppy cocking my head to one side upon being asked if I wanted to go walkies, because this was something I just could not wrap my head around. Triathlon *club*? With an executive board? Group rides? Sunday group long runs? These were entirely foreign concepts to me because I ran and rode to get away from other people. In fact, other people are what *ruin* a good run or ride. Nothing drives me crazier than when someone tries to strike up a conversation during a running race. Exercise is *my* time, my only time to just be alone with my thoughts. The rest of the day is spent with other people. When I run, I want nothing more than to be left alone, even when I'm suffering...especially when I'm suffering. In fact, I believe it is the reason I have always been pretty good at it. Because I don't want anyone to catch me so that we can have a little chin wag, I try to go faster than they do. Joining a club with scheduled practices that were standardized for a whole group to complete, more or less together, is anathema to me. My job has a schedule; the last thing I want is to have to follow a bell during my recreation time as well.

By the time they began spreading their feathers to essentially brag about which races they had done and which they were planning on doing (with the word Kona dominating the discussion), I had mercifully arrived at the front of the line, and needed to switch my focus to the ten or fifteen porta-potty doors in front of me to see which handle went from red to green first, so I could pounce on it before the person waiting at the front of the lines to my left and right. It's like being in the starting blocks for the 100-metre dash. A quick glance to each side to let them know that as soon as that little, filthy, bacteria-ridden, plastic micro-bathroom is liberated, I will be pouncing on it like a cat on a cellar-dwelling mouse.

Inside the cabin, the first thing I always think of is how happy I am that as a child my siblings and I would often have contests to see who could hold their breath the longest underwater. Back then it was just a childish game, but now, struggling to get my wetsuit down past my waist without letting one of the arms touch the toxic chemistry experiment on the floor, shit was getting real...Literally. The second thought I have is that there is some sad fucker, regretting having not completed high school, who is charged with cleaning these things. Have you ever noticed that the level of how concerned you are with coming into contact with someone else's filth is inversely related to just how desperate the need to take a dump is? When I'm at work and feel the urge to go for a post-lunch poop, I find it absolutely appalling that some ignorant prick has left a drop of urine on the seat, and I will invariably move to the next stall to find a cleaner locale to do my business. Inside one of these cabins right before the start of a half Ironman, after having waited for ages, dancing around to think of anything that will distract you from shitting yourself, with a distended, cramping abdomen, your concern about a few microbes is no longer as high. When you've got to go really badly, your DEFCON level preempts your fear of the cooties.

When I left the toilet, I joined the line of lemmings on their way to the beach and ended up at the section reserved for swim warmups, which I wasn't planning on doing. The word 'warmup' itself is a bit of a misnomer when the water is significantly colder than the air and is guaranteed to actually lower my core body temperature rather than 'warm' it up. Also, a warmup is intended to loosen you up and get you physically and mentally prepared to begin the process of focused, high-intensity exercise. The idea of venturing out into open water surrounded by a couple hundred strangers still caused me considerable anxiety, so the less time spent in the reservoir right before the race, the better.

Instead of actually swimming, as the others were doing, my warmup consisted of holding my goggles and swim cap in one hand and walking in just deep enough so that I could pee in my wetsuit without anyone seeing it flow out at my left foot. It's astonishing how quickly the body can produce urine, and how much. I had been hydrating pretty much non-stop since supper the day before, and my bladder was now incapable of containing anything for more than five minutes. There was about one hundred metres of asphalt, grass, and sand from the toilets to the edge of the reservoir, and I managed to take three pisses on the journey, plus two in the water. By the time I found my proper age group corral, I had gone another four or five times. Though I am not an American, I still felt uncomfortably unpatriotic, and highly disrespectful, as I peed my way through the entire national anthem. I couldn't help it, though. I even peed, pretty much at a continuous flow, waiting for our group to make it to the starting archway, while listening to the guys around me pretend to offer good luck to one another, simultaneously hoping they will either drown or get a flat tire.

No one in the 45-49 age group expects to win the race outright, but we all want to podium in our category, even those of us like me, who probably don't have a prayer, and all of us, at least secretly, want to qualify for the World Champs. I know I did. I played the game like everyone else and put on that Oscars smile that is outwardly quite friendly and communicates compassion, whilst, on the inside, screams out terrible things.

I said, "Good luck. Have a good one", to those around me. I even broke one of my personal rules and did something I never do: I not only returned but initiated several high fives, a gesture so overused that it made me almost as nauseated as I get when I hear people use the word 'AWESOME' to describe a bowl of soup. In fact, I found myself combining them. "Have an awesome race, Dude", I offered up with palm in the sky, the universal sign telegraphing that I wish to engage in the high-five ritual. The strangest part of this was that I didn't feel like puking at the thought of what I was doing. Triathletes are such a happy and helpful bunch, and a wave of optimism was taking me over. I felt so full of positivity that I stopped pissing myself, both literally and figuratively. I was no longer nervous and I did not dread the swim. I began to look forward to it as part of the challenge and allure, as well as part of the fun of racing a triathlon. Even when the starter counted us down from ten seconds to go and I pressed start on my stopwatch, I still wasn't nervous. This was...AWESOME!

Then the horn blew and everyone dove in and began thrashing. In all my newly found enthusiasm and alacrity, I had forgotten to position myself to the far left of the line of swimmers, placing my body as close to shore as possible. This had become my go-to strategy, as it gave me a greater sense of safety. As soon as I took my first stroke, I swallowed a little water while gasping for air. The anxiety I had felt in Connecticut returned with a vengeance, paralyzing me, and I stopped moving altogether about twenty metres into the race. I managed to flip over onto my back so I could wait for my entire age group to swim past me.

When it seemed that the slowest person was finally ahead of me, I turned back over and headed left, away from the pack and the race buoys, to my own safe, private parcel of water, and began to swim. I have no idea why, and it was certainly not a conscious strategy, but I began to count my strokes, deciding only to look up to see whether I was going in the right direction every twenty right arm strokes. To my amazement, I never veered off course, and, coupled with the fact that since I represented the outer left side limit of the field of swimmers, requiring my own kayaker to stay with me until the turnaround, my stroke counting acted like a self-hypnotic mantra that kept me calm and anxiety-free. I felt at peace and my stroke felt smoother, though slower than ever before. I would take a stroke and pause as I felt my body glide through the water before my opposite arm repeated the motion. I actually began to *enjoy* the act of swimming. It was graceful. It felt as though I knew what I was doing. Other than the fact that I was almost onshore and could probably have stood up and touched the bottom, I actually resembled a real, confident swimmer.

My confidence grew with every stroke and I found myself, unintentionally, veering back over to the right as I reached the first turn, passing a bunch of people along the way. That's right, *passing* people. Me. By the time I made the turn, I was in the thick of a pack of swimmers in my age group, and it didn't bother me at all. I was getting slapped, kicked, bumped, but it all felt normal and nothing to get worked up about. I was actually smiling and I felt like Rudolph when he finds out that Clarisse thinks he's cute. "I can swim! I can swim!". I was going so well that swim caps in the colour of the age group that started before mine began to get closer. For the first time since starting triathlon, I actually felt comfortable in the swim and it filled me with so much ebullience and confidence that I almost didn't want the 1.9 kilometres to end. Almost.

When it was over, I was having such an out of body experience, with feelings of euphoria painting over the reality of what was actually going on, that on the path from the swim exit to transition, Anne and Owen were waiting to cheer daddy on, but I never noticed them. Anne told me later that I looked directly at her, without having the faintest clue who the hell she was. After I passed them, I was confronted with wetsuit strippers. I didn't know what they were there for, so instead of laying down to let them tug my wetsuit from my soaking body, I just gave one of them a huge hug that lasted just long enough to be awkward. It was a 'good-bye at the airport to someone you won't see again for months' type of hug. Once I released the poor guy, I turned and jogged to transition, with my wetsuit still stuck to my body. Only when I got to transition and realized that I had no idea where my bike was, did I snap out of the fog. Another volunteer noticed the disoriented look on my face and asked me what my bib number was, but I couldn't remember. That's why your number is printed on the wrist band given to you at registration.

When I arrived at my bike, it was time to focus, but I couldn't seem to get my head straight. Nothing made sense. It felt like the first month of calculus class in college. I could comprehend the individual components of what needed to be done, but creating a pattern or series of tasks to *get* them done was beyond me. I frantically looked around to see what the others were doing, but that didn't really help because the visual stimuli I was receiving did not match my personal reality. Nobody else was still wearing their wetsuit. This incongruity snapped me back to reality. "Right. Lose the wetsuit", I said aloud. "Lose the fucking wetsuit".

Easier said than done. I went to put my cap and goggles under my bike but quickly realized that I no longer had them and wondered where they were. I must have dropped them during my hug-fest. There were now several people buzzing by me, pushing their bikes towards the exit, and I was still standing there in my, now dry, wetsuit. I hastily reached back, unzipped and tried to extricate myself from it, which was considerably easier than I thought it would be because it was no longer particularly wet. I just sat down and took it off like a pair of jeans. Still seated, I slipped on my cycling shoes, totally in awe of the guys who already had theirs clipped into their pedals. What a pro move, I thought, and told myself I would do it that way for all future races. With shoes on, I stood up, put on my helmet and sunglasses, and headed out of transition. Unfortunately, though I had seen dozens of people begin to make their way out before me, I went in the wrong direction and tried to exit where swimmers were entering the zone. A friendly volunteer stopped me and pointed me in the proper direction.

I was finally on my way, going as hard as I could for as long as I could, which was my biking strategy for the race. I know that it might hurt me in the end, and potentially destroy my hopes of having a good run, but I figured that it is the discipline that is the most fun because you can go really fast, so just go. Also, this strategy allowed me to catch up with many of the faster swimmers.

My running was solid, so I could back it by dispatching with as many swimmers and cyclists as possible. I knew what fatigue on a run felt like, and, to a certain extent, how to deal with it. I'd bonked before, but never on a run less than marathon distance.

It all seemed to work because I passed hundreds of cyclists throughout the 90 kilometres, and was only overtaken by a handful around the 70-kilometre mark. I was having so much fun. My speedometer even got up to 75km/h at one point, and I never even considered coasting, not once. Not even in the aid stations. Fuck that. I blasted through several Gatorade bottles and may have broken one volunteer's arm. Perhaps I should have paid closer attention during the not so mandatory, mandatory athlete's race briefing. Other than that, the only problem I had during the bike was the bottle cage on my seat-tube somehow came loose and clipped my right pedal every time I got to the top of my stroke on that side. After about a hundred 'clicks' I reached down and tore it off. I lost my balance and ended up in the gravel at the side of the road, but it was worth it because the sound was driving me crazy.

The rest of the bike ride went so well that I never felt any fatigue whatsoever, and the only part I remember was right at the end when I misjudged the dismount line. I wasn't sure whether I was supposed to get off before or after the giant strip of fluorescent tape, so I jammed on my brakes and went over the handlebars. I was so worried I would be disqualified or penalized for breaking the rules, but when I asked the official, with my ass on the tarmac and my bike wrapped around my neck, if I was good, he looked at me like I was a puppy that had just been hit by a tractor, and said, "Technically, you were airborne when your body crossed the line.

Most of your bike is on the legal side, so I guess you're a go".

The temperature had risen significantly and the humidity made the hills seem longer and steeper, but the run was still a breeze. I enjoyed every step and sped by a bunch more competitors without ever being passed. I guess I was experiencing what is known as the 'flow' state because I felt zero pain, zero fatigue, zero anxiety. Everything seemed to be in perfect balance and to, well, flow. Whenever I became slightly thirsty, there was an aid station with a cheery volunteer offering me a cup of water. Every time I felt hot, there was a local dude with a garden hose who didn't wait to be asked before spraying me with cool water. We communicated with a series of winks and nods that I was open to a little drenching. Total harmony.

It was during the second lap that the idea of qualifying for Vegas morphed from a pipe dream to something that could actually, potentially happen. I wasn't entirely sure of where I stood in my age group, but I had sort of semi-consciously been checking the left calf of everyone I passed on the run to see their age. It seemed that I was blowing by plenty of guys with numbers in the 45-49 range, so I started to think that the whole Vegas World Championship thing might actually happen, and I carried that thought all the way to the finish line, where I was greeted by Anne and Owen.

"I think you came in third in your age group", they told me. I was stunned. I didn't really know what it meant. Was that good enough to qualify? How could I find out? What was the proper procedure?

After accepting my finisher's medal and cap and getting some food I never ate, I told Anne that I'd go get my bike and swim stuff from transition before checking in at the information tent to see about awards (I figured there was probably a ribbon or something for third place), and whether or not I qualified. I was really hoping that I had because by this point I had already started to plan our trip. How cool, I thought, would it be to have my bike with me at the airport?

The three of us walked down to the transition area where I gave them each a kiss and said, "I'll just grab my stuff. Be right back. Should be about ten minutes".

I headed for the entrance and was stopped short by a burly, volunteer who was nowhere near as friendly as the others I had, to that point, encountered.

"Where'd'ya think you're going, Bud?", he barked at me, with a large hand placed across my chest. I figured he must be a little slow in the head because it seemed obvious, since I was sweaty, wearing a tri-suit with a bib number around my waist, the mandatory athlete's wristband, and was heading to the transition area with a *finisher's* medal around my neck indicating that I had, you know, *finished,* and simply wanted to collect my belongings and be on my way.

"Just going to get my bike", I said looking down at his hand on my chest as if to say 'remove your hand before I tear your bottom lip off, asshole' (I played Junior hockey in the 1980s which makes the movie <u>Slapshot</u>, starring Paul Newman look like a ride at Disney…That's the default setting). "I won't be a minute".

"It's cuz the race ain't over yet, Bud", he said in a tone that implied that, in fact, I was the slow one. "You can't get yer bike until the last biker is done".

Without thinking, my mouth reflexively blurted out, "You shittin' me?". I didn't mean to sound rude or condescending in any way, I simply couldn't believe that there were people still out on their bikes. Their *bikes*. Not out running, but on their *bikes*. My age group was one of the last to start and I'm not exactly Michael Phelps. It took me an hour and a half to do the run, and I had been farting around for the better part of a half-hour since I finished, and there were still people riding their bikes? What were they doing out there?

"Oh, okay", I apologized, still wanting to punch him hard in the face. "Any idea when it'll open?".

"Two o'clock", he said. I looked at my watch. It was 12:30. I turned to Anne, "Looks like we have a little time to kill".

At first, we just stuck around where we were because that side of transition was in the shade, and watched some of the cyclists roll in. I was struck by what the majority of them were riding. They were NOT racing on dilapidated piles of garage sale, throwaway rubbish. In fact, almost every one of them came in riding the most high-tech, up-to-date, multi-thousand dollar rigs that I would never be able to afford. These machines were absolutely incredible and made my $1500 Giant Trinity look like the entry-level beginner's bike that it was. Somehow, I pictured the bike that people taking five hours to complete a 90k ride would look more like something bought at the grocery store. What I was seeing didn't seem right. They couldn't all have had flat tires or mechanical trouble.

This got me wondering why some people feel compelled to spend so much on gear. Is it simply because they can afford it? I started to think that perhaps I didn't need to feel so brow-beaten by what I saw in transition before the race. When I was waiting around in the bathroom line earlier, I was so intimidated by everything I heard and saw. Maybe, however, they were just as nervous as I was but handled it differently. Perhaps they just like to spend lots of money on expensive equipment, coaches, and downloadable training guides. Maybe, just maybe, I was better off because I did things my way, by myself. It may not have been the best, most efficient, most biomechanically scientific way, but it was what I came up with using what knowledge I possessed. My data consisted, simply, of how my body felt. There were no third parties crunching my numbers (along with the numbers of 50 or 60 other clients), and fitting them into a predetermined formula to tell me what should work best. My training plan was to swim, bike, and run every day until I was too tired to swim, bike, and run. Basically, I got my advice from a Nike ad I remembered from my youth telling me to JUST DO IT, except mine was a little different and was more like: SHUT THE FUCK UP AND GET OUT THERE, PUSSY. Tomayto, tomahto.

After we got fed up watching, we decided to walk back to the car and get something to eat. On our way, we stopped by the information desk they had set up under the giant tent where the meeting had been held, and where the awards ceremony was being put together. On the table were the up-to-date results of who had finished so far, and the number of slots in each age category available for the World Championships in Las Vegas. I noticed that I had, indeed, finished third and that there were three automatic slots for my age group. It appeared that I had qualified, but before getting too excited, I wanted to ask the young woman behind the table how everything worked.

There was only one other athlete at the table with me, so, wanting the woman's complete attention, I deferred to the other gentleman and let him go first. He was slight, wiry, and a little shorter than me, and was leaning over his bike which looked to be worth more than my car, lawnmower, and everything in my basement combined, and his race number was only one digit. For some reason, his face looked familiar, but I had no idea where I had seen him before.

The woman asked, "Can I help who's next?", and I pointed to him. He gave me a wink and a smile and said, "Cheers, mate", with a heavy Australian accent that sounded so cool and confirmed what I had previously thought about Ironman branded races: They were popular and important enough to attract athletes from *Australia*. I mean we were in upstate New York, what would some-body from Australia be doing here if it wasn't for this race? I was super chuffed. After he turned his attention from me, he asked the woman, "Any idea when the cheques will be ready?"

Cheques? What was this dude talking about?

"They'll be handed out at the awards ceremony, around four", she said. "Can I get your name?".

"Gambles. Joe Gambles. Anyway, can I get mine mailed out? I've got to catch a flight".

I was standing next to the guy, the *professional* athlete, who had just won the entire race. Now, I was already a triathlon convert, and this was my new favourite sport, but I couldn't help thinking how cool this was. I turned to him while he waited for the woman to confer with one of her colleagues. He looked at me and asked, "How'd you get on out there?".

At first, I was stunned. There is no other sport like this where you can race on the same course, and largely at the same time as the pros, then, afterwards, chat with the guy who WON. Do you think Tom Brady shoots the breeze with some dude in the bleachers after a Monday Nighter?

"I did alright", I nervously answered. "I mean, I did okay. I had fun".

"Good, good. D'you place well. You know, in your age group?". For some reason, he was actually interested in our banal little conversation.

"I think I finished third", I lied, for there was no 'think' involved. I knew damn well I finished third; I just wanted it to appear like it didn't mean that much, though it meant everything.

"Good on ya!", he continued. "Was bloody hot out there, yah?".

The woman reappeared and he turned his attention back to her, which was a good thing because I am sure I was blushing, having developed a giant man-crush, and I didn't want him to feel uncomfortable. She handed him an envelope and offered her congratulations. He turned to me and held out his hand for me to shake, "I'm Joe", to which I replied, "I know. I'm Brock".

"Cheers, Brock. Nice to meet ya", he said, then he left.

It was now my turn. I asked the woman how it all worked and she told me that I had, indeed, qualified and asked if I planned on taking my slot. When I said, "Fuck, ya", she asked if I wanted to pay now, rather than wait around, which sounded like a good idea and we were done in ten minutes. That is the best system, but, unfortunately, it is no longer that simple.

The rest of the summer I continued to train as I had done before, only now, I did more of it. I even completed another race, in Racine, Wisconsin, where I found out first-hand that humans can withstand fifty-five-degree water, just. I finished in second place with a personal best time of 4:30. It was now time to put all of my focus on the World Champs.

Las Vegas monopolized my thoughts but not because I had any allusions of doing well. The athletes who would be lining up to race there would be the absolute best in the world, at every age category, including mine. They would have qualified at some of the most prestigious races from all over. Sure, Syracuse had been a big deal for me, but it was just Syracuse. Outside of the Northeastern part of the United States, it was not particularly well-known. At least that's the way I saw it. I mean, come on, it's Syracuse, take away the Orange, and what are you left with? These people would be coming from Oceanside, Lanzarote, Geelong, Nice. No, I had no expectations of finishing anywhere near the top, but that was fine by me. As far as I was concerned, just qualifying was the big deal, and that had already been accomplished.

I spent the remainder of the summer experiencing the bittersweet paradox of longing for a cool trip to Las Vegas, while simultaneously hoping it would take a very long time to arrive. Being a teacher, I cherish the summer holiday as I had when I was a child, and I am hard-wired to wish it would never end.

- VEGAS -

As I have said, I wasn't excited to go to Las Vegas because I expected to do well in the race. Yes, I was looking forward to racing so I could see how I fared against the best in the world, but that wasn't what had me so ramped up, nor was it the typical reasons for which Vegas is famous. I have absolutely no interest in gambling and I actually find the whole spectacle of the place abhorrent. It's almost embarrassing to see how much of everything is wasted there. The lights, the money, the bachelor partying (funny movie, though), the magic shows. It's all too much for me. I had been there a few times for the Nike Basketball Coaches Conference, and have never spent a dollar in any of the casinos. What I love is the physical beauty of the landscape that surrounds the city. The desert is clean and unforgiving. To survive there, you need to be tough.

What I really was looking forward to above all else, was walking into Trudeau International Airport in Montreal, rolling my bike box beside me, knowing that there would be plenty of people wondering what was in there. That, along with my aerodynamically engineered helmet attached to my carry-on bag would make me look downright exotic and mysterious. Maybe some would even ask me what it was all for, forcing me to reply, "I'm racing in the Ironman 70.3 World Championships in Las Vegas", with my chest puffed out, then continuing with, "And, yes, I'm fucking charming". They didn't have to know, or even understand that I was a mere 45-49 age grouper, and not in any way remotely close to being a professional. As far as I was concerned, I would let them think what all my co-workers did: they think I must be a pro. Not too many people can boast that they competed in the world championships in anything, which is impressive enough. Add to that the word 'Ironman', and suddenly you're Paul friggin McCartney. Well, maybe not McCartney, but certainly the back-up bass player for Aha.

I left for Las Vegas a couple of days before Anne and Owen were to fly out, which gave me some time by myself to get accustomed to the heat. During the flight, I read through the Athlete's guide a couple dozen times to become completely familiar with where things were and how everything was supposed to happen. In the past, poring over race information like this would invariably make me nervous because there is so much new stuff to learn. This time, it actually brought me a certain level of peace, and I even made a plan based on my estimated time of arrival.

I brought my own bike which, unfortunately, was in several pieces in a box I had rented from the bike shop where I had purchased it. I did not attempt to disassemble it myself, because I scratch the outer limits of my mechanical capabilities changing an inner tube (a task that takes me the better part of a half-hour). Luckily, Nate from the bike shop agreed to box it up for free so long as I 'liked' the store on Facebook, which I agreed to do without having a clue how to go about it. At that point, I was not even on Facebook. Of course, this meant that I would need to find someone who could build it back up again when I arrived. A quick look at the Ironman website the week before had revealed that there would be an official bike shop at the expo that would be able to do it. They would also be able to box it back up after the race for a fee, which included a tune-up. I figured that since my flight arrived at 10 AM and that it was, at most, an hour from McCarran Airport to the race expo, add an hour to collect baggage and rent a car, with a little shopping at the site, my bike should be ready, according to these crude calculations, around 1:30, 2:00 at the latest. That should leave me enough time to get to the hotel and go for a bike ride.

The flight landed right on time and my bags popped out of the carousel in the first batch. Beauty. There was no line at the car rental place, and no one tried to upgrade me. In fact, they threw in a child seat for nothing. Also beauty. Things were humming along just perfectly, the directions to the race venue were spot on, and I found a parking spot worthy of George Costanza in seconds.

On my way to the bike shop tent I noticed, in the tent adjacent to it, there was a place where I could rent race wheels. My Trinity came with stock, standard, regular, run of the mill wheels, and I instantly wondered how cool it would look with a pair of deep-rimmed Zipps attached to it. Not for a second did I factor in how much better the bike might actually perform with the high tech wheels; I had seen athletes with the very same ones take five hours to complete 90 kilometres in Syracuse. Performance was not what attracted me, it was more about how much cooler I would look. In fact, you could have told me they would *add* ten minutes to my bike time, and I would still have paid to have them installed.

I rented a set and brought them with me to the bike shop, filled out the paperwork, and paid in advance. The mechanic gave me a copy of the contract and, without even looking up, she said, "Two o'clock". I looked at my watch and started to do the math. That was a bit later than I had expected, but, if I ate something at the expo, picked up the bike at two, I'd be at the hotel by 3:00, 3:30 at the latest. I could be riding by four. When I didn't say anything right away, she looked up and saw me fumbling with the mental math, then added, "Tomorrow".

I was taken aback by the clarification she offered and became instantly concerned that all my plans were going to be entirely altered for the worse. Just as I was about to enter into full-blown panic mode, I remembered the case of beer I had purchased at the AM/PM on my way from the airport. I was parched when I had started the drive and stopped at a convenience store where I bought a soda, which I downed immediately in the store, and the case of beer to be enjoyed later in my room. I told her I would be right back and sprinted to the car. When I returned, I hoisted the case up and planted it on the makeshift counter they had erected out of a fold-up card table and said, "Two o'clock? You sure?". She took one look at the twelve frosty Michelobs, wiped the sweat from her brow, raised her eyes to mine and said, "Should be done by 10 AM".

The next morning, after picking up my bike and bringing it to the hotel, I decided that once I stopped admiring how cool it looked with the Zipps and taking four or five thousand selfies with me standing next to it, it was time to go for a ride. When I got outside, I noticed that the wind had picked up, so I tried to figure out a route that would have me enjoying it at my back on the way home.

Bringing the bike with those wheels on it down the elevator, with me sporting an aero helmet, was the proudest moment in my athletic life. I felt like Lance Armstrong, and it seemed as though all eyes were on me as I struck my best 'professional athlete' pose. One couple even asked if I *was* a pro. I damn near said yes, asking them if they wanted an autograph, but chickened out. "No, I'm an amateur, but I had to qualify to be here". They looked super impressed just the same.

Now that I was famous, my head barely fit through the elevator doors, but somehow I managed it and made my way to the exit. When I opened the door, the wind hit me with a gust that blew me back slightly and forced too much air into my mouth. It startled me, and the quick, unexpected shock of it made me begin to rethink the whole bike ride idea. I pushed on, however, and straddled the bike, clicked into the pedals, and took about five strokes. The wind hit the deep seventy millimetre rims, and the bike flew out from under me, causing me to fall to the tarmac, facing oncoming traffic. I was about five inches from becoming the fancy, new hood ornament of a light blue Hyundai Tiburon. "Oh fuck", I thought. "Not good".

I tried to put the incident behind me and chalk it up to a simple lack of race wheel experience. Once again, I clicked into the pedals for another attempt, which was also a disaster. I had absolutely no control over my bike, and the only way I could keep it upright was to ride it like it was a beach cruiser. The instant I tried to get into the aero position, resting my forearms on the pads, the bike immediately tried to go horizontal. It was as though I was trying to take a trout for a walk. There was just no controlling the damned thing. The wind was causing the wheels to act like a kite forcing me to swing all over the road, entirely out of control. I decided to abandon the idea, and my big bike ride ended up being a grand total of approximately 650 metres. It did last about 45 minutes, though, so I had that going for me.

In the space of ten seconds, I went from a super confident faux professional triathlete to a terrified weakling who had, apparently, forgotten how to ride a bike, and, just to make matters worse, I had paid $300 for the pleasure of using wheels that ensured I would never finish the bike portion of the race. Good job, Brock. I was fucked. My confidence was totally blown, and I found it difficult to breathe, feeling like I had just contracted COPD. I was hyperventilating, but my lungs simply would not fill, and nothing I tried would permit me to catch my breath. It was as if I had been flown to the top of Everest without having adequately acclimatized, and I could feel my anxiety level rising. I attempted to ignore the problem and fooled myself into believing it had something to do with the hot desert air, coupled with wind so strong it was causing a sand storm. I made the decision to go back upstairs to the room where I could blast the air conditioning and take a nap. Surely a little snooze would calm me down and alleviate some of the stress that was disrupting my ability to collect oxygen.

I woke up two hours later to breathing that was a whole lot closer to normal, but still slightly concerned that I was going to have a hard time riding my bike come Sunday, especially if it was windy. I needed a distraction and decided to find my way over to the athlete's meeting and banquet before driving to the airport to pick up Anne and Owen.

This was no regular mandatory athlete's meeting as there were Ironman legends and dignitaries, as well as local government officials, present, and they all gave speeches. The event was meant to be a big deal, and it looked like it was going to be very interesting, but it turned out that the food sucked and the spectacle itself was a bit of a snoozer. The biggest takeaway from the evening was that it seemed like the room was filled with the fittest athletes on earth. There were no token larger folks just giving it a go. These people looked serious and were all sinew and lung, and I kept wondering how I fit in, eventually concluding that I didn't. I hadn't done the same training as what I overheard these athletes had done, I didn't come from the exotic locales that they did, and I certainly didn't have coaches, like they all seemed to have. When I went to the bathroom and saw myself in the mirror, I noticed that I didn't even have the same 'look' that they had. Everybody at that dinner oozed confidence making me feel meek in their presence, so I decided it was time to leave and drive to the airport to pick up Anne and Owen.

When I saw them, they looked exhausted. It had been a long day, and it showed. The time zone change had them nodding off as soon as we were in the car. With the two of them fast asleep on the ride back to the hotel, I started to wonder if I had done the right thing by bringing them along on this trip. Was it for them or me? I thought of how all of my co-workers were so proud of me and how they all thought I was something special for making it to the world championships. I began to have serious doubts, wondering if all the money I had poured into this trip that I had carved out of my very modest salary, was worth it. Was it selfish of me to be doing this? Had I really needed to spend so much? Were the fancy wheels really necessary?

"Holy shit", I said sort of under my breath, "I'm going to have to give her on Sunday. No more of this 'happy just to be here' bullshit". I came to the realization that I had inadvertently put a lot of pressure on myself. I had worked too hard to just let the race happen.

The following morning I let Anne and Owen sleep in while I drove to the starting area for a practice swim. The venue was a man-made lake that was well manicured and quite nice to look at, but the water was hot and soupy. It was pretty and all, but it felt as though we were on a golf course which gave me the distinct feeling that Happy Gilmore was going to dive in at any moment to retrieve his ball.

For the entire drive over, I tried to convince myself that I would be okay without the added buoyancy that a wetsuit brings. We knew well enough in advance that the swim would not be wetsuit legal that I didn't even pack mine for the trip at all. I hoped that the $400 swim skin I had purchased would keep me afloat plenty enough to keep me off of the bottom of the lagoon, and it took quite a bit to convince myself that the love affair I had developed with my pull buoy over the Spring and Summer had not morphed into a dependency. I had bought it in March because all of the real swimmers at the pool had one, and since the first time I tried it, I found that it was magical. I hadn't swum 25 metres without either it or my wetsuit since, and I no longer had a clue what it felt like to swim 'au naturel'. In fact, I hadn't actually used my legs in the water in months.

When I arrived at the 'lake', I had a feeling it would not go well. There was a line-up to get on the course, and everyone else looked as though they belonged in the water, even without the wetsuit. I actually heard a few people mention that they preferred to swim without one, forcing me to conclude that they must have been dropped as babies because they were certainly a bit fucked in the head. When it was finally my turn, I dove in expecting a fair bit of glide before I took my first few strokes, only that didn't happen. The second my body hit the water, it felt like my legs just dropped anchor and that I was trying to swim vertically, which wasn't good. It appeared I was going to have to not only use my feet, which I was no longer accustomed to at all, but that I would have to kick like a bastard just to remain semi-horizontal. The problem was that when I kicked, I became totally exhausted in seconds.

Somehow, over the previous several months, I had developed the stamina of an 87-year-old coal miner with mesothelioma trying to ascend stairs three at a time. Every muscle in my body was filled with lactic acid and it felt as though there was concrete coursing through my veins. I couldn't breathe fast or effectively enough to get sufficient oxygen to fill my lungs.

My original plan was to swim the entire course once, concentrating on nice, smooth strokes, but since I could only handle about 700 metres before I thought I would drown, the plan was modified. After finishing a quick loop, I exited the water and walked back to the car unable to catch my breath, and with my tail between my legs. How was I going to be able to finish the race, let alone do well, if I couldn't complete the swim? It's a TRIathlon, not a 'fuck about panic session' followed by a duathlon. The anxiety was building with less than twenty-four hours to go, and it was already as bad as Connecticut. Fucking Connecticut.

Searching for a distraction to keep my thoughts far away from anything to do with water, I decided to take the family to Red Rock Canyon. Spending the afternoon in the middle of the desert ought to be a good way to free me from wet thoughts, and I started to secretly hope that I'd get attacked by a Gila Monster and wouldn't have to swim the following day. It would be a good excuse and an even better story.

It didn't work. We climbed all over the most beautiful, red, desolate landscape, but it felt like we were 50 000 metres above sea level, and even a five-kilometre hike was taxing my cardiovascular system so completely it felt as though I was in the Himalayas. Now, I was really starting to worry.

On our way back to the hotel, I insisted we stop at a pharmacy where I was planning to disregard all of my very deeply held ethical principles regarding the use of banned substances, and buy whatever over-the-counter bronchodilator they had on the shelves. I was sure I was dying or having an asthma attack (even though I don't have asthma). I felt so bad that I was actually certain that this wasn't anxiety at all. Anxiety was what I felt in Connecticut. This was different. Yes, I was concerned about the swim, but I knew I would get through it, somehow, even if that meant doing the backstroke the entire way. This was a physical manifestation of a physical problem, not a psychological one. I strongly believed that I had developed acute, rapid onset of asthma, like for real.

The closest Pharmaceutical solution I could find, without a prescription, was the Breathe-Right strips we had been given in our race swag bag. Unfortunately, they did not work at all. In fact, they had the exact opposite of the desired effect, as they pulled the skin so far to the outside of my nose that they actually squeezed my nasal passages shut. It was like being in the extreme cold and having your nose frozen closed.

In a vain attempt to keep my mind off of the problem, I stayed awake all night watching television. I didn't even bother to set an alarm, knowing I was not going to be able to perform well in the race regardless. My honest hope was that by staying up so late, my body would be so exhausted that it would be relaxed, permitting my lungs to open up, but when race morning arrived, I still couldn't catch my breath at all. It no longer worried me because it had been so long since I had a set of lungs full of oxygen that I had forgotten what that sensation even felt like, and the resignation of a certain poor performance prevailed. What concerned me more was that it was going to sound like I was just making up excuses when I explained to everyone why I had done so poorly. I pictured my co-workers rolling their eyes, just like I probably would have done if given the same lame story. But, there was nothing I could do about any of that, so I went through my typical race morning routine, though a little more calmly than usual due largely to the fact that, despite really wanting to do well, I couldn't see how that would be possible or remotely realistic. The difficulties I was having acquiring oxygen were just as limiting to performance as trying to race with a torn hamstring. In other words, it would take a miracle for me to achieve a good result, and similarly as frustrating because my performance would not be tied to my effort or preparation, but to something entirely out of my control.

When I arrived at the fake lake, I managed to get done with organizing my T1 duties quite efficiently and was out of there with plenty of time to walk around and find a place to be alone for a while. I *never* enjoy being around people (particularly strangers, and even more particularly, pesky, perky, athletic, loquacious strangers) on race morning, but on this day my aversion to human contact was significantly heightened. I managed to skirt the left side of the man-made lake and found a small area with three or four Christmas-like trees, surrounded by soft sand, which served two very important purposes. The first was that it gave me the opportunity to be alone, which made it possible to do something I love to do by myself, and that is to freely talk to me. I have always done this, and I'm not sure whether or not it is normal. This was no little pep talk either. I wasn't just saying, "Come on, Brock. You got this". It has never been like that. What I tend to have are full, meaningful, deep, elaborate conversations as though there was someone else there, just with the same name as me. Think Tom Hanks with Wilson, just without the ball. Just me, and well, me. The second thing this secret little spot allowed me to do was poop.

When I ran out of poop and conversation topics, I sat down and stared at the 'lake' for thirty minutes. I said nothing. I thought of nothing. I didn't sing the chorus to any catchy top forty songs. I barely even moved. I didn't get uncomfortable. Aside from breathing, digesting, metabolizing, and ageing, I literally did nothing. I just sat there staring vacantly, eyes completely glazed over.

It was the most peaceful thirty minutes I have ever spent awake in my life, and when it was over, I got up, took a piss, drank some Gatorade, and walked over to my age group corral. I didn't say to myself, "I better get to the swim start; it's getting late". I hadn't set a timer or asked myself, "give me thirty minutes". I just sat and stared, then got up not because it was time to get up but because

I was ready to. I felt incredibly well-rested and comprehensively at ease. It was as though I had slept for days. My mind and body were wholly free of anxiety, and somehow my lungs opened and collected litre after litre of the sweetest, life-giving oxygen. I no longer cared about the race as I normally do. Results did not possess the gravitas they heretofore had. Sure, I wanted to do well, but not necessarily compared to anyone else. I wanted to do my best, go as fast as I could and sustain peak effort for as long as possible, which could have meant finishing last, but it truly did not matter.

All of this was very bizarre to me and I was very conscious of its strangeness, but what was even more out of the ordinary, was that once I arrived at the proper corral, I was starting up conversations with everyone around me, and I was enjoying them. The most mundane stories were, somehow, fascinating. "Oh, you're a hockey referee from Rochester, New York. Amazing". "You say you're a stay at home dad from Chula Vista. Cool".

That half-hour sitting by myself, just a few feet away from my own buried feces, had changed my life, at least temporarily. I was now ready to race, and the swim no longer scared me at all. When my turn came, I dove into the water, headed for the start line, and began swimming. I was not fast by any means, but I never stopped, my feet didn't sink, and I finished in the middle of the pack of men my age. I exited the water feeling as fresh as before I started. My mind wasn't exactly blank, but it wasn't focused on anything specific either. There were so many things going on around me that my senses were working overtime, unsuccessfully trying to process it all. It was a task far too daunting to master. I was so distracted by all the outside stimuli that I left transition still wearing my swim skin over my tri-suit, which, on a normal September Las Vegas day would have meant certain heatstroke. This day, however, was not normal as it was pouring rain, and the added layer of water-repelling fabric turned out to be a bonus. It was working so well that two competitors told me they wished they had thought of it, as I passed them on the bike. In fact, if no one had asked me about it, I wouldn't have noticed I had it on at all. At first, I had no idea what they were talking about, but I made it seem that it was an integral part of my race plan, and rode away shaking my head.

Most of the bike portion of the race was completed in the rain, which was a little baffling to most of us. One of the reasons I was able to get Anne to agree to take time off from work to come out to Vegas at all was because the weather is 100% predictable. We were in the middle of a desert that sees an average of four days of rainfall per year, and it turns out that I had brought Anne and Owen there for all four of those days. How many people can say that? It sucked for the spectators, but for those of us racing, the rain had a welcome cooling effect.

Of course, the sun came out for the hottest portion of the day, just as my run started, which was part blessing and part curse. It was nice to get dry and feel the restorative power brought on by the added vitamin D, but the heat made it much more of a struggle.

The run course was not exactly spectacular, though it was lined the entire length with hundreds, if not thousands, of spectators. Throughout, I kept thinking of that thirty minutes I had spent alone before the start, and how far I'd come since entering my first triathlon. Before I got into the sport, I was in a state of flux. As a young person, I was very athletic and participated at a relatively high level in plenty of sports, but as I aged and completed university, life, as it does with most people, filled up all of my time and energy, leaving very little room for athletics. At Acadia University, I ran cross-country and, thus, dabbled a bit in running as an adult. I even raced the Boston Marathon six times and finished several ultramarathons which I enjoyed for several years, but the sheen wore off and I began an unconscious search for something new. Then, along came triathlon, and now I was competing in the World Championships.

These thoughts buoyed me, and I ran well all the way to the finish line. When all was said and done, I had achieved what I had set out to do, and in the end, the money I had spent to get there had not been wasted at all. I did well enough not to have to rely on excuses, real or otherwise.

Anne and Owen greeted me once I crossed the line with pride. "You finished seventh in your age group!".

I could hardly believe that was even possible, so we checked to make sure. They were right. I indeed finished seventh in a time of 4:43:28. A top ten finish in my first world champs, and the day before, I thought I would need a defibrillator to jump-start my cardiovascular system. I was so happy that I allowed myself a touch of internal cockiness and for a brief moment thought, "This shit is getting easy". The second I thought about it, I regretted it, worrying that I may now be cursed.

A Little Too Comfortable

When I was eight years old, my family took a late summer vacation to Halifax, Nova Scotia. Halifax is a very nice place, and we had plenty of fun while we were there. At least I assume we did; I remember almost nothing about the trip, but what eight year old doesn't have fun on something called a *vacation*, particularly one involving air travel? Looking back, though, I wonder why we went there and not somewhere considerably more romantic.

My father ran the Pension Investments Department at Air Canada, and one of the perks was that he and his family were able to travel anywhere the airline flew, virtually for free. The only caveat was that it was strictly 'space available' only. In other words, we flew 'stand-by'. Having access to the seating plan for every flight, my father could hunt and peck for the flights with the fewest seats sold, increasing the likelihood that we would not get bumped. Sometimes there were flights that went off with very few seats occupied and we would each be able to enjoy an entire row to ourselves. Usually, it was a little tighter and we would sit at the gate on the edge of our seats, waiting for our names to be called.

Being the family of an employee, we were subject to a strict dress code and were prohibited from discussing with the paying passengers how we were able to fly for free. The dress code was in place because there was a certain standard the airline wished to maintain, but it essentially boiled down to no jeans. Men and boys had to wear shirts with a collar which, somehow, included the turtle neck. There is no item of clothing I loathe more than the turtle neck. What kind of sick bastard thought that it would be comfortable to constrict the neck in such a manner as to impede proper airflow? Unfortunately, my mother thought they made her boys look sharp, like Dapper Dan, whoever that was. So that's what we were forced to wear every single time we flew. I don't believe that she really thought it through, however. Think about it: all flights last at least an hour, and sometimes way more than that. The air is stale, the food not particularly nutritious (at least in the seventies). Space is limited and movement is vastly restricted. A turtle neck is destined to make a bad situation quite a bit worse.

The good part was that if there were any seats left in First Class, we would get those. Of course, that meant sporting the turtle neck along with a pair of slacks. Even the *word* 'slacks' makes me want to vomit. They don't sound comfortable at all and I think the word is actually Latin for an itchy, polyester, ugly lower-body garment. And Chinos isn't much better. I think that one of the top five reasons I became a physical education teacher was that I wouldn't have to wear either on a daily basis. I wear shorts at work. Everyday.

The flight home from Halifax, according to my father, was going to be tight. There had been a cancellation the day before, so there were double the number of travellers trying to cram their way onto one plane. When we checked in at the front desk, they told my dad, straight up, that it didn't look good. The flight was way over-booked, so he and my mother had a little pow-wow, and it was agreed that he would stay another night if need be so that the rest of us could make it home for the first day of school. With the agreement made, we hurried towards the gate and my dad checked again with the attendant to see if, perhaps, there had been any changes. It has been my experience that at no point in the history of commercial air travel has anyone ever officially notified the airline that they will be unable to make it for their flight. I have never heard of anyone actually cancelling their ticket. If they aren't going to make it, they just don't show up, which results in a frustrating reality for the would-be stand-by passenger, but it is a reality nonetheless. It is much more likely that there will be a run on open seats at the last minute due to a rerouting problem or an aircraft maintenance issue.

Even at the age of eight, I could tell that it wasn't a good sign to see the gate at standing-room-only a solid hour before the plane was scheduled to pull away, and I could actually see my father age six or seven years right in front of me. He has no poker face, hiding his stress the way a peacock hides his feathers during mating season. He is biologically predisposed to panic and is physiologically incapable of remaining calm during situations that are entirely out of his control. In fact, though he worked for the airline and probably logged more air-time than Chuck Yeager, he is a trembling ball of nerves the night before any flight. It isn't because he is afraid the plane will crash. Once in the air, he's as cool as a cucumber, but beforehand, he isn't exactly chatty. The night before he was scheduled to fly somewhere for business, he could be found sitting in front of the television, in his Y-fronts and black socks, wearing nothing else, other than a thin coating of stress sweat. He would sit on the edge of the couch, crouching forward, polishing his shoes with a very loud, electric polishing brush and a can of Kiwi shoe polish, tongue sticking out of his mouth moving ever so slightly, like a banana slug. He was so consumed with getting his shoes shiny and fretting about not being late for his flight (which he never was because he considered being at the airport three and a half hours before take-off to be cutting it close), that this was the only good time to show him a poor report card or to get a math test signed.

In Halifax, the stress was so great that he had sweat dripping off his forehead and onto his perfectly polished shoes. It was also disturbingly clear that he was sweating all over because there was a significantly darker grey area just above his butt crack on his slacks. He was a total mess until it was confirmed by the woman at the gate that there was only enough room for four of us on the plane. The news that he would not be travelling with us actually seemed to bring him some peace because at least he knew what was going on. Once he learned that the rest of us were 'on', he was able to speak without clenching his teeth and using the F-word for punctuation. In other words, he was visibly relieved.

Unfortunately, though there were enough seats for the rest of us, only three were together, which meant one of us would have to sit alone, next to complete strangers. We didn't need to draw straws or play eeny, meeny, miny, mo, because my mother wasted a total of zero seconds to make her decision. Apparently this wasn't exactly Sophie's Choice.

"Ma'am, there are only three seats together", the gate agent shyly informed my mom. "One of you will be eleven rows behind".

"Thank you very much", my mother responded, then without a moment's hesitation, turned to me and said, "Brock, you're going to the back. You'll be on your own".

Being painfully shy by nature, I was initially terrified. My automatic psychological reaction was to get all clammy and worry, longing to be in my mother's arms. Just as I was about to commence crying, I thought about the situation and decided that perhaps it wouldn't be so bad. I wouldn't have to entertain my little brother, and my sister, three years my senior, would not be able to pick on me for at least an hour and a half. I would be able to eat my entire meal without her stealing the cheese and crackers, far and away the best part of the typical airline offering. In fact, the more I thought about it, the more comfortable I became, and I actually started to look forward to my first 'solo' flight.

Because we were the last four passengers to board, my mom didn't have time to bring me back to my seat before being rapidly ushered into hers. It seemed that as soon as we were in the fuselage, I was on my own. When I got to my seat, I was happy to notice that it was on the aisle, exactly eleven rows, and across the aisle, from where my mother was seated. It brought me comfort that I would be able to see her from my vantage point. I couldn't help thinking, however, that it was a bit odd that, though I hadn't taken my eyes off her from the second I sat down, neither she nor my siblings looked back at all to make sure I was getting on all right. I assumed that she was still stressed and was probably counting the seconds until they would turn off the 'NO SMOKING' sign so she could blaze up with the rest of the fidgety oral fixators onboard.

Before too long, the flight attendants began demonstrating the highly confusing art of clicking and unclicking the seat belt restraint system on the aircraft for both people who have never seen one before. Just as they began telling us that we could use our seat cushion as a floatation device, I noticed that the lady from the gate desk, who should not be on an airplane about to detach itself from the building, was speaking with my mother. I was conflicted because I assumed that the woman was telling her that there had been a change and that I, in fact, *could* sit with the rest of my family, and that I wasn't entirely sure, at this point, that I really wanted to anymore. The woman kept checking her clipboard and pointing in my direction.

For the first time since we boarded, my mother looked my way. She had a very concerned look on her face, and she kept covering her mouth with her hand. I could see that she was reaching the limits of her ability to reason deductively, and was in deep thinking mode. The wheels in her brain were turning way faster than they needed to on an average day, and she wasn't accustomed to it. She looked confused and frightened all at once, and that combination showed up unfavourably on her face. I began to worry about her well-being.

"Maybe", I thought, almost audibly, "they've just informed her that she's in a non-smoking section". That would, most certainly, have caused her to be both frightened and concerned at the same time. Just as I was about to dismiss that theory and come up with a new one, the woman started moving rapidly in my direction until she stopped right in front of me.

"Mr. Gibbs", she said, hurriedly, "you'll have to come with me. Do you have all of your things?".

I responded by instantly bursting into tears. "Why?", I stammered as she began to lead me by the wrist.

"A *paying* customer has arrived late, and there's no longer any room for you on this flight. You will need to deplane".

Even at the age of eight, I understood by her emphasis on the word 'paying', that she considered me to be so low in the airline caste system as to be unworthy of air travel. I could not understand what was going on, and I reached for my mother as we passed her on our way off the plane. She too was crying. I had never seen her cry before, and that made me even sadder. There were no cell phones in the 1970s, and there was no reason for my father to have waited around before leaving the airport. Surely he would have been on his way to find accommodation for the night. Where was I supposed to go? I re-emphasize: I was EIGHT. What the fuck was going on? What were they trying to do with me? I was having a nervous breakdown.

As we were leaving the plane, I assumed God was punishing me for having become too comfortable. I was very scared, but also intensely pissed off. I had done everything I thought was right. I hadn't complained when I was told to wear my turtleneck, nor when I was made to sit alone. I did not cry nor did I make a scene. I said nothing because I could see that the decision to make me sit by myself hadn't been an easy one for my mother. What, then, had I done wrong? What more could I have done?

$$\backslash \quad \bullet \quad \sslash$$

After returning from Vegas, I noticed that I had become somewhat of a celebrity back at work. Of course, that's not saying much, as there are only 600 students and about forty staff members, but I was the Jon Bon Jovi of Westwood Senior High School. There were even a couple of teachers who had tracked my performance on-line and told the others about it in the staff room.

It doesn't take long for news to travel inside a high school. The students can sniff the air first thing in the morning and know that the administrators are out of the building, so all of my classes bombarded me with questions about the race. The staff room at lunch became, embarrassingly, all about me. People were impressed because the word Ironman was bandied about, and everyone has heard of that. In fact, they may not even know that the event is a triathlon, or what a triathlon is, but they have heard of the Ironman. Also, it was the World Championships, which is impressive on its face, and since I finished in the top ten, they assumed I must be a professional. There was no need to explain all the age groups, not because it is any less monumental, but because they are too confusing and would just obscure the actual news of the achievement. There was also no sense using the 70.3 for the same reasons, especially seeing as how the school is in Canada and we use the metric system. In fact, when I have tried to explain the distances covered in a race, my colleagues tend to glaze over in disbelief, asking questions like how many days does it take to complete? and how long are the rest periods?. It's far too confusing.

Though I was slightly uncomfortable, I was definitely enjoying the accolades and the minor celebrity attached to them. It felt nice, not just because they thought I was some kind of athletic hero, but also because they had so many questions about the event, my performance, and triathlon in general, and I was the guy with all the answers. I was floating on a cloud until the inevitable question was asked. I had a feeling it might be, but it took so long coming that I had begun to hold out hope that no one would pose it.

"So what's next?", one of the science teachers asked. "Do you think you're ready to do a Spartan Race now?".

And there it was: the pellet fired from the gun of ignorance. Innocent ignorance, but ignorance nevertheless. It blew up my little balloon of stardom, and I didn't have the energy to give a complete explanation.

"No, I think I'll stick to triathlon for now", was the most polite and politically correct response I could muster. Unfortunately, though, the floodgates were now open, and the questions came non-stop.

"Was it a long marathon or a short one?", posed a math teacher. A MATH teacher!

The cafeteria lady, who was 5'3" tall and wide and deep, felt the need to add, "My son and I are doing a 5k marathon next month in

Ottawa. Maybe we could train together after school". Luckily, she opened herself up for my polite decline when she tacked on, "but we're probably just going to walk most of it".

The Vice Principal proudly announced to all, "My husband jogs too. You two should go together sometime". Jogs.

I guess Andy Warhol was right. Fifteen minutes maximum was all the fame I got before I became jagged. Oh well, I was still very proud of my accomplishment, even if almost no one I knew actually understood exactly what it meant. And what the hell, if I keep training hard, maybe I could do one of those 2k Mud Run marathons someday. If I train *really* hard.

The good thing is that my head never had a chance to get too inflated before resuming full-on training. I took exactly two days off, one of which was due to travel, then returned directly to a long, hard, ten-month, monolithic, unwavering, entirely unscientific, cinder-block of training.

Every week was virtually the same as the last and the next. I know that this is not the best method, but so far it had worked really well, and I refused to change it more out of superstition than for any other reason. I knew it could be done better, but I worried I might jinx myself by altering my approach. The only real modification I made from the previous year was the intensity, simply going harder in all three disciplines. I did two or three, sometimes four, very hard workouts every day, and all days included a morning run done at 3:30, and a bike ride after work, in the basement. The rest followed my work schedule. I swam three times a week, which meant that on swim days I did three workouts at least, plus I taught a few fitness classes at school, so on those days there was added plyometrics, yoga, or weight-lifting tacked on for good measure.

I followed this plan week after week without too much variance, right up to the summer racing season with, as in previous years, only the weather and severe fatigue capable of altering the program. Very few, if any, coaches would honestly recommend such a scheme to a paying client, and the shortcomings are glaring. There were even several occasions where I wondered whether I should tweak things a little here and there to introduce some variety and break through some of the monotony, but invariably decided to play it safe and stick with what I knew. The funny thing is that I didn't stick to the program because I actually thought it was the best way to train. I have a degree in kinesiology, and I would never recommend it to anyone, but when it comes to sports, I am a creature of habit and am apprehensive about making changes to something that appears to be working. I was experiencing more success than I ever thought would have been possible, so, for the same reason that I will NEVER put my right shoe on before the left, I stuck to the plan, such as it was, even though I was perpetually exhausted.

My first race of the year was in June at Ironman 70.3 Syracuse again. Not too much changed from the previous year in terms of my speed, ability, and general fitness, but this time my anxiety level was way more in check. I was nervous because I wanted to do well, but I knew what I was capable of. This year, instead of feeling lost and insignificant listening to my fellow competitors talk prior to the pre-race dump, I knew not to worry. They were just coping with the same nerves as I was, only in a different fashion. Just because they had coaches, nutrition plans, clubs, teams, fancy kit, and better equipment than I did, no longer bothered me as much. In fact, it made me feel stronger because I had none of it and I just knew that, barring an equipment failure or malfunction, based on previous experience, I was going to do just fine.

This time, when I arrived at my age-group starting pen and looked around, I did not see 250 people who seemed designed to scare the shit out of me. They no longer appeared to me as untouchable gods of triathlon. On this occasion, I searched the landscape for the four or five triathletes that I would really be competing with for a podium spot. I felt this new confidence not only because I had done well there the previous year and I was, if anything, slightly faster now, or because I had raced the World Champs and finished in the top ten, but because I had, over the winter, received a letter from Ironman stating that I was now considered an All World Athlete (AWA), which meant that I was in the top 1% of people my age.

Other than the extra confidence it gave me, there really weren't many perks that came with such a lofty-sounding distinction. I received a Gold AWA sticker on my race bib, and I did not have to wait in line during registration, which was nice.

The extra boost of confidence I felt from having had a full year of racing behind me, as well as having done this particular race once before, had a calming effect. My performance was similar, except that I was never in a state of worry. I was able to trust my abilities and training, such as it was. When all was said and done, I finished in second place for the men aged 45-49 and improved my time to 4:30:39, which, once again, qualified me for the world champs to be held virtually in my backyard, at Mont Tremblant.

After Syracuse, I decided to try a race outside of the Ironman umbrella in St Andrews by the Sea, New Brunswick, put on by the Challenge Family. In many ways, it looked just like an Ironman branded event, only with bright red banners. It even had an impressive elite field with Mirinda Carfrae and Tim O'Donnell competing. The pre-race gala was also notable because Simon Whitfield was the celebrity guest speaker. He was quite funny and did an entire set on the weather forecast, which was calling for an actual hurricane. His words were pretty funny on Friday night, but by Saturday they were frighteningly prophetic as we woke to winds that were so fierce that hundred-year-old oak trees had been ripped completely out of the ground all over town. The course even needed to be altered because of damage to parts of the running route. The storm was so bad that we would not find out until race morning whether or not it was still on.

Because of the winds, we were not permitted to leave our bikes in transition over-night, and when I awoke race morning, there was no electricity or running water in the hotel. I assumed the race would surely be cancelled but I made the one kilometre walk up a steep hill to T1 anyway, and encountered scores of other triathletes making a similar tentative migration as well. We all left our spouses and children back at our respective hotels because each one of us was quite certain we would be returning soon, with bad news.

The weather was very calm, but the number of downed trees and fallen limbs that littered the local roads made it look like the site of a natural disaster or a bombed-out village. I kept expecting to see Red Cross vans full of volunteers handing out blankets and juice boxes. None of us making the early morning journey spoke a word to one another, but we managed to communicate, with remarkable collective understanding, via facial gestures and shoulder shrugs. It was eerie, even a bit creepy, but intriguing and calming all at once, and I knew that, at the very least, I would have a nifty little story to tell everyone back home.

The race went on, more or less, as planned, other than the modification to the run course and the fact that there had been limited running water in town, so those who took a little longer to complete the event had to do so with only Gatorade and cola in the aid stations. Luckily, I didn't have to worry because I had a good race and managed to finish fourth in my age group, which included all men 40-49. I enjoyed myself thoroughly and even had the opportunity to high-five Karen Smyers just after the turn-around near the aquarium.

Two races behind me with two great results and it was still only the middle of July. This left me with ample time to continue training for the rest of the summer.

The bike was still the discipline I enjoyed most, and I began to ramp up the mileage doing rides closer to three hours each time. When I first started cycling, I hated it when another cyclist would sit on my wheel for a while, only to pass later on. I didn't understand that this was merely an attempt by other riders to include me in a real training session that would benefit both of us. I simply assumed he or she was being an asshole, trying to show me up. Now, I loved it when this would happen. Unfortunately (or fortunately, I guess), I had improved so much that, if and when I closed the gap on another rider in training, it was because they were significantly weaker, and it would end up being nothing more than an easy pass. Most of the time, it made me feel strong, but I would have enjoyed some relief and I wished they would come past so I could enjoy a little draft, do less work, but maintain my speed. I also worried that they thought *I* was the asshole. There's a good chance that I *am* an asshole, but not in this situation.

By the time of my next race, which took place in Benton Harbor, Michigan in mid-August, I unconditionally identified myself as a triathlete. Sure, I was a teacher, father, son, and a whole bunch of other things, but when asked, 'triathlete' was what came out of my mouth first.

Ever since that first race in Connecticut (in fact it was long before that), I had been searching for more meaning in my life. I had been, consciously or not, desperate for some sort of vehicle or path to deeper happiness. I was in search of something essential towards which I could focus my energy and spirit. There had been a void, and I was finally beginning to believe that triathlon was filling it. My improvement was noticeable and significant, and it happened with ease. When I began, I never thought I would have become as accomplished as I had.

By the time Ironman 70.3 Steelhead arrived, I was utterly confident that I would be able to do well. I checked the finishing times for my age group from previous years, and I knew I could match, or even surpass, them. Even the swim, which like the year before in Racine, took place in the frigid, rough waters of Lake Michigan, was a total non-issue. There wasn't a moment's pause when I thought I might panic. Fifty-degree water was not exactly what I had been hoping for, but it didn't make me unduly nervous. So what, my lips would be blue by the end. Big deal.

Steelhead was memorable for several reasons, not least of which was the quirkiness of the transition zone. It was unlike every other race I had done, where transition took place in a field or parking lot, with, more or less, a square shape, organized in several rows of bikes. If your bike was racked at the very extreme of one end of the row, you could still see the bikes at the other extreme. In Benton Harbor, by contrast, the zone was one long, skinny area with very few rows that went on for the better part of a kilometre, almost requiring an aid station halfway through.

Another memorable feature of the race was that the AWA athletes, of which I was proud to be part, had their bikes racked right near the bike exit, meaning we did not have to run pushing them for a kilometre after the swim. Also, we AWA folks were permitted to share a secret stash of portable toilets reserved for the professionals. This, effectively, meant we did not have to wait in any lines. I had not seen this before, nor has it been the case since, and that's a shame. If Ironman really wants to reward the top 1% of age groupers, give them their own toilet section. That is a way better perk than a pre-race breakfast and a sticker on the race bib. We don't really need a lethal, suitcase identification tag, and I have plenty of swim caps. Just let me take a pre-race shit without waiting in line for two hours.

If it hadn't been for the semi-private toilets at Steelhead, I never would have had the opportunity to meet Lionel Sanders. That's right, I dropped a deuce right on top of a pile of crap left by one of the top pros in the sport, not to mention the eventual race winner that day. The only really shitty part (see what I did there) was that, at the time, I had absolutely no idea who he was. As a matter of fact, he didn't look particularly 'pro'ish at all, and I thought he was just some lost age grouper trying to crash the private shitter line. It's amazing how entitled you feel when given a title. "I'm an AWA dammit", I was thinking to myself. "Who does this prick think he is using *our* honey bucket?". He did give me a smile as he exited and held the door open for me to enter. As I approached, he chuckled and kindly said, "It's not pretty in there. My apologies".

Other than my chance meeting with a Kona contender, and the icy swim, the only other thing I really remember, with any clarity, was that I decided to give the whole 'no socks' thing a go. Some people remember every kilometre of every race. All I've got is that. Well that, and the fact that, though I ran really fast, my feet were bleeding when I was done. My brand new blue racing flats finished the race a dark, rich burgundy colour.

I'm not one for public displays of affection, and I cringe when I see athletes celebrate too vociferously after performing well. I, personally, have never so much as raised my arms in the air after a race, even though inwardly, I am completely losing my shit. I've always preferred to appear as though it was just another day at the office. Age group triathlon is a little different, anyway, because there are several waves of athletes starting at different times, making it very difficult to know where you are relative to others in your category. Of course, you can get a feel for where you stand, based on your times and how your body is reacting to the pace, but what we really want to know, as soon as we cross the line, is how well we placed. By the end of the race, I knew I had done well. I felt great, and, based on the age information scrawled on the calf of the rest of the competitors I saw out on the course, it was evident that there wouldn't have been too many who had finished before me. I really wanted to do a victory dance and spike the football, but all I allowed myself was a brief, quiet, "Fuck, yeah".

I won my age group. My first win. Unfortunately, however, I never got to stand on the podium and publicly enjoy my triumph. In fact, I never even made it to the podium at all because there was a much more pressing concern that perilously needed my undivided, immediate attention. There was no time for "Hey, dig me". The podium would have to wait because I was shitting *through* my tri-suit next to the rear wheel on the passenger side of my car, which was parked in front of a real estate office at the end of a particularly nondescript strip mall.

During the race, I had felt incredible throughout. At no point did I feel as though I was performing outside my capability, and I made a point to remain comfortable the entire way, bringing my effort level up to the edge of discomfort, but never over it. Even the final mile was great. My hydration and fueling plan had been spot on, and I crossed the line knowing I had done well. My time was 4:26:01, and I knew from having trolled the Ironman website that my time would have made me the winner from the year before. After crossing the line and receiving my finisher's medal, cap, and a bottle of water, I headed directly to the tent to grab a plateful of food I never really eat. I was so happy and quite proud of myself.

As soon as the aroma of pizza and burgers hit my nose, the process of digestion of food I hadn't even eaten began in my GI tract, and I went from feeling perfectly fine to 'get the fuck outta my way, I'm gonna shit myself' in less than two seconds.

I left the food tent as fast as I could, running right past Anne, who knew before I did that I had finished first and was ready to give me a big congratulatory hug, in search of the nearest Porta-Potty. There was a bank of them not far from where the podium was being erected, and lucky for me, and everyone within 300 metres of me, the first one in the row was unoccupied. With barely enough time to shimmy out of my race kit before the tsunami of nasty number two raged towards the end of my colon taking no prisoners in search of an exit, I managed to just close the door in time to get almost in the seated position. Close enough was all I could manage. I didn't move a muscle, voluntarily, for a very long time, relying on pulses and contractions in places I had no conscious control over. I'm not exactly sure how long I was in there, but I was salty and freezing cold by the time I exited the cabin.

When I got out, Anne and Owen were waiting for me and asked what was going on and if I was okay. "Let's just go to the car", I said sheepishly and altogether embarrassed. "I need to change".

The ten-minute walk to the car was uneventful and we were able to talk about the race. The monster in my gut had, apparently, been killed, and I was able to concentrate and allow the glow of my win to gently kiss my ego as I prepared my mind to begin the process of getting naked in a public place without getting arrested.

No sooner had I opened the backseat, passenger-side door to shield my ass from the view of innocent passers-by, than I was pummelled by another barrage of intestinal cramps that appeared entirely without a hint of warning, and violently polluted the calm that, mere seconds before, was present. A tidal wave of shit began rolling frantically and burst its way through the door of my arse, like a twitchy gang of thieves Tommy gunning their way out of a crowded bank at noon hour. I had no time to remove my racing kit. In fact, I barely made it into a semi-crouched position before the foul, liquified, burning hot ooze shot out of me with such force, that it completely penetrated the chamois that protects my undercarriage from my bike seat, and onto my racing flats. It was amazing how quickly I went from crusty and dry and covered in salt stains to having wet feet draped in liquid excrement.

I felt so awful that, although I had opened the door so no one would see me changing clothes, I no longer cared at all who saw me doing what. I figured the only crimes I could be arrested for would be indecent exposure and defecating in public, but I also knew that there wasn't a cop in the entire state of Michigan who would be willing to ruin a beautiful late summer dayshift by handcuffing a five foot nine inch, skinny, forty-something, sweaty triathlete, literally covered in moist, runny shit. I figured it was a safe bet they might just look the other way on this one. Surely there must be a drug deal going down somewhere in town or a speeding truck that demanded their attention more than what I had on offer.

You know how they give you those little proxy cards with the race package saying, "this is in case you cannot pick up your gear from transition after the race yourself. This card will permit its holder to retrieve your belongings on your behalf", and you think to yourself, "who does this?". Well, I was very close to needing it that day. As a matter of fact, if I hadn't left it at the Holiday Inn Express in South Bend, I would have had Anne get my bike for me. She did collect my winner's 'trophy' while I had a little lay down on the strip of grass next to the car. Though it wasn't a priority, I hoped the little tree I was next to would shelter me from the sun. It did not, and I ended up with a sunburn to half of my body.

- WORLD CHAMPIONSHIPS 2.0: MONT TREMBLANT -

When I qualified for the World Champs at the race in Syracuse, I hadn't been particularly excited about it. For me, a *World* Championship meant you got to travel somewhere in the world *away* from home. It was supposed to be glamorous and definitely in a foreign land, preferably where the citizens speak a different and novel language that I don't understand. Preferably, anyway. Granted, the province of Quebec fits these criteria for almost everyone else in the world, as it is a province so unique that it came to within a percentage point of seceding from the Commonwealth Of Canada in 1995. Everything about the place is distinct. It is predominantly French-speaking. It has a unique architectural style and cuisine unlike anywhere in the world. There is, to put it succinctly, no place remotely like it anywhere. The problem is that I was born there, grew up there and I still live there to this day. It is wonderful, and there are few places I would rather hang my hat, if any, but because of that, it is not exotic. French is the language spoken most in our house. In fact, my son has a hyphenated name reflecting the wonderful dichotomy that is life in such a special place.

I was so 'ho-hum' about it, that it wasn't the goal I kept in mind throughout the summer. I was looking forward so much more to the following year's Championships to be held in Austria. German language. Schnitzel. Airplane ride. Now we're talking. As far as I was concerned, I would try my hardest and bide my time until then. Of course, by no means did I plan to simply mail in my performance in Tremblant. I was intent on doing my best, knowing that if I could match my time at Steelhead, it would have been good enough to have won in Vegas, by quite a bit, and I knew that Steelhead had not been a 'one-off'. At least with the race in Tremblant, I had a shot at a top ten with, perhaps, not just Anne and Owen watching.

Though the magnitude of the event was never quite lost on me, I just couldn't seem to muster the same type of exuberance I had felt the year before in Vegas. That year, the race was far enough away to require an airplane. This year, it was a ride in a Kia Sportage in heavy, end of summer, Friday afternoon traffic, made significantly more tedious by the fact that Montreal is an island only accessible via a series of overwhelmed, inadequate bridges and tunnels. I live off the island to the South East of the city by about forty minutes, and Mont Tremblant is a resort village about two and a half hours north of the city, in the Laurentian mountains. Traffic from Montreal to the Laurentians is tedious at the best of times, but on a Friday in early September, when people are desperate to latch onto what is left of the summer weather to head for the hills, it was just unbearable. Winter in Quebec feels as though it lasts about eleven months, and, therefore, its citizens get a little itchy when the good weather is nearing its end, making road rage an accepted, even encouraged, provincial pastime. The prospect of a four-hour drive going slower than a Sunday training ride didn't quite possess the same gravitas as hurtling through the air at 600 miles per hour, eating mini pretzels. Mont Tremblant? Meh...

The drive seemed to take an eternity and didn't do much to

improve my excitement for the event. All the major roadways were a sea of loaded vehicles with kilometre after kilometre of endless brake lights. There was little to stimulate the senses beyond the thousands of cavernous potholes, cracks, and patches that characterize the Quebec road system. If it wasn't for the heightened level of awareness required to slalom my way around these not so hidden obstacles, I surely would have been lulled into a dangerous slumber, only to be awakened by crashing into the car a metre away from my front bumper (this actually happened to me once on a road trip to Mount Hood, Oregon. I was so tired that I fell asleep at the wheel and was awakened by the sound the car made as it bumped into the one ahead of me in line at a toll booth. The funny part was that the guy in that car thanked me because he too had fallen asleep, and the bump woke him up).

The closer we got to the town of Mont Tremblant, the less traffic there seemed to be, which caused me to relax a little bit and allowed me to actually begin to feel a bit of excitement for the event. As we drove down Autoroute 117, I thought I saw a road sign with the M-Dot on it, but I brushed it off assuming that I was so exhausted from the drive that it must have been a temporary, home-made poster. We continued for another kilometre, and I noticed it again: a permanent, metal, road sign with a red M-Dot and the distance to the village written on a green section below. "Wow", I thought aloud. "They made a metal sign just for the weekend. I wonder when they put it up". We must have passed five or six of these signs along the highway until the exit for Mont Tremblant. My outlook was really taking a turn towards the positive.

Living in Quebec, I knew that the citizens and government

were proud to host an Ironman and an Ironman 70.3 event each summer, and I had heard advertisements on the radio about the World Championships coming to town, but I had never been to Tremblant in the summer. The images in my head were of snow, skis, and hot chocolate. What I was now experiencing was a permanent commitment by local and provincial governments to advance and protect the sport that I had come to identify my entire personality with, and I suddenly found myself super proud to be part of the host nation for this great event. I was becoming more and more pleased to have a race of such magnitude take place, more or less, in my own backyard. I felt as though I was the guy who knew all the secret crags and breaks, like a local climber or surfer, even though I had never even been on many of the roads where the race would take place.

When we turned off the highway, I had one of those odd experiences where you notice that something in your immediate environment has changed but you can't quite ascertain exactly what is different. It was sort of like when you are on an airplane and it begins its ascent and climbs up, up, up. You don't really notice the pressure building in your head and affecting your hearing. It isn't until you yawn, and the pressure is released momentarily, that you realize you have been half deaf for the past hour.

Just outside of Tremblant, something peculiar was most certainly happening. I was able to hear things much more clearly, as there seemed to be much less ambient, white noise. Every spoken word and song lyric on the radio was much more clear and crisp, like the difference between an AM station and a symphony coming through a Bang and Olafson sound system. For a second I thought I was having a pseudo, Hollywoodesque, Field of Dreams moment of zen-like, metaphysical enlightened clarity. "I must really be in the zone", I thought to myself. A warm, comfortable glow enveloped my body as I pondered a new career in Motorcycle Maintenance, or a move to Tibet until I realized what had happened.

The road surface beneath the car no longer resembled a goat track, like most roads in the province. What we were driving on was like a layer of tarmac-coloured, royal velvet. I could have had an open container of battery acid in my lap, but there was no way it would have spilled. Images of mattress commercials where someone jumps as though on a trampoline while a glass of Cabernet Sauvignon stays perfectly undisturbed right next to him danced around my head. And, the roads stayed this smooth all the way to the village at the Mont Tremblant ski resort, where ground zero for the race was located. I was so pleased that we would basically be racing on a closed course designed, and used exclusively, for triathlon events that, as a taxpaying Quebecer, I was no longer pissed off about. So what if I need a new suspension on my car every year and a half, I race triathlons. I was now actually proud of the conditions of the roads in Quebec. Athletes from all over the world were going to race on the smoothest, most beautifully engineered course anywhere, and I am from this wonderful place. It didn't matter that it was all illusory, because absolutely everywhere else in the entire province, with the very tiny exception of the Circuit Gilles Villeneuve Formula One race track, and, perhaps, the runways at Trudeau International Airport, were piles of shit. These people were going to go home and wonder why *their* local government didn't take the condition of the roads where *they* lived as seriously as Quebeckers.

The closer we got to the resort, the giddier I felt, and I was now officially looking forward to not only racing the event but to the event itself. At each intersection and round-about, we passed volunteers in yellow vests, with the M-Dot displayed prominently, guiding us to the parking areas. Anne and I looked at each other, feeling the nervous excitement brewing as if to say, "This is the shit!".

By the time we had parked the car and began exploring the ski village and the Ironman Village, it was becoming abundantly clear that not only had Vegas been somewhat of an amateur show, but that this was a template that few places would be capable of emulating. Everything was exactly as it should be. The single transition zone (which is a major bonus) was in a perfectly flat, clean-swept, sterilized parking lot, thus eliminating any worry of traipsing through mud and grass. There was no feeling of concern that you might puncture a tire on a stray twig or hidden object. Everything was perfectly square and organized like the circuit board inside your computer. There was a redundancy of energetic, enthusiastic, bilingual, expert volunteers proud to have the entire triathlon world descend on their fair, pastoral corner of it.

Just beyond transition sat the ski village which resembled a vintage, Shakespearian hamlet. Every window on every building had a flower box full of colourful foliage, the streets and pathways were cobbled, and wound intricately and randomly around the squares and fountains. Delicious aromas of gastronomic delight wafted about, filling our nostrils with hints of gourmet poutine and Beaver Tails. Music played loudly, but not intrusively from ubiquitous, hidden and camouflaged, loudspeakers, keeping everyone in a jovial and expectant mood. There was even an open teacup, cabriolet, gondola to take visitors from the lower village to the upper, offering endless vistas of the Laurentian Mountains. Languages from all over the world could be heard, each punctuated by the local French Canadian dialect which, though it sounds natural to me, seemed utterly unique for an Ironman event in North America. Every other Ironman race I had attended so far, was played out entirely in English, so this felt foreign, even to a local like me. I could only imagine how it must have sounded to outsiders.

Even waiting in a long line snaking its way around a major hotel was pleasant. The surroundings were so varied and charming, it did not feel like a chore to simply stand by with thousands of others for our turn to register and obtain our race packages. We felt more like we were sitting in a European piazza, something that thousands of tourists pay to do every day. From the line, you could feel not only the heartbeat of Tremblant but also the magnificence of the event itself. As I awaited my turn, I could not help but smile and feel pride. I wanted folks from elsewhere to ask me where I was from, so I could say, "Yes. This is where I live. I know...I am lucky".

For a day and a half, we explored like any ordinary tourist. I felt none of the anxiety or breathing difficulties I had endured the year before, and I was calm and feeling as though I was both right at home and visiting a spectacular, intriguing, foreign land. Everything seemed so easy, and I was entirely at peace. The only thing causing a minor itch of edginess was the absence of bother, as I kept waiting for the stress to appear and wondering what minor event would be the trigger. But, it never came. The night before the race, I went to bed late, not because I was a ball of nerves, but because I was enjoying myself. From the balcony of our condo, we watched wild deer run off into the darkness, and Anne and I shared a bottle of wine, which is to say she opened it for me so that I could drink the entire thing.

Once I finally went to bed, sleep came easily. The next thing I knew, my alarm was buzzing and it was time to get up to begin preparations to race. This was remarkable because it had never happened before. There weren't seven wake-ups to go pee and no tossing and turning with my mind racing thinking about frivolous details over which I had no control. I never once thought about how devastating a flat tire would be. Unlike every other race whereby I feel nauseated in the morning, forcing down a granola bar and half a banana, this time I awoke starving and ready to fuel up for real. Two bowls of cereal, a pair of cinnamon bagels, and half a pot of coffee later, I felt energized.

Instead of hiding out alone in desperate isolation hoping to escape from fear, I was downright loquacious, bordering on garrulous, talking my son's ear off, pointing at wonderful things passing by outside the window of the car as we drove to transition.

"Look how peaceful the lake looks", I said with Cat Stevens' 'Morning has Broken' playing in my head.

"Look at the mist, Daddy. It looks cold ", Owen said, rubbing the crust from his eyes. He too was looking forward to a good day. Nothing about this experience, so far, resembled any other event

I had done to date, and was, by contrast, exactly how I always thought I *should* feel on race day. Rather than dreading the race, busying myself with all sorts of frivolous tasks to distract me from what was to come and to engage in the futile effort to delay the start, I was eager to get going. The air was cold at eight degrees Celsius, which, luckily, kept me in the car, otherwise I would have been walking around with nothing to do but allow anxiety to creep in. As it was, I tried to have a wee pre-race kip.

Sleep did not come, so I donned my wetsuit for warmth and made my way down to the beach where I found that I wasn't alone. There were hundreds of world-class age-group athletes hanging around having the same morning I was. The atmosphere was festive, perhaps due to the free Red Bull they were handing out like Halloween candy. It was crowded with onlookers and supporters, making it a little difficult for those of us who were trying to get to the water's edge for a warmup. Most everyone was accommodating, though, offering words of encouragement and a pat on the back, making us feel like celebrities, and every kind word and touch augmented my confidence.

Normally, when I enter any body of water cooler than a bathtub or spa, it takes me quite a while to muster the courage to just get wet. I will wade into a lake or ocean inches at a time, watching with bewilderment how others around me just jump in. I'm a peel the band-aid off slowly type of guy in this regard. On this day, however, I pulled on my swim cap, placed my goggles over my eyes, and ripped that band-aid off in one swift motion and dove right in. Maybe the air was so cold that it gave the impression that 69-degree water actually felt warm, or perhaps it was because I was too distracted by the crowds and the beautiful setting, but I began swimming right away, went past several buoys, and headed back to shore. I was actually having fun and was still neck-deep in the warmup area when the fighter jets thundered through the crisp air above us to start the pro race. It was so loud that it actually took my breath away. Eminem's 'Lose Yourself' was blaring through the loudspeakers as the race announcer kept us informed of who was up next. I know none of the words to that song, but the opening guitar riff stayed in my head for the entire swim, like a firefly in a mayonnaise jar.

From the time I exited the lake after my warmup until it was time to start, I had given and received more high fives than at any other time in my life. This must be what Dr. Phil feels like running up on stage. None of this was normal behaviour for me, and even less so because I was enjoying it so much. Every hand I slapped gave me energy, but it wasn't neutral. It felt as though the other athletes were giving me *their* energy. I smiled and wished them luck, and I was truly sincere, but all the while I was looking through their faces and into their souls, with my eyes saying to each of them, "You will not beat me today. I am strong and I will succeed". I wasn't being cocky, I merely felt utter confidence in my preparation and ability. As the announcer gave us the "5, 4, 3, 2, 1, you're off", I whispered, "Let's fucking do this".

I leaped into the water and took up my regular left-side position, expecting, as always, to stay away from the bulk of the traffic so I could swim my own race. As per usual, I sought out my private 'lane', but after about a hundred metres, I found myself drifting to the right, which would normally cause concern, even panic, but this time was different. I *wanted* to be in the mish-mash of swinging arms and violently kicking feet. For some mysterious reason, I was gaining strength from being in the pack. Not only was I enjoying the slipstream of those just ahead of me, but I felt as though I was helping to dictate the pace by constantly touching their feet as if to say, "That's right. I'm right here". With every touch, I could feel their energy leave their feet and enter my fingers as I swam laps inside their heads. I made it so they would be thinking more about the asshole tapping at their toes than about their own race. When I sapped all I could out of one swimmer, I simply moved onto another.

I was actually having fun...during the *swim*. So much fun, in fact, that before I knew how far along we were, my knuckles were scraping the bottom. "What? It's over?", I thought. "Son of a bitch, that was awesome".

The first twenty or so kilometres of the bike were spent in a strange battle of trying to keep warm by pushing harder, only to be refrigerated by the added windchill from the higher speeds. I decided to just accept that it was going to be cold whether I went hard or not, so I tried to rip the pedals off. Most of the remainder of the ride took me by surprise for a couple of reasons. Firstly, I had expected hills, hills, and more hills. We were in the middle of the Laurentians after all, renowned in the Northeast for downhill skiing, but, other than several gentle rollers, there was nothing particularly taxing. Second, though I was pushing as hard as ever, my legs refused to fatigue. Whenever I caught someone, I had no problem pushing past, even when there were five or six cyclists to get by. Once again, all was going way better than planned, and

I started, at sixty kilometres, to picture myself on the podium, because I was passing people by the dozen, and the only cyclists going by me were race marshalls on motorbikes.

Though the scenery was outstanding and the conditions were perfect, I couldn't help but think that we weren't getting the full mountain experience. I was enjoying the ride immensely, taking in the contrasts between the deep green of the boreal forest and the sheer slate grey of the rocks into which the roads were carved, but I had expected, even wanted, to feel my legs scorched by the lactic acid that only sharp, steep hills could provide.

We turned onto Montee Ryan, which headed back towards the ski village and, thus, transition, and I felt we were being robbed of the opportunity to suffer. I also assumed that my cycle computer must have been broken because, by my calculations, we were no more than six or seven kilometres from where I would soon park my bike, but the odometer read about sixty kilometres done. The bike course was going to be short, by a lot. I was thinking that given how well organized everything had been so far, that it was odd that they would have blundered so massively. People were going to be pissed, particularly some of the pros. We turned right at a roundabout going very fast toward the home stretch. Not far from here would be another left-hander towards transition. Or so I thought.

As I approached the street leading to the village, and where my running gear waited, I noticed that nobody was turning, and there was a volunteer with a bright, orange vest directing us to continue straight, under a temporary, pedestrian overpass.

"Aha", I thought. "So we're not done after all".

Almost immediately after passing under the walkway, the road headed straight up, like an asphalt wall. I actually whispered to myself through laboured breathing, "Careful what you wish for, asshole", and I ran out of gears in less than a minute. The lactic acid flooded into my thighs as though it had been simply waiting for a signal, like school-children standing-by for the bell to start recess. It was heavy and burning, and it required so much extra effort just to bring my legs to the top of the pedal stroke.

I loved it. The pain was what I had been expecting all morning. I understood it and embraced it as something to be used to distance me from my competitors because they must have been feeling it as well. Standing and stomping as hard as I could, I heard the carbon of the frame creaking beneath me, and when I looked down I could see that the chainring was warping left and right where it connected to the bottom bracket. My breath was heavy, my mouth agape, and I stared ahead, hunting for the next rider I could pass.

When we crested the final hill, there was a turn-around to head us back towards transition, which meant that the monolith we just climbed at an average speed of twelve kilometres per hour, was about to become a screamingly fast descent. The moment I completed the U-turn, I could feel gravity yanking at me like a four-year-old attached to a Siberian husky. In no time I was going way faster than my comfort zone was accustomed to. I kept thinking that I just pedalled up, up, up, having the ride of my life, and was hoping there were no metaphors for the descent I was presently having difficulty with. The race had been going so well, I was on such a high, having climbed emotionally to a place that delivered sheer bliss, I did not want to have that all come crashing down because the descent was too much to handle.

These thoughts brought temporary concern, but the velocity at which we were travelling, coupled with the twisting nature of the road, did not permit this extraneous thinking to last. My focus narrowed as everything was reduced to staying on the road and keeping my bike under control. The last thing I needed was to lose faith in my ability and flesh from my body. I tucked myself behind my helmet in an attempt to be as aero as possible, leaning into turns with my butt. I could feel the wind slapping my face and bouncing off my bike. Every twist caused a significant amount of turbulence as I hit eighty-five kilometres per hour. I was terrified and exhilarated all at once. At one point, I was going so fast that, as I had to pull to the left to pass another rider, I was forced to sit up because I was losing control and coming dangerously close to the athletes still climbing the other side of the road with their heads down. Every move was so risky, and needed to be executed with precision to avoid ending up in an ambulance. This was the most fun I had ever experienced in my life, but it was also extremely stressful. I was happy to see the final turn towards transition ahead and removed my feet from my shoes early in anticipation.

All that remained was the run. "I've got this", I told myself, because, of the three disciplines, I was most confident about my running. Swimming and cycling are too open to outside influences with equipment and technique being paramount. With running, I could get through on guts, looking good was not necessary. Balls I had, grace...not so much. After changing into my running shoes and grabbing a few gels, I got up from the plastic chair and ran as fast as I could to get back on the course at a pace below four minutes per kilometre, and way higher than I would be able to maintain for long. My breathing was laboured and I began to struggle more than was safe at such an early stage.

"Slow the fuck down!", I chastised myself. "Concentrate on being smooth. Focus on your hands". This is a trick my running coach at Acadia University had taught me. All I needed to do was pretend I was holding a hollowed-out Easter egg in each hand, between my forefinger and thumb, to get me to relax. It worked not only because it forced me to ease the tension in my hands and arms, directing the blood back to the legs where it was needed more, but also because it redirected my thoughts from going fast to going well. Distraction is an excellent tranquiliser. It quells stress and transforms an overactive mind into a serene one. Sometimes anyway.

Once I managed my tempo and rid myself of all extraneous body movements, I zoned out and just ran, passing scores of runners without really acknowledging what it all meant. I do not know how to meditate, but during the run, I was only peripherally aware of where I was geographically or temporally. It's weird: I knew I was in a big race, but it didn't matter at all. I knew I was running and enjoying it. There was fatigue, but it was good fatigue, necessary fatigue, and again, I liked it. I liked it a lot. I was in a state of flow, existing not just in the now, or some other temporal plane, but in both simultaneously. Something was stimulating the part of my brain that releases dopamine and other pleasure hormones because I was becoming more of an addict with every step. As I ran, I passed other competitors, while onlookers hollered encouragement, birds chirped, vehicles revved engines, streams trickled, the sun shone brightly, and squirrels crossed our path. I noticed none of it; at least not deliberately because I was in a peaceful trance that nothing seemed capable of penetrating.

Well, almost nothing.

Most of the run was on a walking path that is closed to vehicular traffic. It is a serene and idyllic, brilliant escape from the business of everyday life. It is a sublime place to forget your worldly worries and simply enjoy nature. As I approached the final kilometre hidden from the public on this wonderful path, getting ready to trade its tranquillity for the roar of noise and action on the town streets, one thought, one uncomfortable feeling snapped me out of my metaphysical reverie with the violence of a sledgehammer to the forehead or an elastic band to the scrotum.

"I gotta take a shit! Like, NOW!".

My gut cramped up as I, ultra-consciously, puckered up my sphincter, closing it as tight as I could. Suddenly, my perfect form was replaced by the straight-legged, flat-footed, forward-leaning gait of a ninety-year-old with advanced, stage four osteoporosis, in dire need of a shit. I hobbled along, abdomen in full cramp mode, shit-hole tight as a drum, until the course left the cover of the forest and headed out onto the street. Lucky for me, and everyone within close proximity of me, there was an aid station right there, and I sprinted (sprinted in my mind, anyway) towards the first porta-potty I saw. Once inside, I Houdinied my way out of my tri-suit before I even had a chance to lock the door, and opened the flood-gates.

The sounds that emanated from my bowels were so guttural,

alien, beastly, and loud, that I did not recognize them as having actually come from me. I defecated with such force, and I unloaded such a prodigious heap of waste, that it piled up high enough to touch my butt cheeks. It was, quite obviously, vile and disgusting, but luckily, it took a mere twenty or thirty seconds to complete the job, making me feel instantly better. The cramps were gone, my breathing improved, and my racing kit felt a little looser. I lost what felt like a third of my body weight in about thirty seconds. Now that's what I call an effective weight-loss program.

When I opened the door to the cubicle, the smells that escaped with me were so awful and, quite possibly, toxic, that two volunteers who were there to pick up bottles and cups discarded by runners with terrible aim, were forced to abandon their post, dry-heaving. One of them remarked to the other with a disgusted look on his face, "Tabernacle, c'est quoi cette affaire-là?", which, loosely translated, means, "Fuck me, what was that?"

With that liberating episode behind me, I took off and tried to recuperate my previous pace. The short break had stiffened my muscles slightly, and I wasn't quite able to get back to the mental state I had previously enjoyed, but thankfully, I was still booking it. I latched onto a Mexican athlete who appeared to be considerably younger than me, and we basically paced each other doing a fartlek workout the rest of the way. It pissed me off initially that he kept coming around me and taking up the position directly in front instead of keeping to the side he had passed on, but I soon figured out what was happening, and returned the favour. Without the luxury of a common language, we communicated an agreement to share the workload without having to say a word. There was nothing to lose by cooperating because we were in different age groups, and we managed to stay together until the village, where he eventually fell back.

The twisting, cobbled streets were lined with a cacophony of screaming fans. It was an incredible, noisy experience made even louder by the narrowness of the pathways that were hemmed in by hotels, auberges, shops, and restaurants. There were no open spaces whatsoever. In the village, we climbed up a long hill to the upper section where the ski lifts began, turned right, and headed down towards the finish line. From above, I could catch glimpses, as we wound down the cobbles, of the finish chute, and I was filled with pride. I knew I had nailed the race. Other than a brief shit stop, everything went so well and my performance was the best I could have given on the day.

As I crossed the finish line and glanced at my watch, it revealed what I had thought. It said 4:24:05. I was ecstatic and I couldn't stop smiling. I rarely openly celebrate, but I did manage a slight fist pump. "Podium, baby", I thought to myself. "Fucking podium, for sure".

Making the podium at the World Championships was a dream, and I analyzed my time, doing some quick mental math based on what I remembered from the times of previous years for my age group. I knew that 4:24 would have been first place in Vegas the year before, by about six minutes. As I received my finisher's medal and strutted towards the food tent, I tried to hold back the thoughts that I might just be the 45-49 age group men's world champion. I felt *that* confident about my performance.

As I descended the cobbled hill leading away from the food tent to where spectators were gathered, I felt like Gulliver surrounded by Lilliputians. I searched for Anne and Owen. I knew that Anne would have already checked out the official results, so she would already know which step of the podium I was destined for. When I finally spotted her, she was smiling and had her hands in the air in a victory salute. As I got within earshot of her, she called out, "You got twentieth place. That's so good!".

She might as well have taken a hockey stick to my testes. I was absolutely crestfallen and was entirely incapable of hiding it, though I tried. I immediately retreated inside myself, so upset.

"Not possible", I said to no one in particular. "There must be some mistake. Just not fucking possible".

I had worked so hard, trained so hard, raced so hard and I had the race of my life. Twentieth place? Fuck off, twentieth place. I had given so much of myself and I was being rewarded with twentieth place? I did my best, but my best wasn't good enough. I did everything I was supposed to do. I hadn't made any mistakes.

Apparently, like in Halifax where there was no room for me on the flight, in Tremblant, there was no room for me on the podium. There was no twentieth step. My heart now shone one tiny light dimmer.

FEELING NUMB

"DID MY SKIN GET THICKER OR AM I
JUST GROWING NUMB?".
—INDIANA DRONES

I've had a few bad days in my life, but most often they have occurred since I have been an adult, and, if I'm being honest, with very few exceptions, they have been the result of my own stupidity.

I grew up in a middle-class Canadian suburb, to parents who did not get a divorce and with two siblings, one older and one younger. That is to say that my problems were chiefly what we now call First World Problems. Getting red Nikes instead of the green ones I asked for, is not the same thing as sharing a bowl of rice with the entire village after having hiked for twenty kilometres on bare feet to fetch fresh water. Having said that, First World problems affect First World kids in profound ways as well. We are sometimes hurt or scarred by events in our lives that others might find pedestrian and insignificant. Small problems can change your life in huge ways.

Mine changed in grade five.

Before the start of October of the year I entered the fifth grade, my life had been meandering down a smooth, happy path the way a young boy's life should. I did well in school, and I had enough good friends to organize a pickup game of baseball, football, or whatever, in about five minutes (without a cell phone or the internet). Days were spent playing children's games and living the carefree life of a reasonably popular, athletic, healthy young lad. About the worst thing that would ever happen was scraping a knee or getting the shits from eating too many unripe apples we swiped from one of the local orchards that surrounded our town. My mother used to tell me I would end up shitting through the eye of a needle at thirty paces if I ate too many. I never tried the eye of a needle part, but we did get a heavy dose of the skitters every August. Until grade five there hadn't been anything big, traumatic, or sad enough to make any singular day stand out as being particularly awful. I had yet to have the 'worst day of my life'.

The day my life changed started out quite well, actually. First off, it was a school day, but I didn't have to go. It doesn't matter whether you are in kindergarten or working on your Master's thesis, nobody is upset when there is no school, snow day or otherwise, and now that I am a teacher, I love it more than ever.

Though I do not recall having been told prior to that day that I had a morning appointment with the eye doctor, I wasn't about to complain. Normally I disliked morning appointments, even ones in the city because my mother would be annoyed enough with the break from her daily alone time that she would not want to extend it for the full day. Usually, it was an in and out, followed by a quick drop off back at school, doctor's note in hand. This one, however, had a different feel to it that I couldn't quite stick a pin in, but, hey, I figured if I played my cards right and did enough strategic delaying and foot-dragging, maybe I could get the day extended. As it was, we were already in bonus territory because the annual eye doctor appointment was a cakewalk. With the regular doctor, there was a better than even chance he might try to impale my arm with a vaccine hidden inside a needle designed to tranquilize a silverback. And the dentist? Don't get me started on that bastard. I can guarantee he wasn't breast-fed. The strange thing about the medical field is that you 'go to' the doctor, but you 'visit' the dentist. This is a conspiracy to make the dentist seem human and not entirely sadistic. You visit an old friend. You visit a sick relative. You visit your grandparents in Boca Raton. You *endure* a dentist appointment, usually just barely.

What made the eye doctor appointment even more innocuous was that it was nothing more than an annual formality, a mere checkup. Like having your snow tires removed in April, it was just something you needed to do. I had not been experiencing any eye pain or loss of vision and I wasn't sick, so there was no imminent emergency. This was going to be the old reading of the chart of letters, descending in size from top to bottom, and always beginning with E. Blind people could get at least one right. After that, I would look through a contraption that made it appear like I was the chief navigator on a submarine. Add a happy meal from McDonald's, and you have the perfect antithesis to a typical day at school.

"We're going to the eye doctor, you say?. Friggin bonus!".

I was so stoked at the thought of my day of legal truancy, that I was distracted from a couple of key hints that this might not be the 'routine' check-up I assumed it was. For one thing, it hadn't occurred to me as strange that, for this annual trip, my siblings were not invited. No 'stay at home' mother of three children makes separate appointments for each child. Also, being a fifth-grader, I didn't keep an appointment book whereby I jotted down important dates. Had I been that type of person, I would have surely noticed that my last 'annual' checkup with Dr. Wise had been, in fact, just three months prior to the present 'annual' rendezvous.

The appointment began, as expected, with a dimly lit room and Dr. Wise rolling around on a stool.

"Now read it again with the left eye covered", He would ask. Easy peasy. He ran me through the customary battery of tests, and after ten or fifteen minutes, he asked if I could 'hang out' in the waiting room while he spoke to my mother, which was your standard eye doctor protocol. "We should be at Mickey Dees in twenty minutes", I assured myself.

It took quite a bit more time for my mom to re-emerge from the dim room than I had anticipated, and I began to get a little antsy. I wasn't worried, per se, just hungry and curious as to the reason for the delay. When she finally reappeared, it was in the company of the good doctor, who was right by her side, which was a little strange because she would normally come out alone, hurrying me to grab my coat so she could get outside and have a smoke. Assuming Dr. Wise just wanted to say 'good-bye', I gave him a knowing nod, but he didn't bid me farewell at all. In fact, he didn't say anything. My mother looked at me like I was a mangy, but pathetically cute, stray puppy, and said, "Dr. Wise wants to run a couple more tests on you. Shouldn't take long. Come on", and she pointed back towards the dim room.

Now I began to get a little concerned. This had never happened before, and as he and I headed back into the exam room, I studied his demeanour for a clue as to what kind of news he was about to deliver. Unfortunately, he was as incapable as I am at masking concern. His mouth uttered the words, "It'll just take a few more minutes", but his body language said, "You're fucked, mate". I half expected to hear, "This is going to hurt me more than it will you". Yah, right. Fuck off it is. It never does.

Once back in the examination room, Dr. Wise ran me through several other tests, with one in particular that stood out, not because it was painful or exhausting, but because I was powerless against it. All my life I have been able to battle my way through things. I do not always make it through with grace or as the winner, but I've never been unable to do something I have put my mind to. This one, however, was no contest and it was so bad that I had to assume that the equipment Dr. Wise was using was defective. It had to have been.

The test involved peering into a microscope-ish contraption with two ocular lenses, one for each eye, like binoculars. This particular piece of equipment works by showing a different image in each eye-piece. Through one there was a horizontal row of digits ranging from zero to nine, while the other showed an image of an upward-facing arrow pointing randomly somewhere along a continuum of the same length as the row of numbers in the first lens. The theory behind the mechanics of the apparatus, and the sense of human vision, is that, though we have two individual and independent eyes which see two different images, they work together to synthesize them, creating a third, entirely unique, one. With this piece of equipment, the combined image is an arrow pointing up at a number along the continuum. It is this combining function that permits us to see in three dimensions and allows us to perceive depth.

I learned that day that I was destined to roam the earth getting only perfunctory meaning from the physical world. I failed the number arrow test horribly because when I looked through the view-finder, I saw alternately either a string of digits or a random arrow. The two never appeared simultaneously.

"At which number is the arrow pointing", Dr. Wise kindly asked.

Knowing I was going to answer wrong, or that he was trying to trick me, I decided to answer with total honesty. "What arrow?".

"The one underneath the numbers", he replied, trying unsuccessfully, to mask his concern. I was desperate to see the damned arrow, and panic was sneaking its way through my veins, and any second I was going to start to cry. In an attempt to hold back my tears, I closed my eyes briefly and kept my right eye closed while my left eye witnessed a miracle. The magical arrow appeared. The feeling of elation was almost overwhelming, though fleeting.

A nano-second after noticing the arrow, I became aware that it was pointing upwards at...nothing. The numbers had completely disappeared along with the joy, and hope, I had felt only a second before.

Now I did the only thing I could think of. It was my last option. I lied.

"It's under the three".

For a few seconds, I thought I had actually guessed correctly, because Dr. Wise turned the lights on, thanked me, and said I could go back to the waiting room.

Unfortunately, however, I hadn't.

From the doctor's office, we met my father and made our way straight over to Barlowe and Barlowe Opticians, where one of the namesake brothers forced dozens of eyeglass frames onto my face, each time announcing, with rapidly waning enthusiasm, "These one are you". Every set he tried was 'me', apparently. The strange thing was that other than the colour, each frame was exactly the same as the previous one.

"How about these blue ones", he said, trying to convince himself more than me. "These ones are you".

They weren't, so he reached for the same model, but in bright red. "How about these? *These* are you".

Another miss. I was thinking, "No they're fucking not", but instead just shook my head, no. He continued with green, light green, grey, charcoal, white (are you fucking kidding me, white?), burgundy, and black.

"Black. Good old basic black. These are *you*".

None of them were me, and I left the room exhausted and crying, leaving the decision to my parents because, let's face it, they were going to end up choosing what they wanted anyway.

When they came out of the showroom with my new frames and showed them to me, I assumed that the smile on my father's face indicated that what he held out for me to see was a joke. In his hands lay the ugliest set of shit brown, faux aviator frames that were mocking me with their sheer hideousness. Some people say beauty is only skin deep. That may be true, but ugly goes right to the fucking bone. They were absolutely horrible, and made worse by two features my father actually paid extra for. The first was a tightly fitting, wide, black, elastic strap, designed to hug the frames so tightly to my head that the nose bridge cut off my ability to breathe nasally.

"Now you can wear them when you play sports", he said proudly.

"Fucking yay", I thought, sarcastically.

The second feature slipped my notice until we walked outside into the bright sunshine. Normally, skies this bright would cause me to squint and even close one of my eyes, but now there was no need because the lenses actually knew to tint to a darker shade when outside. "Oh, fuck me", I morosely thought, almost out loud. "Now I'll never get to eat my own lunch at school ever again".

Dog shit, oversized frames that were way too big for my head coupled with tinted lenses; throw in a late 1970s, pageboy haircut, and I looked just like Elton John. At least that's what most people thought. For the better part of the next two years, I endured every insult a bespectacled grade-schooler could. Four-eyes, Coke bottles, Poindexter, you name it, I heard them all. It would be nice to say that I rose above the teasing and taunting, and became stronger as a result. I'd like to say that I got over it all and turned this unfortunate situation to my advantage, but I cannot. Every single verbal jab hit me squarely on the chin, and all of it hurt.

The real pisser of it all was that I never noticed any improvement in my vision. I still couldn't go to a 3-D movie (if they had existed, that is). Not one thing had changed. I got headaches, just not quite as bad. None of it made sense to me, especially the reason, if one existed, why my parents decided to make a difficult situation even worse by purchasing lenses that went dark in sunlight. I was having a hard time with the standard level of teasing, but whenever I stepped outside in the daytime, where every young boy wants to be, my glasses would tint and every kid in the neighbourhood, would add 'Stevie Wonder' and 'Ray Charles' to the other names they tormented me with. The one I hated the most was started, and certainly perpetuated by, Joel Ruttenberg.

Every smallish town has their own version of Joel Ruttenberg. Being bigger and stronger than most kids his age, he was the town bully. He grew hair on his face and legs earlier than the rest of us, but, unlike the typical, "Hello McFly", type of bully, Joel was no dummy. In fact, he was, and probably still is, quite intelligent. Before I wore glasses, I had been fortunate enough to largely fly under his radar, scarcely even being noticed, due to the difference in our ages. Once the glasses became part of my existence, however, whenever he saw me he would call out, in a merciless, malicious, taunting fashion, "Hey, Elton baby".

Now that I am older, and a teacher, and have children of my own, I know that I should not have let it bother me. I know that, in fact, I could have used it to my advantage. It is so much better to be actually noticed by a bully than to be ignored by anyone. These are things I know now, but back then I hated it. I mean I really fucking hated it. When anyone else attempted to tease me, I was pretty quick with the old, "Fuck off, asshole. You're ugly and stupid. I can always take my glasses off. You're still gonna be a dumb shit". Saying that to Joel would have been both factually incorrect and suicidal. It is one thing to be the target of an insult, and be emotionally scarred by it, but it's a whole other level of torture to have to take it with a smile and say, "thank-you" to the abuser. I knew that if I let my discomfort show, he wouldn't stop there. This was way before the era of pink shirt day, and I could not have felt more impotent than if he just chopped off my nutsack.

For two years I took the abuse almost daily. *Two years* I waited for Dr. Wise to tell me I would no longer have to take the punishment. Every few months my mother and I would go back to his office only to have him say my eyes weren't ready yet, which made no sense because when I was just two years old, I had undergone surgery to straighten my crossed eyes for good. Turns out 'for good' means until grade five. This is what happens, I guess when your mother smokes during pregnancy.

Near the end of my two-year sentence, a few of my friends and I decided to take advantage of a beautiful summer day to head over to Helen Park for a friendly game of pop 500. Unlike an actual game of baseball, pop 500, much like 'scrubs', allows for weaker hitters to have the chance of being in complete control of where and how they choose to hit the ball, as the skill required to connect with a pitched ball is mitigated by tossing it to yourself. We were having a good old time until the middle of my second or third at-bat. Amongst the regular sounds of leaves rustling in the breeze, birds chirping, the odd lawnmower humming along in the distance, and the sounds of children playing, I heard something that made all of my nerves leap to attention, causing all of the hairs on my body to straighten in an attempt to escape from the goosebumps pushing up at them.

"Hey, Elton Baby!".

It was Joel bellowing from the street behind home plate. The only sound I made, apart from the bat hitting the ground in front of me as it dropped from my, now very sweaty, hands, was me whispering to myself, "Oh shit. Game-over". I bent down slowly to pick the bat up off the ground at my feet as Joel and his pals rolled right up to where I was standing, dismounted their bikes, and crowded me from the plate.

"No fair, Elton Baby. It's so bright out and you're the only one wearing those stupid shades", Joel said as he motioned forcefully to snatch the bat from my hands. For some unconscious, instinctive reason, I yanked the bat away, thwarting his attempt. Reflexes are supposed to be nature's way of helping to keep us safe from dangerous situations. Unfortunately, in this particular instance, the opposite was true. The moment I pulled the bat away, I immediately wished I hadn't, for Joel had lunged so aggressively to yank it from me, that, with the bat no longer there, he stumbled backwards, tripped over his bike, and fell on his ass.

At any other time, this type of physical comedy would have had me howling with laughter. Not so now, and before I could beg for his forgiveness, he was upright, with his face millimetres from mine.

"Bad move, Elton Baby. You think you're fuckin' funny? You think you're Rodney Fucking Dangerfield?".

Assuming the questions were rhetorical, I froze instead of

answering, while most of my friends, who moments before were having such a good time, scattered like cockroaches to get the hell away from the park. Joel pushed me hard to the ground and put his foot on my chest, not allowing me to move at all. This particular indignity was made all the worse by my glasses remaining fixed perfectly in place by the stupid elastic strap. Not only was I about to get the shit kicked out of me, but I was going to have to do it wearing a set of dog shit brown, tinted glasses, secured firmly to my head that made me look exactly like, well...Elton Baby.

Trying to decide what to do, I settled on laying there motionless. Should I scream to alert someone in one of the neighbouring houses? Should I attempt an escape, and run like a bastard? Perhaps I should start crying, hoping for mercy. These thoughts took about a quarter of a second to dismiss as folly. The best I could do was just shut up and hope that whatever Joel had in mind would be over quickly.

Once he realized I was not going to squirm around and flop about like a fish out of water, Joel removed his foot from my chest and replaced it with his knee, for what I figured would be a more efficient position from which he could commence pummeling my face. Deep down, part of me welcomed that fate because that way, at the very least, my glasses would get shattered and I could avoid future scenarios such as this one.

But he didn't punch me. Not once. Being both intelligent and sinister, Joel had something altogether different in-store. He had no interest in mashing my face, which could get very messy. He was patient, wanting to savour the moment. This was something he wanted me to remember forever, and the longer the punishment took, the more control he could feel, which is exactly what this whole episode was about: control.

He kept one knee on my chest, with the other on the ground to ensure there was no way I could fidget my way loose. With his right index finger, he firmly tapped a spot in the very centre of my forehead, the way a blackjack player taps the table to indicate his desire for another card. Bracing for a hard punch, I could not help but feel the liberating relief that resulted from such a gross anticlimax.

That was it? That was the big beat down? At first, I thought perhaps he was just tapping a spot as though he was taking aim for the fist, or bat, that would follow. Nope. He just tapped that one, small, hard, very bony spot. It seemed so innocuous that I began to think that perhaps, like the Grinch, his heart grew three sizes that day. I couldn't understand what the point of it was, which I now know, was an integral part of the torture process. All he did was tap; I felt no pain at all. I kept thinking, "What's the catch?".

The 'catch' was that he didn't stop after that initial tap. Or the second, or tenth. Not even after the hundredth. He continued to tap once every second or so for about an hour. That's sixty minutes, or, if you're counting, three thousand six hundred taps to an ever softening cranial plate. For the first five or ten minutes, I felt no real pain at all. From that point on, however, with every succeed-ing tap, the pain grew until it felt like I was getting a one-hour root canal done on my forehead, without a sniff of novocaine. It was absolutely excruciating. My eyes poured tears, but I made absolutely no sound whatsoever. Noise would simply compound the agony. Every so often, Joel would lean down close to my ear and ask menacingly, "How's that feel, Elton Baby? You like that?".

Just as bad as the immediate physical pain was, the mental and emotional torture of not having a clue as to when, or if, it was going to end, was almost worse. The abuse lasted so long that the pain switched from acute to chronic and back again, several times. Every new tap brought me closer to the very real possibility of permanent damage being done, and it went on so long that I wondered if it would end before one of us died.

Once he realized that I had reached some sort of threshold and that there was no way he could further augment the intensity of the pain he was inflicting, Joel became bored and just stopped, saying, "See you later, Elton Baby", and he rode off as abruptly as he had arrived. He didn't even have the god-damned courtesy of breaking or stealing my glasses.

The pain in my head did not abate immediately just because he had stopped tapping at it. In fact, I woke up each morning for several days with a deep, migraine-level headache, which was a sinister irony that was not lost on me as the glasses were prescribed to eliminate my previously recurring headaches.

$$\backslash \quad \bullet \quad \sslash$$

I assumed, after placing twentieth at the World Championships in Mont Tremblant, that, though I had posted a personal best time, the work I had done to achieve it had been inadequate. It was not good enough, and therefore, neither was I.

Every piece of training literature I have ever read, including, if not specifically, triathlon training literature, strongly recommends taking a significant chunk of time completely off from heavy exercise at the end of the season to allow the body, which has been undergoing significant stress for many months, to recover. Pretty much the worst thing you can do is attempt to train as hard as the lead up to your final race in a desperate bid to hang on to form. Knowing this, I did exactly the opposite, not because I thought twentieth place was bad, but because during the race I had it in my head that what I was doing should have been good enough for the podium.

Was I punishing myself? Probably, but it was more than that. Most intelligent competitors would be partaking in an off-season of some sort, so I figured that if I kept training instead, I would be able to enjoy a little head start on building up my form for next season. Plus, I had never rested before, so why would I start now? While others took time off and properly recuperated, preparing their bodies to begin the long process of assembling the suitable aerobic building blocks which would enable them to perform well months down the line, I pounded my already exhausted body harder than ever.

Each day I tried to do a little bit more than the day before, effectively working harder than I ever had on a body that was the least well prepared for what was being demanded of it. Every session was more difficult than the last, but not merely because I was pushing harder. I was pushing harder because the results I was hoping for, and expecting, were not coming. In fact, the harder I tried, the slower and less powerful I became. I was getting worse, which somehow didn't mesh with the 'no pain, no gain' era I grew up in, whereby it was largely understood that the higher the work volume and intensity, the better will be the results.

In the eighties, we knew nothing of periodization or training cycles. To my generation, there was simply 'work harder', which is the reason Nike came up with JUST DO IT in the first place. Most of us were too ignorant to believe otherwise, and blind machismo ruled the day, as the best athletes regaled us about how they succeeded and excelled because they were willing to work harder and longer than the next guy. They went the 'extra mile', woke up an hour earlier, and stayed at it a little longer. More was better. We were inundated with images of guys like Rocky pounding back a dozen raw eggs, wearing a baggy, grey, cotton 'sweat-suit' and sprinting up multiple sets of stairs. Back then, there could be only one obvious reason/solution for why I wasn't improving. It was because I wasn't working hard enough or long enough. I was just being a pussy.

So, why wasn't it working? Today, coaches and trainers know better. I knew better, but I ignored the voice of reason and reverted to what I had heard as a kid, and what I had always done in the past. Instead of waking up at 3:30 in the morning to get in that first workout before work, now, I decided 2:15 was better. Work always trumps rest, and sleep is for the weak. Train, train, train. The more I trained, the more fatigued I became, but instead of recognizing the fatigue as a cue to back off and allow time to recover, I understood it as the obvious, logical, even desired outcome. Tired is good. I would then compound the problem by assuming that if I was in better shape, I wouldn't get tired, so I worked even harder, and cut out anything remotely resembling an 'easy' session. Off days simply did not exist.

From September through February, I kept this up, working more and more each week, getting slower and slower, and feeling more and more deeply fatigued. I was sore all over, all the time, and my hips and legs were in a constant state of toothache type pain. My breathing was laboured where it hadn't been before, and I could feel my heart pounding against my rib cage when I ran. The same thing happened at night, which went counter to what I understood about being fit. I had always assumed that the better was your physical condition, the lower should be your heart rate, and the more quickly it should return to the resting state after hard work. My resting heart rate wasn't significantly different from my threshold working heart rate, and it became impossible to sleep.

Perhaps because of the lack of sleep (or, frankly, the complete absence of any sort of deep sleep at all, ever), I could not concentrate at work and found myself being irritable and short-tempered with my students. The smallest thing would send me into a tirade, and I felt sorry for the basketball players I coached for the workouts I put them through. I couldn't remember where I put anything, and I blamed everyone around me for making me forget. In late September, I caught a cold that never went away until the Spring. The symptoms lasted so long, I no longer viewed them as symptoms of a problem, but as the new normal.

Worse than any of the physical malaise I felt, was how it was making me feel mentally and emotionally. Growing up, I had often been overcome by long periods of grey where I never felt good inside. There always seemed to be a cloud constantly surrounding everything I did, and nothing seemed to excite me much. The only way I ever found to raise myself momentarily out of these periods of extended funk, was through sport. I may have been depressed all day, or all week long, but it rarely occurred during hockey practice, and certainly NEVER during a game. Sports have always been my solution, but now it was more cause than cure. I wasn't living up to my own expectations which made me feel inadequate and, initially, wanted me to dig deeper and work harder. Increasingly, however, I came to dread the work. Though I never stopped training (never even eased up at all), I no longer *wanted* to train, and dread took over when it was time to leave my bed, where I had lain awake all night. The desire to run was approximately equal to a visit to the dentist or to writing a college midterm exam I hadn't studied for.

But, I kept running every day, despite having no desire to do so, which scared me because I knew that soon the lack of will to move would win, and I would simply stop altogether. Bodies in perpetual motion do not know how to stop, but once they do, it is difficult to get them moving again. The concept itself is utterly confusing. I was having so much trouble trying to wrap my head around having zero desire to do the one thing I loved the most, and which helped to define who I was, and I knew something was going to have to give eventually because there was too much constant, chronic pain.

Swimming and biking were fine, and I had no trouble conjuring up the gumption to get off my ass to do them. The problem was that by the time I began having trouble, it was too cold outside to bike, and swimming was always done indoors in the pool. Neither of these activities, from November to April, allowed me the kind of primal freedom that running normally offered. I never ran indoors. In fact, 95% of the running I did was on trails in the local mountains which left my body tired and sore, but it had always been a good sore, the kind that could be worn like a badge of honour. Now, however, I hated the thought of heading out the door to run because it hurt so much that it took way too much physical and emotional effort to take that first step. Instead of freeing me from things that brought me down, running began to bring the darkness back, every single day.

Up until this point, I ran seven days a week, five of which were during the predawn darkness with a mere tunnel of light coming from my headlamp to illuminate the path. Everything outside of that narrow beam was complete, deep, beautiful darkness. When on the trail at that time of day/night, there wasn't another human being for miles and miles, and I thrived on the solitude. My focus was narrowed to what I could see ahead of me, and whatever existed in the velvety blackness on my margins, was mysteriously comforting. I knew there were things out there (I could hear coyotes, deer, owls, insects, rodents, even the odd fisher), but, for the most part, that's where they stayed. I took comfort in the fact that they could see me even though I could not see them, and they never bothered with me. The creatures seemed to know that I needed to be alone. Now, however, running at night terrified me. I became acutely aware of how dangerous it was to be physically and emotionally alone surrounded by complete darkness both outside and within. I was becoming afraid of the night like a child concerned about the monster living under his bed, terrified that I might get injured and because I no longer wanted to run, I was afraid I would never want to again. I was frightened that I would lose the freedom running had once given me.

As autumn turned to winter, the snow fell heavier than in recent years, and the trails became deeply blanketed, which normally would bring a different running pleasure, with every outing feeling like an adventure, as though I was forging my way across the virgin arctic wilderness, like Shackelton or Hillary. The deep ache I now felt was painfully exacerbated by the depth of the snow, and post-holing became too much to handle. For the first time in decades I moved from the trail to the road for my daily runs, which meant that now, in addition to the pain, there was no sense of adventure to keep me interested and distracted. I was amazed at how many human beings are out on the streets at four in the morning in their cars. Running was now not only painful and frightening, but it was also ugly and something I had to share with other people, if only from their vehicles. Unless I am in a race, I do not share my running, and protect it like a hungry dog with a bone.

Every morning I ran, and every session was a struggle. My effort level was higher than ever while my performance had scarcely been poorer. From late November through the first week of March, I stayed awake at night fretting about having to run in the morning.

On Sunday, in the first week of March (the March Break from school), I had planned a twelve-kilometre tempo run, which filled me with fear and dread. The run started exactly the same as all the others had for the previous several months, with the road slightly slippery and covered in slushy, salty, dirty snow, making every step a frustrated, inefficient slog. The route I took was a right-hand turning loop that covered the twelve kilometres with four major ninety-degree turns, like a giant rectangle.

The first of these right-hand turns came about three kilometres in and consisted of turning off of a rather busy street onto a downhill, residential road. The busy street had a sidewalk to run on while the road was tarmac covered in icy slush. As I approached the turn, I remember telling myself to be prepared for the change in surfaces, knowing that the road would most likely be a little slicker after the turn. As I planted my left foot and threw my right leg into the turn, not much went through my mind and I readied my right foot to hit the pavement. It landed on what appeared to be clear, black asphalt but turned out to be what we refer to in the Northeast as black ice, causing it to slide rapidly leftward, taking out my left leg. Human beings are hard-wired to instinctively avoid falling down and all kinds of unconscious things happen to avoid it and correct it once it has begun. Reflexively, my brain started the process of negating what should have been a relatively harmless, semi-controlled slide into the snowbank, and jerked my right leg so abruptly and forcefully that it tore my hamstring from my pelvis, and I felt, and heard, a 'pop'.

If you have ever heard that sound, you know that it is followed instantly by sharp pain and the word 'fuck' issuing from your mouth, reflexively. When I heard it, I certainly felt pain, but not right away. It was momentarily delayed by the feeling of an intense, complete, unmitigated, soul-cleansing relief. I don't know how long it took for my tendon to make the sound (probably less time than it takes to blink), but in that microsecond, weeks' worth of thoughts raced through my mind. Every ounce of chronic musculoskeletal misery that I had been struggling with since late September vanished in that single 'pop'. The mental anguish I had dealt with was gone, and I felt free. The emotional battle between wanting to train hard to get fast, and knowing that it was causing daily pain, was gone. It was as though I had been granted a pardon by the running Gods, and I knew in that instant that, for a while at least, I would not 'have' to run, and that was so liberating. Finally, I had a valid, guilt-free excuse to take well needed time off. The 'pop', of course, meant injury, which also meant that I could not run. It meant I could finally take a rest.

Just to confirm to myself that I was actually injured and not just hurt, I attempted to complete my loop. In the past, I have done things while out running that resulted in very localized, sharp pain that initially I thought would put me out of commission for a while, but after getting back up and on my feet, turned out to be nothing more than a painful annoyance. Once, while running from the summit of the Pain de Sucre trail on Mont St. Hilaire, I caught a root with the big toe on my right foot. Because I was travelling so fast and had gravity helping me out, my foot hyper-extended so far that I had a perfect copy of the pattern of the sole of my shoe imprinted on my right calf. That hurt like hell, but I got up, hobbled around a bit, uttered several sentences containing words I would never use in front of children, and finished my run.

This time, however, that was not possible. My right leg simply did not permit me to run. Even walking hurt, and for the first time ever, I did not finish a training run.

A second after feeling the euphoria of relief, I regretted it. As the wave of elation ebbed, it was instantly replaced by guilt, and I went from knowing I no longer *had* to run, to worrying about not being able to run. It made me think of the students I coached on the cross-country running team. "Sir", they would begin to whine, particularly when the weather was a little inclement, "do we HAVE to run today?" My reply was always the same and they heard it so often that I rarely was able to complete it before they finished it off for me. "We know, we know. We never HAVE to run. We GET to run".

I had definitely been training too hard, and I absolutely should have taken at least a couple of weeks off after Tremblant. Having since researched the symptoms and outcomes of athletic burnout, I have come to the painful realization that every single one had manifested itself in me. I also felt the guilt of knowing that it was all avoidable. Two weeks off was all I would have needed. "Oh, well", I thought. "I'll get them now".

Two weeks, in fact, was the maximum I figured it would take for whatever was wrong with me to heal itself. No doctor had been given the opportunity to diagnose what the problem was, nor was I planning on ever giving one the chance. I hadn't actually been to a doctor since I was seventeen when it was a requirement to play for my college hockey team. In fact, if I'm honest, I figured the problem would most likely be gone in a week. Maybe even less. Still, at a bare minimum, I wouldn't have to run for a few days.

The day following the incident was a Monday and the first day back at school after a week off, and it felt very strange to drive to work without having first run for an hour. Since walking felt fine and there was no discolouration or 'hot spot' on the back of my leg, I hopped on the spin cycle before the first bell of the day and cranked out a long, steady session, completely pain-free, assuming I had overreacted about the pop and felt a little disappointed that my 'big' injury had been a sham.

"Dammit", I thought, "now I'll have to go running tomorrow".

When tomorrow came, I laced up my running shoes, and after a couple of preliminary, superficial, cursory stretches, I headed for the door and began to run. It took no more than three steps before, BAM!

"Holy shit!", I shouted out loud. The pain in my hammy was back with a spiteful vengeance. It was so sharp that I actually fell down. "What the fuck?", I wondered because that had never happened before. I'm no doctor, and I still wasn't ready to see one (that's what WebMD is for, isn't it?), but I began to worry that it might be more than a couple of days before this got any better, so I decided to shut down the running, no matter how good my leg might feel, for exactly one week. The biking hadn't hurt, so I could keep that up, and I never used my legs when swimming, so that would be okay as well.

Midway through the week off, my leg felt so good that I went back to leading my grade eleven fitness class in a high-intensity plyometric workout without even the slightest discomfort, giving me some psychological relief. If I could do that, I wondered, surely the problem had worked its way out, but I still refused to run until the following Tuesday, ridiculous though that may have been.

Tuesday morning I geared up, did my perfunctory stretching routine, and headed out. Again, BAM! The pain was back. Now, I'm no genius, but I knew something was definitely wrong. What normal people say is insane, we 'insane' people just call perseverance, gumption, get up and go, balls. Normally I had pretty big balls when it comes to this kind of stuff, but my leg really hurt this time. This was something that might actually require more than the 'walk it off' that had managed to fix virtually everything else to this point. The decision was made to give it another week.

The following Tuesday yielded the same results as the previous one, as did the one after that. And the one after that, after which point I reluctantly decided it was time to go to the doctor. Unfortunately, I had no family doctor I could call on. You tend not to have one when, apart from a mild STD scare in university (which turned out to be nothing), the last one you visited was a pediatrician. I don't think Dr. Nugent was still alive, and even if he was, I doubt he'd be taking appointments for middle-aged pseudo-athletes too stubborn to have an adult doctor of their own. It's just as well, from what I remember, Dr. Nugent had the most putrid, wrench-bending breath, and he was a real close talker. So, I lined up at six in the morning at the local clinic and saw a totally disinterested general practitioner who looked at me scornfully, and after telling me that I, and everyone like me, was foolish to be exercising as frequently and vigorously as I was, she even found the space and energy to chide me and my ilk for crowding up the local roads with our bikes in the summertime. I just knew that the five-minute exam she performed, without touching any part of my body whatsoever, and without even asking which leg it was that hurt, was inadequate at best, and didn't fill me with confidence that I would soon be on the mend.

"Probably sciatica", she said, disinterested. "What did you expect at your age?".

I had done some online research myself and had ruled out sciatica in the first thirty seconds. My degree in philosophy would surely not get me a job at the Cleveland Clinic, but it was adequate to rule out friggin sciatica.

"Could you possibly give me a referral to see an orthopedic surgeon?", I asked, a little annoyed at having wasted a couple precious hours and a sick day from work. That, in fact, was all I really had gone to the clinic for in the first place. She didn't seem to appreciate my question, assuming, correctly, that I was second-guessing her, and sneered disdainfully down at me.

"I've been practicing medicine for thirty years. It's sciatica", she said with absolute conviction. Then, under her breath, she added, "...probably. You don't need a referral". It was this 'probably', along with the fact that I had none of the major sciatic symptoms, that had me wanting to see a specialist.

I received no referral and left the clinic with a prescription for Naproxen, a sore hamstring, and a hollow vacancy in my gut where, earlier that morning, hope had taken up residence. Once home, I popped two tablets of the Naproxen and within twenty minutes was fast asleep on the couch. I woke up three hours later, foggy and depressed.

For the next several weeks, I followed the same pattern: I ramped up my cycling, never going less than twice a day, and swam three to four times a week. There was also some light gym time thrown in here and there.

Once a week, I would lace up my running shoes and hope for a miracle, but never getting more than five minutes into it before the pain caused me to stop. It hurt quite a lot, but that wasn't really the whole problem. All athletes are capable of dealing with pain. My principal obstacle was that my right leg fundamentally would not extend anatomically properly to allow for running to occur. Something was blocking the muscles from working as they were biomechanically designed to do.

What ensued was a spiral into depression. Though I was still able to train and stay fit, I could not run, which was what I had turned to when I could no longer compete in the sports I had done as a younger person. Running was not only something I had used to define who I was, but was also the lens through which I permitted the outside world to see me. From the moment I started to run daily, it had been decades since I permitted myself the luxury of two days off in a row. Weeks and weeks would pass without a single proper rest day. There simply was no true understanding of my life without running, and unless I went each morning, I had no idea how to approach the world I experienced around me, nor was I able to recognize exactly who I was supposed to be. My deepest thoughts came to me while I ran, and I solved so many personal and professional problems and disputes because of the clarity of mind that the act of running provided. For so long, it had been my altar, my confidant and soulmate. There was no single activity that I had spent more time doing, and none I would have preferred to undertake.

I had read a quote somewhere that I recited to myself weekly since I first came across it which read: "Every morning in Africa, a gazelle wakes up. It knows it must outrun the fastest lion or it will be killed. Every morning in Africa, a lion wakes up. It knows that it must run faster than the slowest gazelle, or it will starve. It doesn't matter whether you're a lion or a gazelle, when the sun comes up, you'd better be running".

Every morning, soon after waking up and before the sun rose, I ran. I ran from troubles and from problems. I ran to escape mentally and emotionally, to recover from the pain of divorce, and even the death of loved ones. I ran to recuperate from minor illnesses and niggling pains. I could always count on running to clear my mind or to fog it up, whichever was necessary. Above all, I ran to challenge myself. Simply put, I ran to stay alive, at least in a metaphorical sense. Furthermore, triathlon, my newest love, consists of swim, bike, and *run*. I am sure there are some great swim/bike events out there, but I don't like swimming that much. If I were forced to give up swimming, I could survive just fine, but life without running, however, was not life as I understood (understand) it.

For ten or so weeks, I endured a complete loss of self and I had never felt so low. I was depressed because I could not run, and seeing other people do it, made everything even worse. When I would ride the turbo trainer in the basement, often I would watch Youtube videos of triathlons and ultramarathons, but ended up being consumed with a combination of jealousy and awe. It had been so long since I was capable of running, that I found it difficult to relate to what I was seeing. It was almost like watching a Hollywood movie where you see actors doing things that are not humanly possible, like James Bond. It's a whole lot of bullshit, nobody does that stuff. No one can. I experienced the same sort of disbelief when watching people run on the internet. It was all mere fantasy.

Every week that passed I would try something different to distract me and cure my injury. I tried creams, stretches, exercises, exotic foods, vitamins, massage balls. You name it, I tried it. During the week I was able to train the other disciplines without a whisper of pain or discomfort, so at the end I would attempt another run, only to be disappointed once again. From Monday to Saturday I thought I was making progress, only to be completely crushed once Sunday came around. I was like Sisyphus rolling his giant boulder uphill all week long, getting it almost to the top of the precipice, only to have it tumble back down every Sunday.

Pretty much everyone told me to go get physiotherapy, and Anne constantly said I should go see my friend Yannick, who is a massage therapist with the Canadian Olympic Swim Team. I have never been a physio type of person, and have always looked upon people who need it as weak. I have seen scores of my students use a note from the physio to get out of PE when I knew there was absolutely nothing physically wrong at all. And don't get me started on massage, which to my thinking was for people who actually listen to motivational speakers, eat too much granola, believe the latest diet trend will get them looking like a supermodel, and most likely have witnessed an alien abduction at least once in their lifetime. I really like my friend Yann, but what he did for a living, I believed to be a bunch of poppycock.

As the weeks passed, I became more and more desperate for healing. Months before the injury, I had registered to race in Syracuse again, which would take place, as always, in late June, and I had even already booked a hotel room that could not be cancelled. I was locked into a commitment I fully intended to live up to, but time was running out, so I eventually gave in and made an appointment with the physiotherapy clinic near work. For four weeks or so, I would drive over there where they basically did nothing more than affix electrodes to my hamstring, and load me full of electricity, until I resembled Jack Nicholson in "One Flew Over The Cuckoo's Nest". I brought along a pack of Juicy Fruit with me whenever I went and offered a stick to every technician who 'worked' on me. Not one of them ever took any, and no one figured out the reference, which made me question their intelligence and, hence, their ability.

The appointments were once a week, and at the end of each session, whoever had been assigned to my file told me to go out and do a run as soon as I got home. Every one of them was baffled the following week when I would reveal that the furthest I could go was 200 metres. Either their regular clientele were not actually injured (as I had always suspected), or these particular physiotherapists were shit. Friendly, but shit.

On my last visit, the Thursday before the race in Syracuse, I lost all hope of getting miraculously cured, at least at that clinic, when the therapist hooked up the electrodes to the calf muscle on my left leg causing me to question whether she had actually completed high school. After letting her in on the big secret that it was the hamstring on the other leg that I was having trouble with, and finishing the session, I didn't even bother to attempt a run. It was officially time to start hoping for a miracle.

When I got home, Anne told me, one more time, that I should go and see Yann which, of course, I didn't. Instead, I packed up the car and left for Syracuse, alone. Anne had decided weeks ago that she and Owen wouldn't be joining me. "Just as well", I thought. "Might be a disaster".

Once I knew I would be alone, I felt less guilty for not booking the same Hilton Garden Inn as the previous year. I was a little concerned that since the new place I chose was on Carrier Circle, it might end up similar to the first time we went to Syracuse, but in the end, I figured it should be okay because this one was a Ramada and not the Super 8. That's what I *thought* anyway, but as my mother used to say, "You know what Thought did, eh? He Thought he farted but he shit himself". She always had a way with words.

As I pulled up to the hotel at the address on my booking slip, I realized that thought had most definitely soiled himself badly on this occasion. The first thing I noticed was that the Ramada sign was covered, poorly, by a flapping piece of plastic/ canvas-like material with the words, 'Howard Johnson' written on it in orange and blue. The awning, under which I parked my car so I could run inside the office to check-in, was missing a pillar and, thus, the roof was caving in on one side.

Once inside the lobby, I noticed that the carpet was torn, didn't meet up with any of the walls, and the brownish patterns weren't patterns at all, but stains. Vomit stains. The room itself smelled like a cross between cat piss and weed, and the furniture was filthy and would need an extensive upholstery make-over just to be considered threadbare. The Ramada sign behind the front desk was covered by a piece of cardboard with "HOJO" scrawled across it, in Sharpie. There was no hiding the fact that this place was presently undergoing a change in ownership and management.

As I checked in, the large, balding, white gentleman, wearing a pair of jeans and a bright green FUBU sweatshirt, looking like a decidedly nonSlim Shady, and sporting a yellow name-tag pinned to his chest that read, 'Carl: Super 8 Motel' (Huh?), was finishing a box of Popeye's chicken and seemed to be both surprised and annoyed that there was an actual customer in the lobby. I was quite relieved that I had already paid in full, and patently refused to give him my credit card for incidentals, which visibly pissed him off. He finally gave me my room key (an actual key, not a card), and told me I was in the far building at the back of the property. When I thanked him, I decided to ask if the hotel had, in fact, recently changed owners, assuming by the haphazard look of the signage and the apparent non-existence of renovations having been started as of yet, that it must not have been too long ago.

"Bout a year and a half ago", he said, exhaling the smoke from his cigarette at the same time.

"Oh", was all my shocked spirit could muster in reply.

As I drove around to the far building, I wondered if the door to the building itself would be locked and if my room key would grant me access because I was given only one key, but as I got closer, I realized that the key question was moot. The door at the entrance was open and hanging by only one hinge. I may not be the most perceptive person alive but I was beginning to get a bad feeling about this place.

Deciding to leave my bike and luggage safely locked in the car, I entered the building to find and check out my room. The number was 225, indicating it would be on the second floor. I was slightly relieved about that because at least the murderer who I was convinced would be visiting me later that night, would be tired from climbing the stairs or scaling the wall to reach my window. The second I entered the vestibule inside the doorway on the ground floor, I was overcome by the sheer strength of the aroma coming from the 'air freshener' they were using in the building. It was similar to the odour in the lobby, only way stronger and minus the cat piss. Apparently the Ramada Inn/HoJo had hired Cheech and Chong to keep the place smelling fresh.

At the top of the stairs, I turned left and noticed that my room was at the end of the hallway. The smell of marijuana had abated somewhat but was replaced by cigarette smoke, which I found a little disconcerting given that the entrance to the building sported a large NO SMOKING sign, as did the wall facing the top of the staircase.

I found my room and reached for my key, but as I brought it to the lock, I noticed that the door was ajar. Normally, I would have assumed that housekeeping was still inside finishing up the final touches, but, from what I could gather so far, maid service was, quite evidently, not much of a thing here. I pushed the door open and peered inside, straight ahead, where there was a small table with a lamp on it with the words NO SMOKING painted on the shade. Next to the lamp was the television remote glued to the table. Conveniently, the TV was already switched on and showing an educational film about how to perform oral sex on three people at once with both hands tied behind your back. Next to the remote, and under the NO SMOKING lamp, was an ashtray that contained a lit and smouldering cigarette dangling precariously from one of the edges, getting ready at any moment to set the place ablaze.

There was no logical explanation for this. I decided that the prudent move would be to staunch the cigarette and report it to the front desk, not that I would expect much action from the 8-mile wannabe there. Just as I approached the table, I looked to my left at the bed. On it was a scantily clad prostitute seemingly asleep, with one leg on the floor and one hand hanging over the edge with another lit cigarette dangling between two fingers, and ready to drop to the floor.

"Uh", I said, clearing my throat. "Excuse me?".

She awoke entirely unstartled, which I found rather unsettling.

"Hey baby", she said, sounding as though her throat was full of marbles, and rubbing the lack of sleep from her eyes with the cigarette hand. "You all set?".

"All set for what?", I asked, trying not to sound rude.

"To party, baby. Come on now".

"I'm sorry", I said, trying to swallow the vomit that was now in my mouth, and backed my way towards the door. "I must have the wrong room. Is this 225?".

"That's right, baby. Mmhh, hmph".

"I still think I have the wrong room. Sorry to disturb you. I'm gonna go", and I sprinted back to the lobby, leaving my car parked where it was.

FUBU was on the phone and didn't appear to be too happy that I was bothering him again. After I explained the situation, he left the room, pulling out his mobile phone and asked me to wait a few minutes. He returned about fifteen minutes later, assuring me that my 'suite' (that's what he called it) was ready.

When I returned to the 'suite', the prostitute was gone and there were no lit cigarettes, but the room, otherwise, looked exactly the same. The bed was not made, which was fine because, since I hadn't had a tetanus shot recently, I was not planning to sleep on it. There were no less than five cigarette butts floating in the toilet. The windows were literally bolted shut, and when I attempted to close the door to the room, it wouldn't because the door itself was ever so slightly larger than the frame. The TV worked, though, and there was free porn if I wanted it. So there was that.

Normally I like to arrive in the race city two days before the start of the competition, but I could not have been more relieved that, in an attempt to save money, I decided to show up on Saturday this time. There was no need for a crystal ball here: The Ramada/Howard Johnson Carrier Circle was a bad omen that, considering the state of my hamstring and the fact that I hadn't run since the first week of March, I found entirely unnecessary.

I'm not exactly sure whether it was because I really had no business starting the race on Sunday, knowing there was scant likelihood that I would finish, or if it was due to all of the second-hand weed smoke I inhaled all night, but I wasn't the slightest bit nervous when race morning arrived. It didn't take long to get ready because I wore every piece of clothing I packed, in addition to the three plastic race bags, in an attempt to stave off getting a staph infection from the bed. It would have been difficult to explain to Anne how I contracted a sexually transmitted disease in Syracuse from filthy bed linens.

I really did not believe I would be capable of finishing the race, and that alleviated my normal race morning nerves. There was absolutely no stress, and it was actually quite amusing to watch all the other competitors fret over every feature of their pre-race preparation and rituals. Seeing the first-timers made me smile because I knew what they were going through. I could actually see and feel the curiosity and wonder as they tried to study what the veterans did. I remembered well what being that guy felt like and wanted to tell them that the race was going to happen whether or not they were nervous. The race didn't care whether they had done the work, or not. I wanted to tell them, "either way, you have to do your best with what you've got. You will not fail or look foolish unless you give it less than what you have, and if you have less than the others, so be it, you will have a starting point for the next race. If you never race again, you will have done more than most people who are too lazy to get up and try. Just relax".

As soon as I finished the thought, I told myself to try to remember it the next time I was going to race for real.

It turns out that there is something to be said about controlling your nerves and remaining calm on race day, because I swam better than ever, finishing in just over thirty minutes. As I exited the water and looked at my time, I was pissed-off knowing it was probably all for nothing. I shook my head after having been stripped of my wetsuit, forgetting about my injury, and just bolted, instinctively, for transition, running as I always do, and because I was on autopilot, I felt no pain. Getting to my bike as quickly as possible was all that mattered. Only when I clipped my helmet, leaned one hand on the handlebars (I've never been a hand on the seat kind of guy. I like to be in total control of the steering mechanism at all times. Sure, I whack my shin against the pedal from time to time, but that's part of the fun of triathlon. No pain, no gain.), and *ran* for the exit, did I realize consciously that my leg did not hurt. I began to have a little hope thinking that perhaps I could finish this thing after all.

The bike was an effortless two-wheeled sojourn going faster than ever before. My legs accumulated lactic acid on the climbs, and it was flushed away on the descents. Parts of the ride were challenging, for sure, but overall it was an easy outing that was way more fun than difficult. Most training rides caused more discomfort than this. Nearing the end of the ninety kilometres, I began to do some maths. Assuming I could run, if I was capable of performing at my average half-marathon speed, I was on pace to have the fastest race of my life and I would easily win my age group, beating the winner's time for the 45-49 category for the past four or five years. Again, I had hope.

I dismounted, leaned on the bike again and guided it through transition to my spot, and as I geared up for the run I kept thinking, "I'm pretty sure I can do this. My leg feels great. Let's go".

With shoes and race belt securely fastened, I grabbed my hat and gels and took off towards the exit. As I ran, trying to wedge the nutrition in my rear pockets and adjust my cap, my running style, as it always does at this point in the race, resembled that of a toddler who has just shit himself. It's the same stiff-legged form I have while running with my bike. It isn't pretty, but it doesn't last long because once I get out on the course, my gait always begins to take proper shape as the stride lengthens and the power is generated by the proper 'running' muscles. All through transition I kept thinking everything was actually going to be okay. The injury was healed, needing the exact amount of time off it took to get to this day. I began to feel so happy as more than three months of not being able to run miraculously came to an end, and the weight that time had placed on my morale was lifted, making me feel light and smooth and efficient.

With these thoughts dancing around gleefully in my head I exited the transition zone and made my way out onto the course where it took all of ten or eleven paces for me to go from hopeful to despondent. I felt a sharp pain in my hamstring and I was unable to extend my right leg the way it needs to in order to run. Apparently, healing had *not* occurred. I was not fine and I was not going to win my age group.

In fact, there was very little chance I could finish the race at all, but I was not ready to quit just yet and I decided to risk deeper injury attempting to run through the pain.

Unfortunately, pain was not the only limiting factor. There were two bigger issues, largely outside of my control, than pain at that point: the first was that I couldn't, biomechanically speaking, run, and second, I lacked the patience to walk twenty-one kilometres.

The run course in Syracuse is a double out and back, so I made up my mind to complete at least one of them. I probably would have done both, but I could not stand the fact that most everyone in the race, as well as those watching it, assumed that I was too tired to run or that I lacked the fitness or was simply too weak of body and spirit. Spectators lining the side of the course would cheer on those around me, then, upon seeing me walking, would instantly change their tone, their faces would change expression from joy to sadness, and they would offer me a commiserating pout. They took pity on me, saying, "You got this. Not far now". I hate pity, and I really wanted to tell them all to fuck off. I did not want, nor did I need, and I certainly did not ask for their sad faces and sombre tone.

My pride took a big hit that day as the walking caused zero physical pain, but every single step led me deeper and deeper into despair. Once I reached the turnaround, I seriously began to be plagued by the thought that I may never be able to run again. I mean how long does it take to heal a stupid hamstring? I had tried everything, shy of massage, to get better. I was lost.

Being a two-lap course, there are two options available to runners as they finish a lap. Option one, for those completing the first lap, is to make the turn and head back out on the course to start the second. The other is for those finishing the entire race. These folks are directed towards the finishing chute where they will end their day and receive their finisher's medal. Knowing I was probably not going to finish the race properly, the night before I made sure to familiarize myself with the correct procedure for officially dropping out of the competition. It is surprisingly simple. All you have to do is get off the course, find the nearest race official and hand them your timing chip while declaring that you are done. As I slowly walked approaching the end of my first (and only) lap, I decided the easiest exit was down the finishing chute where there were several race officials who would be happy to assist me.

Of course, everyone assumed I had done the entire race, despite the fact that I was giving the sign of cutting something short (hand crossing the neck repeatedly, swinging my head from side to side saying, "no, no, no"). Even the race announcer was extolling my virtues, "And here, in third place, from Beloeil (pronouncing it, as always, incorrectly), Quebec, Canada...Brock Gibbs".

I continued to protest saying out loud that I was abandoning the race, and that I did NOT complete the entire 21.1-kilometre run, but no one would believe me. They thought I was just being a typical humble Canadian. We are humble, I admit, but if I just came in third overall, I would have been a little more excited than I was showing. "Fuck me", I thought. "I can't even quit the race properly today".

I looked down at my watch and noticed that it took me one hour and twenty-three minutes to walk ten plus kilometres, which is about as much time as it would have taken me to run the whole thing on a good day. This pissed me off even more because I would have been on the podium had I been healthy, and not just for my age group, but overall. As I neared the finish line, I assumed that the fact that I was walking and gesturing in a manner that clearly illustrated that I did not just finish third, would be adequate to indicate that this was, quite obviously, a premature departure from the race. It was, in effect, a DNF, and it was unnecessary to be told 'Congratulations!'.

Apparently it wasn't because nobody was listening to me. I told everyone at the finish area that I had not completed the race, that I was injured and needed to abandon, but they were having none of it and continued bestowing praise on me. Finally, as one volunteer was placing the finisher's medal around my neck, I gently grabbed her hands and told her, right to her face, that though I was indeed finished, I did not complete the race at all.

She became instantly irate, and chided me, ripping the medal back over my head and tossing it on the table where all the others lay, scornfully saying, "You should have said something sooner.

Now you've made me look stupid".

"I did say so before. Several times, but nobody was listening", I said, wanting so badly to add, "and you look stupid anyway".

She refused again to hear what I said and continued to rant and rave, basically calling me a cheater. It was bad enough that I figured I would never run again, but now I was being accused of being dishonest as well.

About an hour after I 'finished' the race, a storm blew in that was so severe, the race directors were forced to cancel what was left and led the remaining competitors off the course, giving them a DNF and a fifty percent discount on any future Ironman branded event. Unfortunately, I was not extended this offer, but not because I had DNFed before the storm, as you might think. Nope. In their compassionate wisdom, Ironman, probably on the advice of the woman I had previously embarrassed, deemed that the method I had chosen to abandon the race, which was exactly the way it is supposed to be done as per the athlete's guide, was grounds for disqualification. On the results page, next to my name could be found a giant, ugly, DQ, which, if you say it quickly enough, sort of rhymes with, and imparts the same meaning as, "Fuck you".

Though I had booked my 'suite' at the luxurious Ramada Carrier Circle with the intention of leaving Monday morning, I decided that once I retrieved everything from transition, I was going straight home. Because the door to my hotel room did not close, let alone lock, everything I had brought on the trip was already in the car. I also didn't want to return to my room to find Bubbles or Candi, or some other pay-for-play-worker, lounging around my suite, wearing my pyjamas while her John took a shower and brushed his teeth using my toothbrush. As a matter of fact, even though I never returned to the Hotel, I threw the toothbrush out before I left the race venue, just to be on the safe side.

When I returned home late Sunday night I startled Anne, not just because I was ten or eleven hours early, but because I was sobbing. She was sympathetic and attempted to comfort me the best way she could, which is to say she cut through the bullshit and said, in the softest way possible, "Go see Yann!".

First thing Monday morning, I phoned Yann at Centre Kinesis Massotherapy Clinic, and told him everything, starting from my 'accident' in March. Unlike any of the physios I had seen, and in stark contrast to the doctor who refused to refer me to an expert, he immediately asked about how my body had felt for the weeks prior to my injury. I told him about the toothache type of pain I had been experiencing and how I really hadn't wanted to run for weeks and weeks. With this information, which took me no more than five minutes to deliver, he told me I should come in for a massage on Friday afternoon. Then, out of nowhere, he added, matter of factly, "Two things: one, Anne is right. You should have come to me a long time ago. Two, there's no way it's your hamstring, and it's definitely not sciatica".

Huh? He asked me only one question and hadn't laid a hand on me. He hadn't even seen me at all, and he already had a partial diagnosis that was entirely different from no less than five 'medical/fitness professionals'. It has always been my contention that massage therapy was a bunch of hippy, dippy, baloney, intended for the weak gullible, cult worshipping, toga and huarache sandals in the wintertime wearing, outdoor plumbing, compound dweller.

Now, Yann's ready-made, insta-analysis, based upon my half-hearted response to a single question, confirmed it.

"What a load of crap", I thought. "See you Friday".

The session itself was nothing like what I had expected. Other than the aroma-therapy chamomile, vanilla mist diffuser in the corner of the room, and the soothing, soft ambient music playing in the background, the room resembled a warmer version of a doctor's office. There were anatomy posters on the walls and an educational skeleton in the corner, and the massage itself was more like a water-boarding torture session than the spiritual cleansing day at the spa that I had expected. There were no cucumber slices for my eyelids and no Korean woman gently filing the imperfections from my fingernails. What Yann was doing to my legs (yes, plural, he worked on both) was totally excruciating. In less than five minutes I was ready to tell him my deepest, darkest secrets just to get him to stop.

The room was cool enough that when I removed my clothes (let me pause briefly here. When he said to get undressed and lay on the table, I assumed he meant for me to get naked, which I proceeded to do, though uncomfortably. He didn't, however, mean that at all, and was shocked as I lay on my back with my tar paper laying limply on my upper thigh.) my skin became covered in goosebumps. They didn't stick around long though, because Yann had me sweating profusely as he began to mash my legs with both hands. I was lying face down looking through a miniature, padded toilet seat, and grabbing on for dear life to the legs of the table while Yann kept telling me to relax. That was easier said than done because he had, somehow, managed to have his hand buried deep enough into the back of my leg to wrap his grip around one of the muscles there, holding it like the handle of a tennis racquet.

"Yep. That's it right there", he said. "You feel that?".

"Are you fucking kidding me?", I responded, unable to hide my anger. "You're playing Boris Becker with my hammy. Yah, I feel that!".

"Just what I thought. It's one of your adductor muscles", he said proudly. "Not your hammy at all. Tons of scar tissue. I just need to agitate and get it moving along".

He told me that the injury itself had been healed for a long time, but the extensive scarring had been impeding my range of motion and causing the pain. After just under an hour, he asked me to get dressed, left the room and came back drinking a cup of tea and said, "Well, that's that. Don't run on it today. It'll be too tender from the massage, but tell me how it goes tomorrow".

Tomorrow? I couldn't help myself, and I laughed right in his face. I hadn't been able to run for months, now he rubbed me for an hour and figured, boom, I was cured, but he didn't appear to be insulted at all, just a little confused. I assumed he was kidding because I had been to a doctor and a bunch of physio sessions with no improvement. Did he really believe that fifty-plus minutes of deep tissue torment was going to magically turn me into a marathoner? "You think I'll be able to run tomorrow? Like for real?", I asked, not wanting to appear rude but looking totally unconvinced.

He replied in a manner suggesting that I was being silly to even ask such a ridiculous question and that the response was quite obvious, "Of course. Don't go for three hours or anything, but definitely push it a bit. You need to see how well the scar tissue being moved improves your range of motion. Have fun".

As I left his office believing I had just wasted $80, I shook my head wondering how he managed to stay in business. Why would anyone go back to him when he gives advice like that? I hadn't been remotely capable of running for three months, but at least I could walk without any pain at all. Now I was being told to go running even though just shuffling down the street to my car was an excruciatingly painful endeavour.

"He's fucking nuts", I said aloud, looking like the crazy person you often find on the Metro, and struggled to find my keys.

Saturday morning I dusted off my running shoes and headed out the door. In my head, I gave myself, at best, a kilometre before the pain would rise enough to cause me to stop.

Five minutes passed with nothing, and I thought that was pretty good, so I continued, constantly on alert for the sharp twinges to occur. Ten minutes...Still nothing. After fifteen minutes, I was approaching the point whereby I would have to decide whether I would continue on the road or head up the trails of Mont St. Hilaire, and there was still no pain, so I headed for the hills.

After about an hour of absolute freedom, it dawned on me that I hadn't even thought at all about the pain for quite some time. It simply was not there at all and I was so happy. I had found something very precious that had been lost for a long time. Upon returning home, I immediately called Yann who answered the phone by simply saying, "And? How far did you go?". He didn't ask if it was okay or if I felt pain. He knew I wouldn't. He was just curious about how far my fitness level had allowed me to get.

"Fifteen clicks", I said, euphorically. "Yann, you're a magician".

Before I could continue with a million 'thank yous', he cut me off simply saying, "I know".

Months before the injury I had registered for Syracuse as well as two other races: Ironman 70.3 Muskoka, and my first full-distance race, Ironman Lake Placid. For the longest time, I assumed I would have to cancel my involvement in these events, but when I hung up the phone with Yann, I began looking for accommodations in Huntsville and Lake Placid. I didn't have much time either, with Muskoka being in the first week of July and Lake Placid in the last. Basically, I had one week to train for my next race. The good news was that my swimming and biking were solid, so I just needed to do as much running as possible, without doing too much all at once. As it turned out, the running that week went quite well. It was the cycling that ended up causing me some serious pain.

We had planned to leave for Muskoka on the Friday before the race, so I did my last ride on Thursday. I was about sixty kilometres into a 90km ride, and was on the home stretch of a giant loop, when I decided to blow through a stop sign in the historic part of Chambly, Quebec, right in front of the old Fort. As I approached the sign doing about 40km/hr, I noticed a Volvo SUV dutifully performing her three-second pause before continuing on. As I got near the vehicle, between its right side and the sidewalk, I became aware, with grossly insufficient time to react, that the front passenger-side door was being forcefully swung open. Stopping (at least under my own power) was not an option, and I rammed headfirst into the door, which, luckily, had the window rolled down. My bike stopped all forward progress instantly, while my body threaded the window opening like a dolphin leaping through a hula hoop, and I ended up on the sidewalk eight or so feet away.

Volvo - 1, Trek Domane - 0. My shirt and shorts were torn, leaving a healthy dose of sidewalk rash on my right shoulder and hip, and one of my front teeth had been chipped and was quite loose, while another had pierced my lip. Thankfully, though, my bike escaped the incident entirely undamaged. Lucky.

Before I could stop her, the driver of the car was out and rubbing Purell hand sanitizer on my open wounds, basically starting a fire on my shoulder. I had to physically stop her from hurting me further, and she needed much more calming down than I did. She apologized at least fifty times in the space of two minutes, and no matter what I said, I could not convince her that the whole episode was entirely my fault. As I rode home, I could feel my tooth floating around inside my mouth like a Chicklet, but I decided to put off going to the dentist until after getting home from Muskoka.

The race went quite well, and there was no pain from where my hamstring injury had been. Considering the paucity of run training I had been able to complete in preparation for the event, I considered the sixth place in my age group to be quite an accomplishment.

I had about three weeks to prepare for my next race which would also be my first full Ironman. It had been a dream of mine ever since the first race I did, to not only try an Ironman distance race but to do the one in Lake Placid. Growing up, there were only two triathlons on television: Kona and Lake Placid, the latter being a mere two hours from home. I had been flirting with the idea of attempting it for years, but every time I tried to register, it was already full. Finding an open slot in Placid was more difficult than scoring tickets to a Led Zeppelin reunion concert, dead drummer and all.

I had been lucky this time due to my AWA status whereby we were offered to register for bundles of races at once. One of those bundles was a Syracuse/Lake Placid combo package called the Upstate New York Experience, which was opened up for us before the general public. I registered in August 2014. Of course, when I signed up I had no idea I would be injured for the entire Spring of 2015. It didn't matter, though, because I was running again and was making the best of what training time I had available to me. It also didn't really matter how prepared I was because the race was going to proceed regardless. I had no real, immediate idea just how difficult a full iron distance race can be, so I decided to treat it as simply two 70.3s back to back, an approach that gave me the confidence (false or otherwise) I needed just to toe the line. Doing half distance races always left me tired at the end, but never completely spent, so I figured if I took the pressure of performing well off of myself, I could just go smoothly and coast to the finish line where I would finally hear Mike Reilly or someone like him, call me an Ironman.

In addition to this strategy, I also counted on the high I was feeling just to be able to race at all, to get me across the finish line. A month ago I couldn't run, but that didn't matter. This race could be 2000 miles long, if it meant I could run, then I would do it. Basically, my big race plan was to surf my way to the finish line on a wave of ignorance.

You hear all the time that ignorance is bliss. Sometimes, however, ignorance is just, well, ignorance. Nevertheless, being all I had, I was hanging onto it for dear life. Some people were planning to draw on their altitude training, long bike rides and runs to get them through. I had done one long run since the previous August, and that was less than a month ago in Muskoka, and the longest ride I had done all summer was on the same day. Ignorance, and high hopes, were pretty much all I had, and so far they were doing just fine. I had ridden the same wave with success in Muskoka, now it was keeping my mind occupied on anything but how long and painful the race could potentially be. I had done zero Ironman specific training and was counting on cashing in on some residual 'Miracle On Ice' magic from 1980.

Everything had gone perfectly upon arriving in Lake Placid. The weather was great, the people were super friendly, and the place had the feeling that a festival was about to break out. Around suppertime the night before the race, when I normally get nervous about what lies ahead the following day, there appeared out of nowhere, the perfect distraction.

While I was working my way through my third bowl of Ramen noodles, we could hear the sounds of dozens of different sirens and horns from various emergency vehicles. Red lights were flashing everywhere, and when I went to the window and peered out at Main Street, I could see scores of fire trucks, police cars, and ambulances speeding through town. In their wake were hundreds of people relishing the distraction, trying to follow the action to see what was going on. We joined the throng and followed it to the site of the commotion, which turned out to be a raging fire right in the middle of town. There was no one inside the building that was ablaze, and the owner of the business that resided therein stood behind me talking to his insurance company as we watched. I was taken aback by how concerned he appeared not to be. His tone was such that I would not have been surprised if, after hanging up with his State Farm agent, he made another call to book a tee time for Sunday. Looking at him in amazement, I figured that if he could be this calm about a large investment literally going up in smoke, I had no business being nervous about a little exercise.

Once the firefighters had the inferno under control, the crowd dissipated and we went back to our hotel in a state of peace, and after a couple of glasses of wine, I went to bed whereby I fell instantly into a deep sleep. Perfection.

At two AM, my annoyingly weak prostate was no longer capable of sealing off the tiny bladder full of wine, Gatorade, and Pepsi, and I got up to pee, which you might think is no big deal. I mean, how long does it take to go for a piss? Unfortunately, I am one of those people who need to pee every half hour or so once the original seal has been broken, and therefore, I knew I was in for a restless last couple of hours during which my mind was capable of two things: negative thoughts and ulcer producing worry. I thought of all the things that could potentially go wrong during the race: Flat tire, mechanical problem, diarrhea, vomiting, getting lost, alien abduction. You name it, I thought about it.

My mind brought me back to the fire. Was it some kind of sign? Was my race going to go up in smoke like that building? These thoughts were killing me, so I did the only thing I could think of with two hours to burn before my alarm was set to go off: I finished Anne's pizza, Owen's pasta, and a bowl of Raisin Bran, all while sitting in a bathtub full of hot, steamy, water. In no time, I was bloated and burping and starting to feel the onset of some serious acid reflux.

When it was finally time to make my way over to transition, I tried to relive the serenity I had felt the previous night after the fire, but it was no use. In contrast to how calm and peaceful the village seemed to be, I was a ball of nerves. The air was still and there was a complete absence of sound. Even the birds were silent and the streets were devoid of vehicular traffic. The only beings awake were the various triathletes solemnly heading in the same direction. No one spoke, as we were all in a state of introspective, trance-like daydreaming, attempting to do the impossible and visualize the race that lay ahead. All the 'ignorance is bliss' crap that had been keeping me distracted the day before was rapidly being replaced by the agonizing realization that I was entirely un-prepared for the Herculean task that lay ahead. I began to question exactly what I was doing here, and I was upset that I had booked a hotel room so conveniently located that allowed Anne and Owen to stay in bed while I left to prepare for the long day ahead, alone. I was now in dire need of some sort of distraction.

Once I left the transition zone and found my way to the beach, I noticed that so many of the other participants looked just as ner-vous as I felt. This was not like a 70.3 where people are giddy and playful. This was serious business and everybody looked terrified.

When the cannon fired to herald the start, all emotions disap-peared and it was time to simply swim, which I did very well, exit-ing the water with more energy than ever before in a race until I realized that what I had just completed was merely the first of two laps. As I made the Australian exit and headed back into the water, I told myself to either read the athlete's guide or go to the damn briefing the day before the race next time. Miraculously, it felt as easy as the first and I finished relaxed and ready for a bike ride.

Leaving T1, I felt like I could pound the pedals forever. I seemed to have tons of energy and a large number of fans shouting encouragement really gave me quite a boost. I was firing on all cylinders and hammered so hard that I only looked at the computer on my stem for the first time after fourteen kilometres, at the base of a smallish hill. The next time I looked down it read 17.2 kilometres. "Whoa", I thought, "that hill was way steeper than I thought" because it felt like a lot of time had passed to cover only three clicks.

The next section was downhill and the tarmac was not in the best shape, causing a few cyclists to take up the entire road. Several minutes had gone by before the state of the pavement allowed me to safely look down at my computer again, and when I did, it still read 17.2 kilometres. The damn thing was busted and I knew that this was now going to feel like the longest ride ever. I hate not knowing how fast I am going or how far I've travelled, and now I would have to rely on the sporadic mile markers the rest of the way to know how much distance I had covered and how much was left. *MILE* markers. I am Canadian so I *hate* miles. They take way too long to cover.

After a while, I was able to put this minor problem to the back of my brain and simply enjoy the ride. Because this was to be double what I was used to racing, I had told myself to go easier than usual, which was a little difficult to do without any speed data to work with, so I was forced to rely entirely on perceived exertion. Unfortunately when cycling, as with swimming, I have only two speeds (or effort levels): fast (hard) or very slow (easy). I was going fast. Half ironman fast, which at first was fine, but I panicked when I saw several riders coming towards me on an out and back portion of the course, causing me to speed up to a pace that was outside of my comfort zone.

The bike course consists of two laps of the same route with each one finishing with what the locals affectionately (sadistically) call the Three Bears. I am pretty good at going uphill, so I attacked the first bear with vigour. Lactic acid quickly filled my legs, making the second bear a little tougher, and by the time I hit the third bear, I was really starting to feel some deep fatigue.

When I finally reached the top, I realized that I was more spent than at the finish line of any of my previous triathlons. This realization frightened me because I still had ninety kilometres to go, after which there was the minor issue of a marathon to run. I have never had doubts about being able to finish a bike ride, ever. This was new, and I didn't like it very much at all.

I timed my nutrition intake well on the first loop, consuming exactly half of what I brought on board, which was excellent management that I was proud of. I was so proud, in fact, that I rewarded myself by finishing what I had left at approximately twenty kilometres into the second lap. Not good. By the time I reached the base of the Three Bears the second time, I started to get the feeling that I might not be capable of finishing. Other than my first race in Connecticut, whereby I barely even started due to an anxiety attack, the thought of not finishing had never been a remote concern, at least not with an uninjured body.

When I finally crested the last bear, I had thoroughly bonked. On the *bike*.

Before I began to coast into T2, I had started to negotiate with myself, trying to figure out if I should even concern myself with attempting the run, and after considerable back and forth, I decided not to bother, concluding that I would never be able to finish. This way, I could go back to the hotel way earlier and begin the process of drinking my way to a palpable understanding of why things had turned to garbage so early.

I entered transition, and just as I was racking my bike, I was overcome by another profound desire to move my bowels, and the only toilets I could locate were adjacent to where our running gear bags were hung. That was going to have to do, so I took off and actually cut right in front of a lady, yelling apologies as I slammed the door behind me. She may have been a bit perturbed initially at my lack of social grace, but once I got down to business, the sounds I made had her apologizing to me for getting in *my* way.

The experience was so liberating that, when I was done, I zipped up, exited the cabin, and headed to the racks to retrieve my gear bag. I had decided to give it a go and brought my running gear to the changing tent where, to my absolute delight, I found waiting for me a smorgasbord of high calorie, sweet and salty snacks. Figuring there was no way I was going to be winning anything, and that qualifying for Kona, which was never really an option anyway, was not in the offing either, I took my time and grabbed fistfuls of potato chips, and chugged cup after cup of Coke and Red Bull. Watching me in the wedding reception styled tent, you might have thought that I looked more as though I was queuing up at a Carnival Cruise Line dinner buffet than about to run a marathon. With my immediate, number one goal being to find calories, there was no urgency to get back out onto the course, and getting to the barbecue chips before they were all gone was my first priority.

Fully fuelled, I left the tent with enough calories in my belly to provide the necessary cognitive confusion to trick myself into believing the rest of the race would be fine, albeit slower than what I was used to, and the crowds of screaming onlookers buoyed my spirits.

The throngs of spectators that lined both sides of the road in town thinned out the further we got from transition, and with fewer well-wishers to offer encouragement, I could feel my energy beginning to wane, until two things happened. The first was that I noticed, off in the distance and to my right, the ski jump from the 1980 Winter Olympics, which brought mental images of finely-tuned athletes going through the air with the grace and courage of the victorious. Memories of ABC Sports coverage of Olympic glory with announcer Curt Gowdy flew around inside my head, distracting me from what I was presently going through.

The second was that there were a few volunteers handing out salt, which came in tubes resembling, in both shape and size, sticks of lip balm. They asked, firstly, if I wanted some. As a public school teacher, I am bound by contract to accept anything that is offered for free, so I grabbed a stick. Then, as she handed it to me, the volunteer asked if I knew how to use it, which caused me to pause briefly. On the one hand, I thought, "I'm not stupid. I have eaten things before. Pretty sure I can figure this out". Then I began to question that confidence. "Wait a minute. I've never tried this before. Maybe there's something to it". Finally, after wrestling it from her on the fly, I said, "Fuck it", flipped open the cap with my thumb, and downed the entire thing.

The human body is 70-75% water. Mine went from that level to 0% in two seconds. It turns out there is quite a bit of salt in those tubes, so much so that it is difficult to swallow it all. I hadn't realized that before I opened my throat to take it all in. What I also hadn't realized was that, by emptying it in one pull, I would be incapable of absorbing anything at all until the next aid station, which was a mile away. I tried to swallow some saliva, but I had none left and my esophagus felt as though it was welded shut. Sometime later in the race, I was passing another of these salt stations, and I overheard the volunteer ask an athlete if he knew how to use it. He said that he did not, and I instantly, and instinctively, thought way less of him. To me, it was like asking for directions when you are lost or reading the instructions on how to assemble a bed frame from IKEA. I also thought, "Are you an idiot? Dude, how hard can it be? Open your mouth and pour it in". In my defence, I was tired and cranky by this point. She explained that he needed to lick his finger and dab a few crystals with the wet bit and place the fingertip on his tongue. She added, "Obviously, you don't want to just swallow the entire tube in one shot. That would be silly".

Who was the idiot now?

Nevertheless, the salt helped, even if it was just because my attention shifted from feeling fatigue to trying not to die from rapid onset dehydration. Once I finally reached the next aid station and devoured all the liquid I could choke down, I felt fantastic. I reached the turn-around and headed back towards the ski jump at better than 70.3 pace. I was flying.

Then I wasn't. If you have ever bonked, or hit the wall, or met the man with the hammer, then you know that, in addition to being painful, awful, demoralizing, agonizing, it is also very mysterious. Hitting the wall in a long race is very similar to hitting a deer with your car. There is no warning until it is way too late. It's not like you see the deer a kilometre down the road, then play chicken with it to find out who will turn first, only to smash into it because it is as brave and stupid as you are. No, when you bonk, there is no deer in your path at all until suddenly there fucking is, and it smashes your windshield and ruins your day. One minute you are cruising along, feeling great, then, in a second, you are completely devoid of all energy and are reduced to a very slow and pathetic-looking shuffle. Sometimes, you even get to puke and shit yourself, not that you care at that point. There are no glaring warning signs, no equivalent to a 'check engine' light. It just happens, and it isn't glamorous in the least.

In Lake Placid, I was doing fine. I looked up and caught another glimpse of the ski jump way off in the distance, and felt the thrill of victory sensation. Two steps later, there wasn't a spare calorie left in my body for me to use, and when I lifted my head and saw the ski jump once again, the only images that came to me were of poor Vinko Bogataj, the Slovenian ski jumper who crashed horribly every weekend on ABC's Wide World of Sports, while the announcer delivered the tag line, 'The Agony of Defeat'.

My run was only about a third of the way done, and I was

totally cooked. I tried to soldier on, running (sort of) for about a minute, then walking for five until I would reach the next aid station where I would ingest at least one of everything they had on offer, after which I would run again for a couple of minutes before needing to walk.

Though I have bonked several times before, it had only been this bad one other time. The Hellgate 100 in Virginia was a race I'll never forget, mainly because there are large chunks of it that I can't remember at all. Much like the race in Lake Placid, I was probably doomed to fail it as well. As far as the Lake Placid race goes, I was, quite simply, exceedingly undertrained for the distance. A full Ironman is so much more than merely double the length of a half, and the training required is way greater than simply doing twice as much, and needs to be significantly smarter. Nutrition is also very different as I could probably finish an entire 70.3 race on a glass of water and one energy gel. I wouldn't do well, but I would surely finish without walking. A full ironman requires a well-thought-out, strategic, methodical schedule on how much and when to take on nutrition. Also, I had been injured during the time when it would have been wise to figure this stuff out. I really didn't think I would be able to race at all.

For Hellgate, I had just been stupid. It took place in early December, which is reason enough to make it daunting. The summer before, I had run the Devil's Backbone Ultramarathon and finished third overall. I was also the first person to cross the finish line that year from outside of Montana, where the race took place and the only top ten finisher from east of the Rockies. That race had only one aid station at the turnaround and was mostly above

9000 feet of elevation. Right on the race website, it says, in bold all caps, "THIS CANNOT BE YOUR FIRST 50 MILER". Seeing as how it *was* my first 50 miler, and that I finished third, to the obvious surprise of the race director, I felt that the Hellgate, which was in the Blue Mountains of Virginia, and, thus, not above 9000 feet, would be considerably easier, despite the greater length.

It wasn't. Not only was the course itself super gnarly, in an Appalachian Trail sort of way, but I didn't exactly set myself up for optimal performance by driving from Montreal to Roanoke right after a full day of work. The drive took a little over thirteen hours, and we left home around 5:00 PM and arrived at the hotel at 6:30 AM, which sounds fine, a little whacky, but fine, except for the fact that the race was to start first thing the next morning. By 'first thing', I mean 12:01 AM, which meant, in effect, I would start a 62-mile race without having slept in two days. Not smart. Also, during the day, while we waited around for the pre-race dinner and meeting, the area suffered an ice storm bad enough to affect support access for the race. The result was that, due to road closures in the Blue Mountains, support crews would only be able to help racers at half of the original locations.

This did not fill me with the utmost confidence, nor did my first encounter with the race director. At the pre-race dinner, I was lining up to get my spaghetti, and he sidled up beside me and overheard me ask if the sauce was vegetarian. He tapped my shoulder, resulting in me turning to face him. He took one look at my shoulder-length blonde, shaggy hair and asked, in a condescending, nasty tone, "Vegetarian? What's with the hair? You think you're Jesus?".

I had no idea how to reply, or even whether I should drop my cafeteria tray, like I had done hundreds of times with my gloves playing Junior hockey, pull his shirt over his head, and commence throwing punches at his ear, or just ignore him. I extended my hand for him to shake and said, "Hi. I'm Brock...from Montreal".

He looked me in the eyes and squinted, sizing me up as some kind of Canadian, Pinko, Atheist, commie, then looked down at my extended hand. He didn't shake it, and turned his attention to the food he was scooping on his plate, and muttered a totally disinterested, and purposely distracted, "Uh-huh".

As I walked away, totally intimidated, I muttered to myself, "Who the fuck was that prick?".

Turns out the prick's name is David Horton, and he's somewhat of a legend. He blew me off because he's seen thousands of runners, and he knows who will do well in his race and who won't. It took him all of ten seconds to somehow know that I wouldn't finish the race and, therefore, wasn't worth talking to.

Did I finish the race and prove him dead wrong? Nope. The fucker was right. After hallucinating for hours and sleeping (deeply) while running with no conscious memory of how I got as far as I did, I abandoned the race after 80 kilometres. I had shit myself, puked all over my neck and chest. I'd fallen more times than I could count. I got totally lost...twice, and ate bacon at an aid station absolutely convinced it was a Snickers bar. It was the first meat I had eaten in ten years. I was so deeply exhausted that I could not have cared less when the race officials told me that they could not recommend that I attempt to finish.

In Lake Placid, I was beginning to have similar feelings. Inside my head, I was a lone sufferer. I did not want to speak with anybody, not even the well-wishers at the aid stations whose calories were the only things keeping me from going into a coma. I know now that I must have appeared rude, but that was not my intention, as my boorish attitude was nothing more than a survival mechanism. I simply lacked the fuel to power the neurons in my brain to complete the complex matrix of synapses required to utter more than a simple word: "Thanks". Sometimes I would nod my head ever so slightly, or raise my hand in the universal gesture for 'thank-you', but these never happened together or in some proximate sequence. A choice had to be made because there was not adequate energy for all three or even a combination of two choices. Even the act of choosing was too taxing. Whatever response I gave came unconsciously from my autonomic nervous system.

Though I went through all this torture by myself, I was not alone. There were others out there suffering as much as I was, some even more. There were more than twenty-five kilometres remaining and some people were already doing their best Julie Moss impressions with some of them looking like they belonged in a Michael Jackson music video from the 1980s. Many of these athletes were not going to finish, I knew that, but it brought me no comfort. Others would catch a second wind when they cracked open whatever secret nutrition they had waiting for them in their 'special needs' bags. I had no such bag. When I read about them in the Athletes Race Guide, I deemed them unnecessary and not worth the effort. Of course, that was a decision I made on Saturday when I was full of pizza. In fact, I was so high on empty calories that I considered anyone who was preparing a special needs bag to be both weak and stupid and had probably been the type of athlete to take notes at the not at all mandatory Mandatory Athlete's Briefing.

Now, with the grace of a bulldog eating a jar of mayonnaise, I could barely manage a shuffle, looking like Tim Conway in a Carol Burnett Show episode. I actively wished for an act of God that would distinguish my earthly existence, and I thought to myself, "Who's the loser now?". I willfully coveted a special needs bag. If there had been a dude in a Santa suit out on the course, I would have sat on his knee and begged him for one. I wanted one so bad that I even contemplated stealing one from another racer, and had I possessed the energy, I would have fought someone for theirs. Then again, if I possessed the energy, I wouldn't need one in the first place. The worst part of seeing the bags was knowing I still had a full lap to run. There wasn't a molecule in my body that believed I would be capable of making it all the way.

Then I saw Anne and Owen again, looking so happy for me. I should have been pleased to see them, and, in a way, I was. It's just that seeing them cheer me on made me feel like I had to at least try to finish. There was no way I could just walk off the course and lay down, not now anyway. "Fuck", was the only word my glucose deficient brain could process and bring to my lips. "Fuck". There wasn't even enough energy to warrant the use of an exclamation point.

Somehow, again, I managed to pick up the pace to what felt like a sub-two-hour marathon pace, but which probably resembled an ageing caveman. So long as there were well-wishers lining the street, I was somehow capable of a 'run', but as soon as I ran out of people, I ran out of grace and talent.

The rest of the race was an ugly, pathetic attempt at athleticism whereby I could only manage a five to one walk to run ratio. When I eventually crossed the finish line, a completely defeated and de-flated man, I vowed never, ever to attempt another full Ironman again. The only way I would ever get to Kona was as a spectator or a volunteer. And I was serious too. I had only made such an ominous, 'NEVER AGAIN' statement once before, and that was referring to tequila after a rough night and even rougher 'morning after' I will never forget. No, I was done with dreaming of one day running down Ali i Drive listening to Mike Reilly telling me I am an Ironman. It's too bad because that had been a dream I had thought about every single day since before I did my first triathlon, but it was definitely gone.

Nope. I said "never again", and never again was what I meant. Just to demonstrate how serious I was, when we got back to the hotel, before going to the room, I went to the bar next to the lobby and ordered a Tequila Sunrise and downed it in two gulps. It was delicious.

THIRTEEN CHEESEBURGERS

The education system in Quebec is quite different from any other place in North America. Other than the fact that the majority of available public instruction is offered largely in French, the major difference is in the post-secondary school structure. Elementary school begins in kindergarten and wraps up after the successful completion of grade six. After that, students make their way to secondary school (high school), which goes from secondary one (grade seven) to secondary five (grade 11). Before continuing on to university, students must complete a two-year program of study at junior colleges which closely resemble a typical university in that attendance is not strictly mandatory, and work is left up to the students to get done. The only courses whereby attendance *is* mandatory, are those in Physical Education.

Students must obtain credits by completing a number of Phys. ed. classes over their two-year programme, and there is a great variety from which to choose. You can take courses in a major sport or physical activity, from basketball to Pilates, or broomball to yoga. There are even offerings in activities such as 'Walking for Fitness I and II'. The idea is to get people moving and to develop a lifelong interest in a healthy, active lifestyle. The courses, themselves, fall into two general categories: those that last fifteen sessions of about an hour and a half each, or 'intensive' courses. The intensives are held, usually, over a three day period during the weekend, and involve travelling off campus to some predetermined, remote location. Generally, these courses involve pursuits that take place outdoors, usually in natural, rugged environments.

One of my college roommates, Kennie, who was not the strongest student, academically speaking, had decided, with the aid of his advisor, that the intensive courses would best fit his needs. They would free up larger blocks of time during the week for him to place added focus on the academic courses he tended to have trouble with, which is to say, *all* academic courses.

Schoolwork had never interested Kennie in the least and, as a result, he never performed well in an academic setting. I suppose today he would have been diagnosed with A.D.D. and would have had the benefit of an array of aid and personalized education plans designed to draw out his individual proclivities. Back then he was just considered 'special' and was largely left to struggle alone. If, however, Kennie found an interest in something (usually in athletics), he flourished. The phrase, "He's a natural", has been used to describe his performance in a kayak, on a football field, in cross-country running, on a skateboard, playing the guitar, and flattening beer caps with his teeth. So long as he believed it was in his best interest to be good at something, he decided he would be, and it was so. When he put his energy into it, there was little he could not do. There were only two problems with this: first, he had to actually put his mind to something, which turned out, most of the time, to be quite difficult, as he was easily distracted. Second, you could not get him to put his mind to something for him, no matter how good you knew he would be at it, or how much you knew he would enjoy it.

Of all the things he excelled at, none was more impressive to watch than his unique ability to create magic on a pair of downhill skis. There wasn't a trick or maneuver he could not perform with absolute grace. Different and changing snow conditions were handled without any noticeable twitch or perceived difficulty. So, when Kennie told me he had chosen 'Steep Angle Skiing' as his Phys. ed. option for the first half of the winter semester, I was happy for him and bummed that I had already taken the course and wouldn't be there to see him make the most challenging and dangerous slopes on Mount Washington look like a bunny hill.

Having already taken the course, I knew what was required of the students, from organization and packing to being able to hike for hours in extremely cold conditions and sleeping outdoors.

The first obstacle was, of course, qualifying for the trip, which is to say that each prospective skier had to demonstrate an expert level of alpine skiing proficiency. The proving ground for this endeavour was a tiny hill in the Eastern Townships of Quebec called Mont Joye, that was hardly a challenging track, to say the least, but was conveniently located close to campus. Once at the hill, each student was supposed to demonstrate a wide variety of skills on various types of slopes, before finally proving himself or herself on the Diablo, the triple black diamond run. All this took a couple of hours, and there were no exceptions. Mount Washington was too extreme a place to be without adequate skills. 'Absolutely No Exceptions' was a phrase that Kennie never fully comprehended, and he only showed up near the end of the evening at the top of the big run. Having not seen Kennie perform any of the preliminary tests, the instructor informed him not to bother because he had failed to meet any of the require...

WHOOOOOOSSSSHHHHH! Kennie took off before the teacher could finish his sentence, and was at the bottom of the run in under thirty seconds. From his vantage point at the top of the hill, where he could see the entire route, the teacher watched in open-mouthed amazement as Kennie utterly shredded and flattened the terrain, which had been a very challenging obstacle for many of the other skiers in the class. He had made the Diablo look so easy. Not even stopping at the base of the run, he headed straight for the parking lot, unclipped from his bindings, and leaned his skis against the bus, where he waited for the rest of the class.

Had you not seen him perform that night, you would, most likely, not have taken him for an actual skier because he did not dress for the occasion in typical fashion. He wore a pair of jeans and his brother's Greenfield Park Packers football jacket over a Judas Priest concert T-shirt. No goggles, no toque, no gloves. None of the evening's events were that big a deal to him, either. He had been in a hurry, the mountain, if you could call it that, was not that high, and he knew he was only going to be doing one run anyway. He didn't even have a lift ticket. It was a "let's get this fucker over with" type of deal, and therefore, there was no need to get fancy. Kennie wanted to take the course, and he really wanted to see how he could fare on what everyone said was the most challenging terrain in the East, but not so much that he couldn't just take it or leave it. Nothing about it was going to make him lose any sleep. He wasn't nervous at all and existed in a state of permanent relaxation. His entire demeanour could be summed up with a single word: 'Whatever'.

Did he meet the official requirements to take the course? Absolutely not. *Did he qualify?* Of course, he did. Was he excited about that? Not really. Whatever.

The next portion of the course was a mandatory two-hour session held at 8:30 Monday morning, the same week as the Friday departure. At this session, the students watch a slideshow of photos from the previous years to get them both excited about, and somewhat familiar with, the type of terrain they would see on the trip. This would also be the only opportunity to find out what they needed to bring in terms of food, clothing, and equipment. Needless to say, this was a very important seminar and, true to character, Kennie damn near missed it.

I'd like to say that the meeting was far too important for even him to neglect and that he had set two alarms to ensure he would be awake for it, however, that was not the case. He had, in fact, forgotten about it entirely. The reason he had managed not to miss it, was that he thought he had an English class during that block, which he intended to skip, as he did almost every Tuesday morning. Only it was Monday, so when he showed up at the sports complex to avoid class by going for a swim, he ran into several classmates who would be accompanying him on the ski trip, and they ushered him into the conference room where he took a nap for an hour and a half. He completely missed the slideshow, and left the information packet on the table, covered in drool.

When he returned to our apartment after the session, I asked him what he thought of Tuckerman's Ravine.

"What's Tuckerman's Ravine", he asked, puzzled.

"Tuckerman's Ravine. New Hampshire. East face of Mount Washington. Avalanche danger. A hundred and thirty or so people have died there. Winds up to 150 miles per hour. Very steep", I said, getting more pissed off with every word. "Are you telling me none of this rings any bells for fucksake? Don't tell me you missed the fucking meeting". I was dumbstruck.

"You mean we're going to Vermont", he said, beginning to show a little enthusiasm. "I thought we were going further than that. Someone said it was a three-hour bus ride".

I wanted to punch him in the face. His statement pissed me off so much, and I'm not sure whether it was due to his lack of geographical awareness of the world within a three-hour radius of our campus, or his 'ho-hum' attitude towards the trip, but I couldn't handle it. To maintain my sanity, I simply let it go, handed him the plate of french fries I was no longer hungry for, and told him that someday his carelessness was going to get him killed.

The rest of that week proceeded in normal fashion, by and large, with the exception that I was consumed with envy. I was jealous of Kennie because the upcoming weekend should be one that he would never forget. Thoughts of my own trip to Tuckerman's flooded my memory, making concentrating on my schoolwork difficult. I remembered all the challenges and sheer enjoyment the trip had brought me. Even reminiscing about my packing lists was thrilling, as well as how cool I remembered I looked with my loaded backpack, with skis attached to the sides. I could still feel the adventure. The course is mainly about skiing very steep pitches, but it involved so much more than that. The learning started long before my first descent. In fact, it began even before we stepped on the bus.

Each student was expected to be entirely self-sufficient and self-reliant. We were to bring with each of us the food we would require for two nights outside, along with the proper clothing, as temperatures could go way below zero. We would have to hike for about three hours to get from the bus to the Hermit Lake shelters, which offered protection from the elements. Packing wisely was essential. You needed to make sure you would have everything you would require, but not much more because whatever you brought, you would have to carry yourself. I had agonized over my list for hours.

Self-sufficient though we were expected to be, the college was willing to lend out pieces of equipment that you may not own, such as stoves, sleeping bags rated for the winter, spare poles, and even cooking supplies. They weren't going to provide any food, and you had to have your own skis, boots, and clothing, but if you needed to borrow something, all you had to do was to fill out a request form and give them two days notice. We were to bring our own food, but if we needed last-minute items, or fresh items such as fruit, veggies, or meat products, the bus would make a last-minute pit stop at a grocery store across the border in the United States.

My pack had included an 'extra' of just about everything and was neatly and smartly packed with stuff I would need early and often near the top. I was proud of how well-prepared I was for the trip, having done my research, and was very eager, though nervous, for the departure day.

It was with this same sense of nervous anticipation that I began the week of Kennie's trip, although as the week progressed, it began to morph into worry and bemusement. I hadn't seen him making and remaking any lists as I had done. There were no organized piles of supplies spread throughout the entire floor space of the apartment, as had been the case for me. There was no "DON'T FUCKING TOUCH!" labels stuck to any of the food items in the fridge or pantry, and no attempt had been made, as far as I could see, to tune up and sharpen his skis. The apartment was devoid of any of the excitement that had flooded it the week before my trip. None of his roommates felt the need to tell him to shut up about the stupid ski trip, as they had felt necessary to tell me. There was so little preparation going on that I actually asked Kennie, on more than one occasion, if he had dropped the course altogether, which, of course, he hadn't. That would have required going to the Registrar's Office and actually filling out a form.

Thursday afternoon, the day before his scheduled 6:00 AM departure, I could handle it no more, and confronted Kennie, demanding to see what he had packed, grabbing him by the arm intending to have him follow me to his room. He yanked his arm free, and simply said, "My stuff's by the front door".

Feeling a little sheepish, and like an overbearing parent, I muttered an apologetic, "Oh", and walked to the entrance to see what he had packed.

His 'stuff' was there all right. Everything he felt he would need for two three hour hikes, two six-hour ski days, bone-chilling weather in a place with more weather-related deaths than Mount Everest, five or six meals, and two nights in a frozen lean-to.

By the door, I found two skis (not fastened together for easy transport, nor to a pack), two poles, two ski boots, a large pillow (which he informed me, tapping an index finger to his temple indicating his wiley, forward-thinking, was for the bus ride), and his football jacket, which was slung over the tip of his left ski. And that's it.

Though I had known him my whole life and, thus, had seen him do some seriously stupid shit, I was still mesmerized by how stunningly ill-prepared he was.

"Where's the rest of it?", I begged. "You've got no food here".

"I'm gonna be wearing the rest", he replied, looking at me like I was stupid, "and the dude said we're gonna stop for food on the way".

I do not know for sure what an aneurysm feels like, but after hearing that statement, I thought I had a pretty good idea because my eyebrow began to twitch in searing pain.

"You're going to starve to death", I said, "that's if you haven't already died from exposure. You're never gonna make it", I continued, growing angrier by the second. "Not even you can survive what's in store for you this weekend".

I wasn't sure what was upsetting me more: the fact that Kennie was preparing to die on the mountain, OR because his behaviour was making me sound just like my father. Kennie just shrugged his shoulders and asked, "Whatever. Can I borrow your gloves?".

My desire to punch him squarely in the face was overshadowed by the sense that I needed to save his life first. I turned and headed back to my room to gather some things that might mitigate his demise. When I returned to the living room to hand him my backpack containing bib snow pants, gloves with a windproof mitten over shell, toque, goggles, sleeping bag, and a pair of woolly socks, Kennie was asleep on the floor with crumbs from my last Pop-Tart on his chest and chin. The TV volume was on full blast and was playing a 'Cheers' rerun. I launched the pack into the air, sending it on a trajectory that would, hopefully, intersect with his forehead, and, as it did, he woke up and said, "Norm!". I felt like pissing on his jeans right there, and scolded him, pointing my finger in his face, "I hope you fucking freeze to death".

When I awoke the next morning at around seven, the first thing I did was walk over to Kennie's room, fully expecting to find him sleeping like a dead man, but he was gone. Scotty, one of our roommates, came in and told me he had already seen Kennie head out. "I woke him up an hour ago. He's gone on his ski trip".

So there it was. Kennie *had* managed to accomplish more than I had expected he was capable of and actually made it out the door, on time, no less. This was about a centimetre shy of a miracle. Perhaps, I thought solemnly to myself, he would survive the weekend after all.

Well, he *did*, in fact, survive, but barely. He did not freeze to death, as I thought he might, and he managed the slopes, I was told, like no one before ever had. He hadn't wiped out or broken his neck, or any other bones, for that matter. In fact, nothing about the potentially severe elements of Tuckerman's Ravine had threatened his well-being in the slightest. He had made it home in one piece and, seemingly, no worse for the wear.

On Tuesday, two days after his return from New Hampshire, we were forced to put him in a taxicab with directions for the driver to take him to the nearest hospital. It appears that Kennie had contracted a bent over in seething pain, bloated stomach, yellow-eyed, pissing from the ass, dizzy variety of food poisoning.

He hadn't packed any food before leaving on the trip, not a sandwich, apple, oreo...not even a single gummy bear, so it was not from any questionable food item he had squeezed into his pockets from home. The bus had made its customary stop to pick up last-minute food items one may have needed to round out a well-planned menu, or in Kennie's case, to create one from scratch. But, it is unlikely that he would have purchased anything there that would go bad and put him in the hospital because he was far too lazy to cook anything. Pop-Tarts might taste better when actually toasted, but that's an unnecessary extra step he was never willing to make. Those of us who hadn't been on the trip that weekend were confused as to what might have made him so sick, so we began to survey people who had been with him and who might know just what he had ingested.

"Did any of you guys see what Kennie bought at the grocery store that might have made him sick", we asked. "Like, did he buy some sketchy-looking ribs or something and eat them raw?".

"Kennie didn't go to the grocery store", someone replied.

What the hell were these people talking about? Unless he drank his own piss, which would have not been a surprise at all, how could he get food poisoning from eating nothing?

"What do you mean he didn't go to the grocery store?", I demanded. "Did he not eat all weekend?".

"No no", they said, "the dopey bastard went to McDonald's instead".

They said 'instead', and not 'as well'. When I had gone on the trip, many of us went to McDonald's to get a cup of coffee or maybe some breakfast. Having known Kennie as long as I had, I wasn't shocked to find out that he had decided to buy all the food he would need for the weekend at Micky Fucking Dee's.

As it happened, he had purchased thirteen cheeseburgers and one hot chocolate for the entire trip. That is pretty stupid, but nothing compared to how he chose to make this veritable buffet of epicurean delight last for the duration of the trip.

Upon reboarding the bus, take-out order in hand, he sat down and consumed ten of the thirteen cheeseburgers, washed down with the hot chocolate, before the driver put the vehicle in gear, and placed the remaining three in his inside breast pocket where they stayed for the rest of the trip. He had not eaten again until around 4:30 on Sunday afternoon, because he wanted to save the remaining burgers for the bus ride home. He had kept them next to his warm body for the duration of the trip because he feared a wild animal would steal them from the campsite, and because they were already cooked. Everyone knows that cooked food isn't as tasty when it gets cold. By the time he actually placed the bacteria-infested sandwiches in his mouth, the two silver dollar sized pickles were not the greenest part of the burgers.

I guess I was wrong when I said he'd get himself killed on the ski trip, but I was close.

\\ • //

After my Lake Placid debacle, I needed to find a redemption race, something that could make me feel as though I was at least a marginally capable age grouper. I found what I was looking for in the Challenge Maine half ironman in Old Orchard Beach. The course was outstanding with an ocean swim from a giant beach start. The bike took us through rolling farmland that had a 'lobster shack on every corner' feel to it, and the run was almost entirely off-road. It was an out and back, which stayed largely on a nice, wide pebble-covered path. It was exactly what I needed. It felt so short compared to the Lake Placid race, and my results reflected just how comfortable I was there, finishing second in my age group in a time of 4:24. As far as I was concerned, I was back and feeling quite confident...maybe too confident.

Due to the fact that I had been forced to take off so much time from running in the Spring, I decided not to take any days off after Maine, to make up for it. There was an off-season from racing, but not from preparing to race. The strange thing is that, though I didn't feel that I deserved any time off, I did not want to push anything either. My training was relentless in terms of the number of workouts, but none of them were hard. As soon as I started to push it a little, I would always back off, and all I could think about was how awful it had been to be unable to run. I never wanted to go through that again, so I never went particularly hard. You could say I was training not to lose instead of training to win.

From September to January, I ran every single day, just not hard and not far. The weather would judge where I would go and for how long. All of my cycling during that period was done indoors, with most sessions lasting about an hour, and I would swim twice a week, doing 2000 metres straight each time. Unlike in previous years whereby I would have the goal of qualifying for, and attending, the World Ironman 70.3 Championships, this year was all about not getting injured. The 2016 World Champs were going to be in Australia, anyway, and it didn't matter how much I trained, I assumed that a trip to the Sunshine Coast would be fabulously above my teacher's pay grade.

In January, while invigilating a math exam, I decided, just for kicks, to investigate how ridiculously expensive a flight to Australia would be, expecting Travelocity to confirm my prediction.

They didn't. The prices were almost affordable, so I checked what it would cost to fly AND stay in Mooloolaba, where the race was to be held. Again, it appeared to be just about doable. The students writing their tests could have been cheating like Vegas card counters for all I knew, as my attention was nowhere near the classroom. I was now completely focused on trying to figure out how to qualify.

My life had serious focus once again, but a small part of me was a little concerned because I would now have to allow myself to go hard in training, and that worried me. The last thing I wanted was to get injured and relive the previous Spring, which made me very tentative when training because now the stakes were higher.

Not only did I not want to miss out on any races, but I NEEDED to be healthy for the first race of the summer so that I could punch my ticket to Australia.

That first race of the season was in Syracuse again. Redemption. Qualification. Pressure. I felt it all, and my performance on the bike suffered a bit as a result. Luckily, my age group third place was enough to snag a slot for the big race. The moment I arrived back at my hotel room in Syracuse, which was thankfully devoid of boogers and prostitutes, I booked my entire Australia trip, almost maxing out my credit card, but feeling wholly satisfied. With my head in the clouds and an entire summer to look forward to, I decided to try to qualify for the following year's World Championships as well. That way I could have a little peace of mind throughout the winter and concentrate on being healthy and getting faster. Again from my Syracuse hotel room, I went on the Ironman website, found a race, and registered for the Ironman 70.3 Timberman in New Hampshire. Now, with my credit card fully maxed out, I could concentrate on preparing for two very important races. I felt awesome. Skint, but awesome.

The rest of the summer went well. I finished first in my age group in a Rev3 event in Williamsburg, Virginia, and first at Timberman, which successfully qualified me for the 2017 Ironman 70.3 World Championships in Chattanooga, Tennessee. Though I placed well in both races, I was a little upset with how long it had taken me to complete them, both being about ten minutes slower than I had expected, but I did win, so I guess everyone else sucked as well.

I had never before been so excited for a race as I was with

Australia. Even Vegas paled by comparison, though the feelings were similar in that the excitement was less about the race and more about the trip itself.

When the day came to begin travelling to Mooloolaba, the 2016 Summer Olympic Games were still fresh in the minds of the sporting public. Yann, my massage therapist, had been lucky enough to work with the Canadian Women's Swim Team in Rio, and he brought me back an official Team Canada podium shirt, which I decided to wear for my flights. The shirt, combined with the fact that I had my aero helmet attached to my carry-on nap-sack, turned me into an instant, though entirely anonymous, celebrity. Several strangers stared at me and I could tell some were trying to work up the courage to come talk to me. One couple eventually asked if I was on my way to a competition.

"I'm headed to Australia for the Ironman 70.3 World Championships", I replied nonchalantly as though it was just another event in my busy professional schedule. Judging by the reaction I received, you would have thought I told them I was Usain Bolt on my way to a huge track and field competition. They peppered me with questions and others joined in, not allowing me to just sit in peace. Maybe, I thought, the shirt was a bad choice after all. I had been a celebrity for about a half-hour, and it had already become tedious. After signing two autographs that were going to make their recipients very upset once they Googled me and found nothing more than a copy of my Master's thesis and a 'Rate My Teacher' entry from 2003, I made a mental note to change my shirt on the flight to San Francisco.

The San Francisco flight was a manageable length, at around

five hours, but it was just long and 'domestic' enough to leave me starving upon arrival at SFO. After finding the proper gate for my next flight, to Sydney, I needed to hunt down something to eat. In no time, I found a Starbucks and anchored myself into the twenty-minute queue, leaving me a window of ten minutes before boarding would begin. Halfway through the wait, I developed an intense urge to urinate, which turned the last ten minutes into a bit of a pee-pee dance/shuffle.

Just as I reached the front of the line and prepared to give my order, I heard my name being called. The voice over the public announcement system told me to check into the gate immediately. I am sure that the teenager working the cash was not expecting "Son of a bitch!", as the response to her, "Can I take your order?", but that's what she got, followed by a hasty apology as I took off down the stairs to see what was so damned urgent. When I arrived at the gate, the ticket agent asked to see my visa to enter Australia.

"Pardon me", I asked, "my what?".

Apparently, Canadians require a visa when travelling to the land down under. I did not have one, and given my severe desire to pee not two minutes ago, I was surprised that I almost shit myself.

"No problem, Sir", the agent calmly announced, "you can purchase it here. It is one hundred Australian dollars". Phew.

The next flight, from SanFran to Sydney, was long. Really, really long. Like driving from Montreal to Phoenix nonstop kind of long. It was so long, in fact, that I watched Seinfeld. All of it. It was a delightful distraction, but I was left wondering what to do with the remaining nine hours. Did I mention it was long?

There were two strange things about that flight. First, considering it took more than seventeen hours, I didn't sleep for one minute. Normally, even for a flight from Montreal to Toronto lasting an hour, I am dead to the world before the plane extricates itself from the jet bridge. I have had flight attendants scold me for sleeping through their 'safety' briefing, which is ridiculous anyway because if we go down, the seat cushion will be using me as a floatation device, not the other way around.

The second thing was that the flight was full and the only words I uttered the entire time were "Yes, please", when asked if I wanted wine with my meal. I sat five centimetres from the woman next to me for seventeen hours, and we never exchanged hellos, which suited me fine. I hate small talk, and because she never addressed me, I did not have to pretend to care about the minutiae of her life. At the same time, however, being a guy, and thus possessing the inborn proclivity to be at least slightly narcissistic, it pissed me off just a tad that I did not appear charming enough for her, at the very least, to exchange pleasantries. I wasn't expecting her to ask me to join the Mile High Club with her, but she could have said "Hello". I mean it's one word, not the Gettysburg Address.

I don't normally stress out too much at airports because it is a personal policy of mine to be ridiculously early for flights and, when booking, I always make sure that layovers are a minimum of two hours in length to allow time and space for unexpected delays and disturbances. Unfortunately, there wasn't much choice at my price point for this trip. My layover in Sydney was a mere ninety minutes, and I knew I would have to clear customs as well as change terminals for my flight to Brisbane. Ninety minutes was going to be tight, so as soon as I deplaned, I did my best O.J.

Simpson impression (Hertz rental car advertisement, not alleged wife stabber) and sprinted through the terminal. It worked, too, because I made it to the security check-point queue before everyone else, and, as it happens, I needed the extra time I had been able to bank.

I made it through just fine, despite not having to take off my belt, but the security agent was taking issue with my bag. When he realized that the bag was mine, he gruffly grabbed me by the arm and dragged me to a secondary screening area where he questioned me about its contents. After describing everything I could remember was in there, he informed me that the x-ray machine, which he told me 'never lies', picked up an image that led him and his team to believe that the bag contained explosives and we would have to wait for an expert.

Thankfully, the expert was directly on hand and the matter was cleared up almost immediately. I still have absolutely no clue what items appeared to be particularly incendiary in the bag. All I had in there was a laptop, a book, and an extra t-shirt. Oh, and a bundle of candles and a wad of Silly Putty with a string attached to an egg timer. Some people are so sensitive.

By the time I reached the condo I had rented, it was 4:00 PM local time, and two calendar days after I left home. My plan was to get a pizza, unpack, and check out the beach and surroundings. One out of three would have to do, because I picked up a pizza and opened the door to the unit where, once inside, I fell onto the sofa and went to sleep for a quick nap.

I awoke at 4:00 AM the following morning, ravenous. I ate an entire medium pizza, drank two litres of Pepsi, and got myself ready for a run up the coast. It turns out you need more than ten minutes to properly digest that kind of volume. The run was the worst I had been on in years, but the scenery was pretty, and it was cool to see kids going for a quick surfing session before school.

After my 'run', I headed off to the bike shop to pick up the Giant Trinity I had rented for the race, half expecting it to be a child's beach cruiser with a basket and a bell. It turned out to be an excellent, race-ready piece of engineering, far superior to the bike I raced on back home. They even fitted me perfectly to it, and it had an integrated hydration system, which my bike back home certainly did not. The bike was so nice, in fact, that I decided not to ride it until race day. I guess all the travel, lack of sleep, and completely different time zone altered my judgement to the point where it resembled that of a kindergartener. You know, the 'special' one who sits alone in the corner, eating paste.

The two days that remained before the race were a total fog that no amount of food, wine, or attempted sleep, could clear up. I went for two runs, walked on the beach, and watched a ton of Australian television, which, by the way, is vastly superior to what we get from the U.S. back home. Ideally, I would have had two weeks, at least, before the race to acclimate and train on the course. Unfortunately, the event took place, as it always seems to do, just as school is getting started back home, and it is frowned upon for teachers to take time off right after the summer break (in fact we need special permission). I had exactly one week, that's seven days, to get to Australia, race, see whatever I could, and fly home. I recommend more than that, if you've got it, that is.

By the time race morning rolled around, the fog in my head

had cleared, and I felt ready, though, after having read Bill Bryson's book about Australia, I was pretty sure I would be eaten by a shark just moments after having been killed by a box jellyfish. The way I saw it, there was less than a fifty percent chance that I would even survive long enough to make it to T1 where there was sure to be a den of poisonous snakes waiting for me under my bike.

During the swim, when I wasn't darting my eyes in every direction on the lookout for blue-ringed octopuses and stonefish, I was thinking about hopping onto my rental bike. I had never before been given the opportunity to ride a truly top-end piece of machinery, and I was anxious to experience just how much faster it was than what I was used to. As it turns out, it was quite fast. As a matter of fact, it was so fast that about 300 metres after leaving transition, the entire integrated hydration apparatus just fell off and was immediately run over by forty or fifty pissed off athletes who were trying to get ahead of me.

"Well, it looks like I just bought a hydration system", I announced to the guy yelling at me for littering the road, "Wonder what that's gonna cost me".

And cost me it did. Almost instantly, I became very thirsty, but I had to wait for an aid station. I 'drank' three vanilla gels instead.

Putting the hydration problem out of my head, I tried to concentrate on going as fast as I could. Along the highway, I was booking it, going faster than I had ever gone on a flat stretch of road.

At one point, we left the motorway and headed out into the country-side where we encountered some very steep hills. Normally I enjoy hills, both the part that goes up as well as the going down bits, but in this race, I had trouble with both, on the first hill of the day.

On the way up, I dropped my chain three times. On the third time, it became completely jammed, which cost me twelve minutes, most of which was spent with me standing doing nothing other than shouting, "fucking stupid piece of shit", over and over again. Of course, this did not do anything to get my chain unstuck, but it sure made me feel better.

Chain issue resolved, I roared down the other side, trying to gain back as much time as possible, adopting a full Chris Froome danger tuck, which seemed to work, judging by the blurriness of the scenery to my left and right. The only problem was that at the bottom of the hill, there was a sweeping right-hand turn that I would probably not be capable of negotiating safely at full speed, so I grabbed a handful of rear brake to scrub off a fair amount of it. I must admit that I pulled a little hard on the brake lever, but I'd done that many times before, and it usually results in a pretty fun rear-wheel skid, Tokyo Drift style. Unfortunately, that didn't happen this time.

Here's a bit of free advice: if you are from North America and you rent a bike in Australia, take it for an easy spin before participating in an important race, such as the Ironman 70.3 World Championships, just to learn its various idiosyncrasies. You see, they drive on the left-hand side of the road over there and, apparently, that means they put the rear brake lever on the left side of the handlebars as well. This, of course, means that the right-side brake lever controls (you guessed it) the front wheel brake, which, when jammed hard, sends the rider perilously into the air. When

I grabbed the right brake, the front wheel stopped spinning instantly, and because I had been going very fast, the laws of physics took a huge shit on me. I found out that a body in motion wants to stay that way, even when the vehicle it is attached to, comes to an abrupt halt. Luckily we were riding through the countryside by then, so when I flew over the cockpit, I cleared the road, the gravel shoulder, and the fence demarcating the edge of a farm field. I landed rather softly, after a few tumbles, in a cushy patch of tall, green grass, and several "fucking stupid piece of shits" later, I was back on the bike and fighting to regain position.

When I finally made it to the run portion of the race, I decided that I would need to push it to make up the time I had lost on the bike. My pace was so high that I was unable to hold in all the gas that had been building inside my gut since breakfast, and I was farting like an old lady at a Bingo hall after polishing off a giant bowl of boiled onions. The Australian guy behind me was being tortured but didn't quite have the pace to pass. He did manage to say, "Never trust a fart on a long run, Mate", which made me believe a poop stop was imminent. The cramps started and I began looking for escape routes to hidden alleyways, corners, hedgerows, anywhere, frankly, that I could hide for a moment to pop a squat and have a dump. The farting continued and the release of gas seemed to keep the cramping at bay long enough to get me to the finish line with no more than a Hershey squirt on my chamois.

I ended up finishing 29th in my age group, which isn't that bad, but I was ten minutes away from being in the top ten. Stupid fucking piece of shit chain.

Though the flights home took about the same amount of time

as the ones to Australia, I was totally spent by the time we landed in Montreal. The strange sensation of spending fifteen hours on a flight only to land at the same time we took off, gave me a 'free' day, but the fatigue I felt was deeper than any I had ever experienced before, and it lasted for weeks. Every day I woke up and tried to run or bike, only to stop after five minutes, completely exhausted and unable to continue. For the first time ever, I was going to be forced to take time off without being injured.

Worse than the physical funk my body felt, was the mental and emotional depression it caused. I am not the most chipper person at the best of times, but take exercise away from me, and I tend to get more than a little prickly. Each day that passed, I fell a little deeper and deeper into a depressive gloom that became more and more difficult to escape. Nothing worked. I tried to get back to my regular 'off-season' training regimen, but it didn't make things any better. I would get up at 3:00 AM, just like I had always done, put my running gear on, and head out the door to complete a little warmup before the real running would start. No matter how badly I wanted to be able to go longer, that ten-minute warmup was all I could muster.

After weeks and weeks, I eventually lost the deep fatigue, but I no longer seemed to possess the mental fortitude to get my body to work, and my fitness was hemorrhaging from me like blood from a wounded soldier. I still loved the idea of triathlon, but it just wasn't happening. Something needed to transpire to get me going.

Then, one Saturday morning, my son asked me, "Daddy, have you ever been to California? I'd love to go there. It looks really fun".

Boom! That was it. I was going to plan a trip to California for the following summer, but I needed some sort of legitimate excuse to get us there, so I researched to see if perhaps there was an Ironman event I could try. I seemed to recall having seen something called Vineman on the Ironman website before, so I typed that into google and, lo and behold, there was a race at the perfect time. Ironman Santa Rosa. Another full Ironman...Yay. Though I had vowed never to do a full-distance race again, it gave me something to work towards. I now had a purpose, and, initially, I didn't worry too much about what I was training for, all that mattered was that I was moving again, finally. I was able to get up and run in the morning, spin at some point during the school day, and toss in a couple of swims every week. As mundane as that routine was, I was able to keep it up until around March, when I knew I would have to start ramping up the volume significantly.

Sometimes when there is so much that needs to get done, you have trouble figuring out where to begin. Often this problem results in just blowing it all off, or simply doing the easiest stuff, just so you can at least say that *something* is being accomplished. That's how overwhelmingly daunting the task of Ironman training seemed to me at the time, as so much needed to be done that I could only focus on small bits at a time. It was as though I was tasked with building an entire house from the ground up, and I decided to spend most of my time choosing curtains in my favourite colour instead of pouring the concrete for a foundation and getting the major structure actually built.

In the end, I decided to train as I always had, and to hope for the best. At least, I figured, I would be better prepared than Lake

Placid because this time I could go running in the months leading up to the race. There was no way it could be as tough as the last time.

When I went to the Ironman website and clicked on the Santa Rosa race, the pictures were beautiful and the course description was so tantalizing, making everything seem right, so I pulled out my credit card and began the process of officially registering. There are so many steps allowing the prospective triathlete the opportunity for second, third, even fourth reflection. They gave me every chance to come to my senses and say, "Fuck this, what was I thinking?", before the final click of the mouse. I looked at each step carefully, and as I hovered the cursor over the CONFIRM icon, wondering whether or not I was sure about this decision, I was reminded of an event that happened years ago when I was living in Vancouver.

I was driving home one night after my four to midnight shift as a janitor at the Coquitlam Centre shopping mall, and I was tired, hungry, and in desperate need of a little television time before going to bed. I was piloting my Chevy Cavalier station wagon down Como Lake Boulevard when I got behind some dude in a Jeep CJ. It wasn't just any Jeep CJ either, this one was jacked up so high, it required a step and a special handle just to get into the damned thing. The owner, I was certain, was definitely compensating for something...something small.

Como Lake has a traffic light at every one of its many, many intersections, and if you are unlucky enough to hit a red light on the first one, unless you intend to break the land speed record for a station wagon, you will most likely be stuck at every red light for the rest of your journey. On the other hand, make the first light, and you can ride a green wave all the way home.

As I neared the first set of lights, it appeared as though I might make it on the green, but it was going to be close. I got to within metres of the intersection when the light turned yellow. Being from the province of Quebec, I instinctively understood that yellow means it is time to stomp on the gas with both feet and squeal through, sort of trying to avoid pedestrians, and I prepared my right foot to press down hard on the gas pedal. Unfortunately, Jeep CJ guy, not being from La Belle Province, did not possess the same mental wiring as I did, and hit the brakes, causing me to lock my seat belt and let out a rather aggressive, "FUCK!".

Gathering my dwindling composure, I settled in and began to construct a plan to get around CJ Guy, and waited for the light to turn green again. When it did, I stepped on the gas but had to stop short, because CJ needed to light his cigar and didn't notice the change in colour as quickly as I had. He was, quite obviously, not in the hurry I was. Bastard. Due to the added delay, we were now destined to miss the next green as well as the one after that, placing me firmly under the influence of full-blown rage, which I openly displayed using all the typical techniques ranging from arms raised overhead, screaming obscenities at the windshield and beyond, gesturing with my hands like a traffic cop using the internationally accepted sign for 'move ahead', all the while screaming, loud enough to be heard by the drunk, homeless man outside, "FUCKING GO!".

CJ saw all of my ranting and raving via his rearview mirror, and decided to respond by channelling his inner prick, and figured he'd mess with me a little. He began to slow down near the following two or three intersections, even when he could have made it through under the green, forcing us to come to a stop. Then, when the light turned back to green after the wait, he would pause until it turned yellow before proceeding. After a couple of these sequences, I was adequately livid and resolved to mash this fucker's head in at the next red light.

At the next stop, I jammed the car into park, almost tearing the shifter off in my hand, opened my door, and stormed towards the Jeep, seething. When I arrived, red-faced and veiny-necked at his vehicle, I did not hesitate to grab hold of the handle next to the driver's side door, step on the step, grab the door handle with my left hand, and rip it open with vigour, fully intending to instill fear deep into the soul of CJ.

The very second I opened the door and caught the briefest glimpse of the driver, I sensed instant regret, for inside the cab was a mountain of a man, weighing no less than 250 pounds (255 if you count the tattoos). He was bald and had a long, scraggy, ZZ Top beard. He wore sunglasses, even though it was about 12:30 AM, jeans with a skull and crossbones belt buckle, and nothing but a black, leather vest covering a small portion of his muscular upper body. In his mouth was a partially-chewed, half-lit cigar stub, which did not mask the foul smell emanating from his body and breath. He never averted his gaze from the windshield, in an act of total indifference to my presence. His left hand was at twelve o'clock on the chain-link steering wheel with his right hand firmly clutching the silver, monkey skull shifter head. As I looked at his left ear in abject horror, in a low baritone, he very calmly posed the following question to me: "You sure you wanna do this?".

I was quite sure, in fact, that I did not wish to proceed with my initial plan, and politely replied, "No sir. Sorry to bother you. Enjoy the rest of your night". I then stepped back, gently closed his door, and jogged back to my car, got in and locked all the doors.

The second I clicked on that CONFIRM tab for Ironman Santa Rosa, I whispered to myself, "You sure you wanna do this?". Truth be told, I wasn't at all, and the training regime I had been following reflected that. All I really wanted was to go to California.

When race day finally arrived, I wasn't worried in the least. I had put thinking about it out of my head for so long that everything simply felt the same as a 70.3, which, I assumed, was appropriate considering I trained for it exactly the same as I would have for a race half as long as I was about to attempt. The vibe and appearance of the Ironman Village was similar to what I was accustomed to, so I figured that comfortable familiarity was a positive omen of good things to come, and that had me feeling relaxed.

Due to this relaxed state, the race was nowhere near as difficult as I imagined it would be. It was staggeringly worse. In Lake Placid, there had been a legitimate excuse for my poor performance and the physical torture I had been through. I had hardly done any running all Spring. Santa Rosa, on the other hand, was entirely my fault. I looked for something, even someone, I could blame for my lack of fitness, but there was only me. Some things are so obvious that we overlook the true meaning of what they are and refuse to believe that what appears to be so simple, despite searching for a complex, hidden meaning, actually is just that: utterly simple.

I remember years ago visiting the Brooklyn Museum and

stumbling upon a rather provocative piece of contemporary installation art. I stared at it for quite some time, moving around it to look at it from several different vantage points in an attempt to figure out the piece's hidden, true, profound meaning. I searched my memory of the hundreds of literary works I had read for help, drawing upon Kafka and Kierkegaard, Chompsky, and even Dr. Seuss, but I was totally stumped. I was convinced that there must be some hidden meaning to what I saw sitting in front of me, under a cube of plexiglass.

The piece itself was a regular-sized human turd, on top of a white, plastic, perfectly square box. That was it. There had to be more to it than just that, I wondered. Lost in thought, the guy standing just to my left (who turned out to be Philip Seymour Hoffman), seemed to be having the same dilemma as I was. After ten or so minutes, he sighed, shook his head, leaned over to me, pointed at the work of art and said quietly, "It's a piece of shit".

I don't believe he was passing judgement, per se. He was simply making an accurate observation. There was before us a piece of shit sitting innocently and inoffensively on a box. That was all it was, in a truly phenomenological sense. It *was* shit, right there for all to see.

There was no good excuse for my performance in Santa Rosa. It was shit, borne out of a serious lack of proper training, and it was all my fault.

I spent the rest of the holiday licking my wounds and trying to start over with my training. I had been caught up so much in outcomes for so long that I had lost sight of the enjoyment of the sport, and once I figured this out, I was free to just swim, bike, run, and enjoy myself again. Even though I had the Worlds in Chattanooga coming up, I managed to ignore numbers and targets and just do what I love to do, and it was working out so well.

Then we went to the Griffith Park, where I went for a run and jammed my knee going down a really steep hill. The pain was sharp and localized, making me think that it would be temporary and wouldn't affect my performance for the rest of the summer, but as it turned out, I was wrong again, and the result was no running for the final month before the big race.

I ended up finishing an upsetting 100th in my age group. My knee hurt. I was exhausted, and I was sick of triathlon. Something had to change with regards to how I had been approaching the sport, as well as my future involvement in it. Up until this point, I simply swam, biked, and ran in some random combination every single day. There was no real rhyme or reason, and certainly no science to any of it. I just always went as hard as I could until I was exhausted, every time. After Chattanooga, I decided that either I would take up a different sport, or I would approach this one more intelligently. I decided that this new approach would begin with some time off.

ONE STEP FORWARD, TWO BACK

"IT TAKES A LOT TO CHANGE A MAN. HELL,
IT TAKES A LOT TO TRY. MAYBE IT'S TIME
TO LET THE OLD WAYS DIE".
—JASON ISBELL

In 1995, my fiancée (now ex-wife) and I decided that, before moving back to Montreal from Vancouver, we would first take a few months to backpack around Europe to explore our relationship and find ourselves before life got too messy and busy. Actually, *she* decided we were leaving Vancouver, an idea to which I was totally opposed, and she really had no interest in bumming our way around Europe (a dream I had wanted to make a reality for a very long time) but conceded that to me when she saw how upset I was to be moving away.

By and large, the trip was great, but there were a couple of low points, with one being of particular note because it almost ended our ten-year relationship.

We were on a train from somewhere to Nurnberg, Germany,

and being a time long before mobile phones were a thing, we were leafing through the <u>Let's Go Europe</u> travel guide to see what was worth visiting upon arrival, when I had the sudden urge, as is often the case, to go to the bathroom. I don't know if it is the same today, but back in 1995, the travel guides suggested carrying your important stuff, such as passports, money, tickets, wallet in a pouch around your neck and close to your body. I, of course, bought the biggest one I could find and, though heavier and bulkier than what most people carried, was able to accommodate all essential items, plus a few snacks, guidebook, journal, my girlfriend's documents, rail passes, small groceries...whatever. When I got up to go to the bathroom, I left the pouch with my fiancée to watch over.

Cleaning out my bowels took a little longer than I had anticipated, and as I finished up we were already in the station in Nurnberg. My fiancée was waiting outside the toilets, and we disembarked together. Once we left the station and made our way across the street towards a small, green area, I asked her to hand me my pouch so I could check out the guidebook.

"What do you mean, your pouch?", she asked, parenthetically implying that I was an idiot.

"My pouch. My blue pouch with EVERYTHING in it", I replied, starting to panic and wondering why she would make such a stupid joke. "I left it with you when I went to the shitter".

"Well, I don't have it", she said, with the kind of calmness that only someone who believes they are totally innocent, or who doesn't actually give a shit, could have. "You must have left it on the train".

With a quick "Fuck me", I took off with my seventy-litre bag strapped to my back like a packhorse, in the direction of the station, desperately praying to a God I only really believed in at times like this, that the train was still there.

The platforms were at the top of one of the longest sets of up and down escalators I have ever seen. Looking up from the bottom and seeing that neither one was moving, I chose the closest one and started climbing as fast as I could, looking a little like a Sherpa. The pack, like my breathing, was heavy and my legs were exploding with lactic acid as I forged my way upward. I needed to get to the platform to find the train so I could search it for the pouch, but getting to the top of the escalator was becoming a much more difficult and immediate task. Everything depended upon my reaching the platform, and I was giving it all I had, but as soon as I got to within eight or nine stairs from the top, the escalator began to move in the wrong direction. The stairs were going down, and I was working as hard as I could to go up.

It seemed that there was a sensor at the top that detected when someone was ready to descend and would turn the escalator on. A train had, apparently, just arrived and there was a crowd of passengers making their way downstairs to the exit, forcing me to ride with them. When we neared the bottom, most of them began to walk the rest of the way, and eventually, the stairs stopped moving again. When they did, because I was not thinking straight, I began climbing up anew instead of just going to the bottom, moving to the right and riding/running up that escalator. Stupid, I know, because as I approached the top again, the same thing happened. This time, I fought the crowd and muscled my way up, but my legs were exhausted and my pack kept bumping into the people who were trying to ride the stairs in the proper direction. I fell face first and tumbled fifteen or twenty stairs downward, where my heavy pack teamed up with gravity and brought me to my ass. I continued downward for another thirty or so steps. When I regained my balance, I again attempted to run against the tide, making almost zero upward progress, until I ran out of energy and I was brought down once again.

Due to my panicked and increasingly hypoxic state, I kept trying to ascend, only to get within a few metres from the top before falling back to the halfway point. I tried over and over to get to the top only to be smote by gravity and repelled by a force over which I had no control.

After what seemed like hours, but which was probably more like ten minutes, I gave up and allowed the stairs to take me to the bottom, where I sat motionless while I caught my breath. Once I had sufficiently filled my lungs with enough oxygen for my brain to function at a third-grade level, I figured out the puzzle that lay before me and took the other escalator. The moment I positioned myself at the bottom, the sensors detected my presence and began moving me effortlessly upwards towards the platforms.

When I reached the top, I noticed the train was still there, so I entered it and checked every single seat, and found...nothing.

As it happened, this was not our train. The one we had arrived on had already left for Dusseldorf or Hamburg, or wherever, with all of our important documents and most of our money. I took a couple of 'alone' minutes to sit and try, unsuccessfully, to come to grips with having lost everything, including seven or eight pounds of water weight through all the sweat I had shed on the escalator, before I got up and began walking slowly back to where I had left my fiancée waiting outside. I took my time because I was very tired and because I knew that this was all her fault. If I hadn't taken those extra few moments, I was sure to end up in a German prison on a murder rap. We were only a couple of weeks into a trip I had dreamed of for years, and now, due to the negligence of a girlfriend, who never really wanted to go in the first place, was about to end.

I left the train station and began to make my way back to the square out front and I looked up to see if I could spot her, inwardly hoping just a little bit that I wouldn't. When I found her, she was relaxing on the edge of a fountain with her pack under her stretched out feet, reading from the guidebook.

"An old lady noticed it on our seat and brought it to the station police", she said, with a tone meant to ridicule me for taking off is such a huff. "When you did your Ben Johnson imitation, I found the security office. Your pouch was already there".

I was so relieved that I ignored the implied slight to my lack of intelligence, and gave her a big hug which lasted long enough for the high of instant gratification to wear off and be replaced by the feeling that she had robbed me of the pleasure of being angry with her for screwing up.

I suppose all's well that ends well.

$$\diagdown \quad \bullet \quad \diagup$$

With my terrible placing at the World Championships in Chattanooga behind me, and with a throbbing knee, I decided to shelf running and swimming for the month of September to focus on cycling at a very moderate pace, entirely indoors, to allow the healing process to begin. My knee needed a rest to get better, and so did my ego. This was a new concept for me as I've always done the bulk of my training outside, and never took time off from running unless there was an injury that literally prevented it. Now, my knee hurt, but I probably could have kept on running on it.

It was so uncommon for me to do so much training indoors that, when I told my mother about it, I remember her saying, "What the fuck would you do that for?", only half-jokingly. She never minced her words and always had a hard time tolerating weakness, laziness, or apathy, from her children. "What are you made of, sugar?".

"Ma, I have a really sore knee", I replied, feeling like such a wimp. "I don't want to make it worse, that's all".

"A sore knee", she launched back, with a little more vitriol than normal, and with the joking half now completely gone, "I can't feel my left hand anymore, but I'm not taking time off".

I had no idea, but apparently she had been secretly having trouble with her left hand for a couple of months, so in late October, she went to the doctor who diagnosed the problem as carpal tunnel syndrome and had them surgically cleared out. At around the same time, I started to run again, though on a treadmill. Her hand was being taken care of, and my knee was no longer a problem.

I thought I would hate running on a machine instead of on a trail, as I always had in the past, but now I was thriving on it, and I actually enjoyed being in complete control of my progress. Before,

I had always used merely how I felt as my guide, but now I was able to put aside perceived effort, and focus on the science of training properly. It seemed as though I got a little more efficient and a little faster every week, without noticing the extra effort, and in no time I was able to go at a four-minute per kilometre pace without it feeling like I was pushing it. The treadmill was making my form better and my turnover so much smoother. It also didn't give a shit whether or not I was tired, and it refused to slow down just because I didn't feel like it. If I stopped moving my feet it would just shoot me off the back.

By the time December rolled around, despite the snow, wind, and freezing temperatures, I felt confident enough to try running outside one day a week while reserving the treadmill for the other four. At first, my outdoor times were WAY slower than indoors, mostly due to the fact that I was terrified of putting a foot wrong and slipping myself into another injury. I never, at least initially, took a step that I didn't think deeply about first, but the more I ran outside, the more confident I became, and the less thinking was required. Eventually, I was on autopilot and was able to just run.

This continued until Christmas morning when my autopilot missed seeing a patch of black ice which my left foot hit, causing me to slide, make a pathetic attempt at recovery, and overextend my calf muscle. The result was a familiar popping sound and sharp pain in the belly of my gastrocnemius that I did not recall asking Santa for at all.

After walking the rest of the way home, we packed up the car and drove to meet up with the rest of my family to celebrate an event I was no longer feeling particularly festive about. When we arrived at my sister's house for Christmas dinner, my brother asked what the pop sounded like.

"Sounds like no fucking running for a month", I snapped back, unable to mask my annoyance. "That's what it sounded like!".

I had a couple of glasses of wine and was really beginning to enjoy my bad mood, which was made more acute by the holiday season, so I decided to sit next to my mom and see who could sulk the best. December 25th is also her birthday, which you could just tell had been pissing her off since she was a child because no one really gives a shit that it's your birthday, and they certainly don't wrap your gifts in pink or blue wrapping, that's if there is any birthday stuff at all. December 25th is for Santa, Rudolph, Christmas trees and ugly sweaters. It's always Ho, Ho, Fucking Ho!

This year, though, I figured I could out-mood her, what with the bad calf and all.

She wasn't having any of it, and just stared into space, rocking back and forth in her seat, which was not a rocking chair. She wouldn't engage in conversation at all, saying only, "uh-huh". This was the worst mood I had ever seen her in. She was so pissed off that she appeared to be afraid of herself, which was really weird, almost scary, but I blew it off, had more wine, and looked for someone else I could complain to.

After the first week in January, I started running again as though I hadn't been injured at all, ramping my pace up to four-minute per kilometre without any pain whatsoever. Around this time, my mother's hand, and now part of her arm, were still feeling like they belonged to someone else, so she went to get it checked out. The diagnosis had changed and was no longer carpal tunnel syndrome but, most likely, a mild stroke. Though this was pretty awful news, we all felt a little sigh of relief because now, at the very least, we knew what was wrong. My mom took the news pretty well, feeling that if this was as bad as it would get, she could deal with it. The prognosis was considered 'good', and she went back to functioning as normal, though with slightly hindered left side mobility. She did not appear to mind it too much because she held her cigarette in the right hand, after all, so she could smoke, work the TV clicker, drive, and cook. All things considered, she was good.

My mother was happier than I had seen her in months and I was running again. For a bitter cold, piece of shit, long, dark, Quebec winter, things were just peachy, until, of course, I decided to give a zero-drop shoe a try. Why? Well, because they look really cool, and all the badass trail runners wear them, so it seemed. Being fifty doesn't necessarily stop you from trying to look cool, so I strapped on a pair of Altra trail shoes and jumped on the treadmill going hard right from the moment I pressed the START button. Before I got past my second kilometre, my right calf snapped with that familiar pop I had heard from the left side about a month earlier. Now I was going to be off my running feet again.

At around the same time, my mother was feeling pretty good and went to the neuro doctor to have an MRI scan done to ascertain the extent and severity of any damage caused by her stroke. It turned out, however, that it wasn't a stroke at all, but far, far worse. I will never forget the fear I saw in her eyes when I showed up at my parents' house after work to see how the appointment had gone. She looked terrified, staring at the television vacantly.

"What's up", I said, trying to lighten up the mood in the room.

"I have a brain tumour", she softly replied, staring at me as though she couldn't tell I was there.

Suddenly, my calf didn't hurt so much, and I was having a hard time trying to figure out what to say. I didn't want to show how shocked and devastated I was, and I certainly did not want her to feel any worse, if that was even possible.

"Good", I said, trying to emit confidence. "Now they can cut that fucker out and you'll be able to move your arm properly again".

She didn't fall for it. Neither did my dad, and I certainly knew it was bullshit. It was a good try, but bullshit nevertheless.

That was February 23rd, my sister's birthday. I started running again on the 24th. Pain or no pain, there was no way I was going to be able to process such horrible news without the dopamine hit that only a good hard run could deliver, so I put all of my energy into training, and I was doing it wisely, balancing hard days with easy days. There were long, 'zone two' workouts and more strenuous, 'threshold' workouts. I experimented with varying intensities, and I could feel my body getting stronger, my lungs more efficient. The improvement in my fitness was very noticeable, and I was, wisely, resting more than I ever had, enabling the hard work to absorb.

Unfortunately, there was an inverse relationship between my gains and the health of my mother. She seemed to get noticeably worse by the day. Her dexterity was all but gone, she needed a walker to get around, and someone had to carry her up the stairs. She could no longer cook, change the channel, clean herself, but she was able to smoke, though. Watching her deteriorate right before my eyes was so difficult, and the worst of it was that someone who I had seen as tough as nails my whole life, simply could not hide how afraid she was. She had always been so strong, so tenacious, and now was as frail as the petal of a flower, and she knew that she wouldn't last very long. It was a very trying time.

On Tuesday, March 13th, my dad brought her to the hospital for a routine biopsy. She was scheduled to be back home no more than a few days later, so she could live out the rest of her life, such as it was, and however long that might be, surrounded by her stuff and in her own home. I went to work early that day and brought my brother along so we could run side by side on our separate treadmills, and talk about mom. Thirty minutes into our one hour run, my calf gave way again, but I wasn't angry this time. For some reason, I just had a feeling that this was supposed to happen, and I simply stepped off the machine and decided, right then, not to get back on until my body was truly ready, however long that would take. It really didn't seem to matter as much anymore as my whole life's context had changed. Luckily, I was able to swim and bike, so I had an outlet for the deep sorrow we were all feeling.

The surgery went well, and I left school early to meet up with my sister, brother, and dad at the Montreal Neurological Institute. When my mother came-to, she was in good spirits and was quite hungry. She actually looked pretty good, except for the horseshoe sized (and shaped), Frankenstein scar on her head. It appeared she would be going home very soon, probably the following day.

We all stayed with her until about ten that night when my sister left to bring my dad home for a well-needed rest. About twenty minutes later, my mom began to complain to me that something was wrong with her tongue. She had never felt anything like it before and the sensation wasn't painful but she looked to be very frightened. I decided that it would be best to get a medical professional in the room to check it out, so I leaned over her to press the button next to her bed to alert the nurse. Just then she started to cry and tremble. The moment the nurse arrived in the room, my mother began to have a series of terrifying, violent seizures. Her body thrashed uncontrollably on the bed, tubes were being ripped from her arms and the alarms on all of the machinery in the room were going off loudly all at once. My brother and I did our best to hold her down while a team of doctors injected her with several syringes worth of drugs to try to get the seizures under control.

After a terrifying and emotional half-hour, the drugs began to take effect and they moved her to the Intensive Care Unit, where she would spend the better part of the next few weeks intermittently lucid and feeding via a tube. She was grey and struggled visibly for every breath. She was also eternally thirsty and the only pleasure she displayed was when one of us would wipe her face with a cold, wet cloth.

"That's beautiful", she would just barely whisper, then battle, unsuccessfully, to stay awake.

She suffered massively for three weeks and died very unpeacefully on April 8th, my son's ninth birthday. The next day my calf didn't hurt anymore; it had finally healed.

Since the end of summer, I had felt like Charlie Brown getting up a good head of steam, trusting everything was fine, only to have Lucy jerk the football away just as I was about to kick it.

On the morning of April 8th, I wished my son a happy birthday. That afternoon I said good-bye to my mother forever, and on

April 9th, I kicked that fucking ball...hard.

By the time my first race of the 2018 season began, on June 24th, I had managed to get myself in the best shape of my life and I knew that, so long as I didn't have any mechanical issues, I was fit enough to win my age group. I had trained properly and thoughtfully for a change, going harder than ever, but in control, and my body seemed to withstand the pressures and stresses I placed on it. I was determined to let nothing slow me down.

The swim at Ironman 70.3 Mont Tremblant went off without a hitch. I was in and out of transition in no time, but when I got on my bike and held onto my aerobars, I immediately noticed that the left one was loose and moved upward when I pulled on it. It became, effectively, nothing more than an armrest for the entire bike leg. It took me about ten minutes to adjust my technique and I began to fly, passing dozens of riders along the way.

At kilometre sixty, a motorcycle pulled up beside me. I looked over at its occupants, believing they were cheering me on, when the woman seated behind the driver, playing the part of passenger and 'race official', informed me that I had been drafting and had incurred a five-minute penalty to be served at the next penalty tent. I looked at her, then at the virtually empty road ahead. There was no one in front of me for about 200 metres, but I was too upset to even curse.

I made it to the tent, waited for two or three minutes to be handed a stopwatch, watched it count up to five minutes, took off and went as hard as I could, managing to still finish fourth in my age group...just four minutes behind the guy who finished first.

His name was Brock also. What are the odds of that?

My next race was almost exactly a month later in Santa Rosa, only this time it was the 70.3, so I was ready for a little redemption.

Back in high school, we used to have mid-year exams just before Christmas break which were quite formal and felt exactly like 'finals'. Taking place in the gymnasium, there was row upon row of seemingly endless little desks at which students of all grade levels wrote various different tests, from Physics to French, and Economics to Ecology. Everyone was very nervous about these exams and the stress was always palpable. This was the time of year when we would collectively pray for a fire or blizzard that would have school cancelled, letting us out of an exam. These prayers, unfortunately, were never answered until tenth grade when the power went out thirty minutes into my chemistry exam. For the next fifteen to twenty minutes, utter chaos ensued and the decision was made, by the Principal, to cancel the exam. That year Christmas came a few glorious days early.

In Santa Rosa I was ready for the whole race but, as it happened, I only needed to prepare for two-thirds of it, as they cancelled the swim due to fog. When the cancellation was announced, I immediately had two very clear thoughts: 1. It occurred to me that for the first couple of years that I competed in triathlons, I would have leaped for joy upon hearing the news that there would be no swim (much like I had done during my exam in the tenth grade). 2. Where was I going to pee? You see, I never line-up to use the bathrooms at a race for number one. That would be stupid. Number two is a whole other story, but peeing can be done standing up almost anywhere, so long as A. it's outside and B. you're wearing a wetsuit. I always hide inside my 2XU rubber toilet before the race and let her rip. It always drains down the left leg and exits via the left ankle. All I have to do is pee and move around because nobody looks at your ankles, especially when they are busy thinking about the race ahead. Now, however, there was no swim which meant there was no need to wear my wetsuit and, thus, I had nowhere convenient to take a piss.

The new starting procedure for the race was time trial style, with four competitors leaving together every few seconds. The bike course begins ever so slightly uphill before going down over a long bridge. When I got to the front and started, I found it hard but it was uphill, so I thought nothing of it. When we started to descend, people were passing me in a tuck position going too fast to pedal. I, on the other hand, was turning the pedals like crazy and I wasn't even in my hardest gear. Clearly, it seemed I didn't have the legs that day. I struggled the entire length of the bike ride thoroughly pissed off that I had, quite obviously, lost the form I enjoyed three days prior. I was forced to work so hard just to keep moving that it never occurred to me that something might be wrong with the bike itself, other than maybe a flat tire. And it wasn't that. I checked like a million times.

When I dismounted my bike after ninety kilometres, I fully expected the run to be just as bad, and felt horrible because I had planned to use this race to qualify for the following year's World Champs in Nice, France. After that bike ride, however, it was clear that I wasn't in the great form I thought I had been. To my surprise, the run turned out to be kind of easy. I felt strong and fast and my legs turned over with ease and very little fatigue. I couldn't understand what had happened because my form was miraculously back. It didn't make any sense.

I ended up finishing fifth in my age group which wasn't good enough to qualify for Nice but I did have the fastest run of anyone in my category. That made me feel a little better but I was still disappointed and perplexed as to what happened to my cycling form, and when transition opened allowing us to retrieve our bikes, everything suddenly made perfect sense. I gathered my things and began to roll my bike towards the exit, but the back wheel just skidded on the pavement. It wasn't spinning at all. As it turned out, I had installed the wheel improperly when I assembled the bike in the hotel room the previous day. I had never bothered to apply the brakes after spinning the wheel to make sure it moved, but once I did, which only happened for the first time, since assembly, on the bridge at the start of the race, they stayed stuck to the wheel.

Two races and two total disappointments later, I had nothing to show except excellent, unused form. Both times I had done something stupid and had allowed my mind to lose focus at key points, denying me of the results I had been hoping for. I did not qualify for Nice and I was very unhappy. I had spent the better part of the previous three years either exhausted or injured in the childish pursuit of attempting to validate my self-worth through the sport of triathlon, constantly refining my approach and redefining my purpose. There had definitely been periods of pleasure and times when I felt that I had, indeed, found myself in life and in the sport.

Unfortunately, a destructive pattern seemed to be developing, as the harder I tried and the more I wanted to succeed in the sport, the more I allowed myself to be defined by it. Since I was experiencing ever waning success, I felt that my value as a person was diminishing as well. Since September I had studied how to train more efficiently, adopting more intelligent methods and working harder than I ever had before, but none of it was good enough. The results were not there. Though I had been alive for fifty years, it was like I was eleven again, feeling as though life was not fair. It didn't seem to reward me for my effort and sacrifice of time, health and emotional well-being. I was being told, once again, to get off the bike I did not receive on my birthday.

I began to wonder whether it was time to give it up and begin a new search for something that could make me feel good, but then I thought about it all. My lack of success this time around was my own fault and had nothing to do with fairness. I made several mistakes that could have been avoided but that were not cause for regret. So I didn't qualify for Nice; now I had the opportunity to try to achieve that goal somewhere else. Was winning really the reason I was spending so much time and effort with triathlon, or was there something else to it all? Placing well does feel great, but there is so much more to the sport than that. Triathlon is an organic community of like-minded people who love both being a part of a group while enjoying the alone time the sport allows. Whether we stand on the top of the podium or in 237th place in our age group, triathlon forces us to push right up against the limit of what we are capable of. As in life, we lose far more often than we win, but the triumphs weigh so much more than the disappointments, and through the defeats we are able to learn and improve.

I was disappointed with my results in Mont Tremblant and

Santa Rosa, however, I wasn't about to give up on a way of life that had helped shape who I am just because I rode too close to the guy in front of me or because I didn't properly align a wheel. It was time to put the negative thoughts aside and concentrate on what was to come next.

My next race was the 70.3 World Championships in Port Elizabeth, South Africa, which, unless I won, would not get me a qualification spot for the following year either, but was really cool nonetheless. Though the race was super surreal in many ways, as well as super fun, the thing I remember most was having my bike NOT arrive with me. This experience, though very stressful, reinforced one of the reasons why I love the sport of triathlon because, as it turned out, I was not the only athlete to make it to South Africa sans bicycle. There were hundreds of us including the reigning world champion, Daniela Ryf.

Several of us sat around together in the tiny Port Elizabeth airport, which is about the size of the gymnasium where I attended elementary school (and with a security detail less strict than a pre-occupied, teenage babysitter texting her boyfriend and taking selfies to post on Instagram), filling out official-looking forms none of us had any real confidence would miraculously reunite us with our bikes. I sat next to Daniela and actually shared a pen along with pleasantries. She is the world champion and potentially the best long-distance triathlete ever, whereas I am a fifty-year-old age grouper. Her bike is worth more than my car and my bike and my television put together whereas I purchased a five-year-old, second-hand Quintana Roo CD 0.1 on Kijiji for $1300 from a starving McGill University nursing student. She was paid to ride her $15 000 Felt, but we were in the same predicament and discussed the issue like we were pals preparing for a Sunday morning café ride. I don't know for certain, but I don't think Lebron James is put in the position to have this sort of thing happen to him very often. I'm almost certain he doesn't fly commercially at all. Daniela, the world champion many times over, was in coach with the rest of us.

Normally, having a piece of my luggage lost, especially one so fundamentally important as my bike, would cause me to become overwhelmed with stress, resulting in a certain horrible mood. Knowing that I was not alone in this setback made me feel slightly better and when I realized that THE top professional was seated there, alongside me, with the exact same problem, I felt not only better but like I was part of a small, exclusive community. In fact, if I'm totally honest, I was a little let down the following day when I received an email notification from British Airways that my bike was waiting for me at the airport in Port Elizabeth. I no longer felt special. One email had taken me from being interesting to just one of a few hundred 50-54-year-old males hoping to go fast enough not to finish last.

Race day turned out to be memorable for a few reasons. Firstly, it rained the kind of rain you really only see on television when there is a monsoon in some far off, exotic place, like Africa, for instance. Second, the race day portable toilets had attendants who cleaned and deodorized the cabins after each use, making for a surprisingly pleasant pre-race turd cutting. And finally, though the weather was terrible, many of the roads were not truly worthy of a world championship, and the views were so spectacular that there were times when I sat up just to check them out, I still managed to finish in around four and a half hours, good enough for tenth place in my age group. Tenth best in the world is pretty impressive on its own, but add to it that just prior to starting I had the opportunity to take a shit in a fresh clean vestibule, and you've got yourself a pretty damn good day out.

Fortunately, my bike made it home with me on the same flight, giving me one last opportunity at Ironman 70.3 Atlantic City to qualify for Nice, and it turned out to be my best racing achievement ever. For some reason, I was filled with confidence and the moment I got out of the water after the swim, I knew it would take a truly great performance by someone to beat me. I wasn't being cocky, I was just sure. I knew right away that I was going to love that race. I managed to finish first in my age group with a time of 4:26 in the lashing rain. I had finally punched my ticket to Nice and all the negativity I had let get to me after Santa Rosa was gone.

When I arrived home from Atlantic City, I checked my email. Waiting for me was a message from Wattie Ink inviting me to become a member of their Elite Team. It had taken some time, but I finally felt like I had arrived. The journey I had begun six years before was finally starting to make sense, and I actually began to get it.

Triathlon isn't just a sport that is about winning and losing. It is, above all, about balance and balancing. Hard days versus easy days. Swim days versus run days. Work versus training. Family versus practice. Racing versus participating. Fuelling versus fasting. Spending versus conserving. In order to be successful at both triathlon and life, regardless of what those two things mean to you, a balance that keeps you engaged, excited, content, curious and challenged must be found. This needs to be accomplished while remaining mindful of the importance of the people around you that make it all possible.

I remember seeing a woman carrying a cardboard sign at Ironman Lake Placid that read, "If you're still married, then you aren't training hard enough". Of course, I giggled when I first saw it, but it does highlight a problem that an alarmingly high number of triathletes face, not having learned to balance triathlon with what is truly important.

I have come to understand that if you pursue something too hard, you can lose sight of why you are searching. Often it is better to stop looking and just let it find you. It took me six years but I finally realized, though I was desperately searching, I hadn't found triathlon. Somehow, by simply letting go, it found me.

ACKNOWLEDGEMENTS

First and foremost I need to thank Anne. Without her support, I would never have found the time or energy to complete this, Owen, for whom this book is written, Felix for putting up with all the noise from the turbo, PJ and Chris who were the silent audience for whom I was writing, Lori whom I have come to know so much better in the last couple of years, Dad whose acceptance I still seek constantly, my Wattie Ink family for accepting me as a real triathlete, my coworkers who think more of me than I deserve, Jessa who read this before anyone else and who set me straight about much of it, Peter Miller for the numerous conversations about the content, Sean Snow for being my first triathlete friend and mentor, Heather Jackson for showing real interest in this project, Adam Hill for taking the time to read this, and of course, Mom.

About The Author

Brock Gibbs is a high school physical education teacher from Montreal, Quebec, Canada. Feeling too old to partake in the sports he had successfully engaged in as a teenager, at the age of forty-five he took up triathlon. After almost quitting his first race due to a panic attack in the swim, he has worked through several injuries to have won his age group at several Ironman branded events throughout North America. He has also finished in the top ten at the Ironman 70.3 World Championships on two occasions. Having earned the distinction of Ironman All World Athlete, he is in his second year as a member of the Elite Squad of the number one amateur triathlon team in the world, Wattie Ink.

Sean Snow is a 31 time Ironman finisher from Concord, New Hampshire. He has competed in 15 World Championships, including Kona five times. He has raced in the last five Boston Marathons and continues to raise the bar for other amateur endurance athletes, chasing age-group wins in races of various distances simply for the sake of competition. His biggest fans are his wife, Pam and daughter, Steph, herself an accomplished endurance athlete.

Printed in Great Britain
by Amazon